CLASSIC WALKS
Great Britain

by Bill Birkett

The Oxford Illustrated Press

Photography by Bill Birkett
(unless otherwise stated)

© Bill Birkett, Ronald Faux, Tony Greenbank, Cameron McNeish and John White (as credited), 1987

Reprinted 1989.

Printed in England by J.H. Haynes and Co. Limited, Sparkford, Nr. Yeovil, Somerset.

Published by:
The Oxford Illustrated Press Limited, Sparkford, Nr. Yeovil, Somerset.

Haynes Publications Inc., 861 Lawrence Drive, Newbury Park, California 91320

ISBN 1-85509-203-4

British Library Cataloguing in Publication Data:
Birkett, Bill
    Classic walks in Great Britain.—(Classic
    walks series).
    1. Great Britain—Description and travel
    —1971—Guide-books
    I. Title   II. Series
    914.1'04858   DA650
    ISBN 1-85509-203-4

Library of Congress Catalog Card Number
    87-80506

All rights reserved. No part of this book may be reproduced or transmitted in any form or by any means, electronic or mechanical, including photocopying, recording or by any information storage or retrieval system, without written permission from the publisher.

Contents

ACKNOWLEDGEMENTS

For those who walked a few of the miles with me or offered information I would like to thank:

Mike Ansel, Martin Battersby, Jim Birkett, John Cleare, Greg Cornforth, Paul Cornforth, Geoff Crackett, Ronnie Faux, Mike Feeley, Roy Garner, Tony Greenbank, John Hargreaves, Eric Jones and staff, Ted Lean, John Lockley, Willie McCloud, Cameron McNeish, Richard Oldfield, John Quine, Jon Rigby, Stewart Sykes, Neil Towler, Graeme Wallace, John White, Ruth and Gerry Williams.

For correcting the manuscript I would like to thank:

Jim Birkett, Susan Lund, Jon Rigby and Jack Williams.

For the use of published material I am indebted to Fell & Rock Climbing Club.

Thanks are also due to Paul Renouff of Photo Scope for black and white photograph printing, and to Olympus for use of their light and thoroughly practical camera equipment.

To Susan, the prettiest walker I know.

INTRODUCTION

Britain is an infinitely varied and beautiful island. Its topography, flora and fauna, history and peoples all change dramatically with their different geographical locations. It is a land of high mountains, rolling hills and flat plains; of deep slow rivers and high tumbling waterfalls; of naked black rock and of plentiful golden corn; of snow and of sunshine; of wilderness; of tiny villages and sprawling cities. An insular and independent nation, Britain is strongly influenced by, and surrounded by, the sea. A country whose peoples are remarkably separate in nature yet united in spirit; where a number of different languages are indigenous and remain in current usage and where each small area has its own dialect. From the dramatic stone circles of prehistory to the modern-day motorway this is a land richer in the remnants of man's progress than most. Now peaceful, Britain has a long and bloody history.

Alongside man there exists the wild Britain, a world of rich and varied flora and fauna. In the skies you may see the huge golden eagle or the diminutive wren. On the land wanders the great red deer and the tiny shrew and in the waters brown trout flash and salmon jump. From the most delicate fern to the stoutest oak, Britain is a wonderful land; magnificent and free.

There is no better way to explore this land than to walk. Walking is a means of discovering many things and simply by putting one foot in front of the other you will find freedom; the freedom of Britain and freedom of spirit. CLASSIC WALKS IN GREAT BRITAIN is both a guide to and appreciation of thirty-one of Britain's finest walks.

The book describes 19 day walks and 12 long distance walks (which can take anything from three days to three weeks) selected from the length and breadth of the British mainland and the Island of Skye. The aim of the selection is to provide a full holiday or a long weekend of walking with a minimum of travel between. In addition to the day walks in any specific area I have described a suitable centre which can be used as an effective base from which to tackle all the walks in that particular area. On the multi-day long-distance footpaths the walk is effectively divided into days that take you from one suitable halting point to another.

The format of the book is designed to do two things: firstly it is a concise and clear guide which, along with the map will help you quickly and simply locate and execute the walk and secondly it is a literary and photographic appreciation of the walk and the area through which it passes. In many respects a walk is not just an experience of the different physical features but of an adventure shared by others. The essays are written to capture this adventure and Ronnie Faux, Tony Greenbank, Cameron McNeish, John White and myself have described the walks, on a personal basis, to achieve this end.

Before discussing in detail the layout of the book and explain how best to use the information provided I think it prudent to explain how I came to construct this book on great British walks. It is very obvious to me, but in this world of increasing specialisation and polarisation it may not be apparent to some. It is simply because I love the British countryside.

I had a most fortunate childhood and was brought up in the heart of the English Lake District — deep amidst the fells. My parents both loved the outdoors, my father was (and is) an expert ornithologist and botanist and my mother provided the sandwiches and filled the flasks. Really there were few days when I wasn't out and about in the countryside. On summer and spring evenings, and sometimes the very early mornings, after and before my father went to his work at the local slate quarry we were out together on the fells — observing the peregrine falcon or searching for a rare fern.

Weekends simply meant two full days were spent out of doors but with the Ariel Red Hunter motorbike and sidecar we travelled further afield — to Yorkshire or southern Scotland. Holidays most often saw us in the wild and rugged Highlands of Scotland although I remember we did travel to Wales or Cornwall occasionally. On the old motorbike and sidecar in pre-motorway days the journey itself was quite an adventure!

From a very early age I had two great passions: one was climbing (I just naturally climbed anything that didn't move), and the other was photography. I'm not quite sure which came first, the climbing boots or the camera, but both were early acquisitions at an age when most boys preferred model cars. Retrospectively, I suppose, it was an extraordinary childhood for not many people are fortunate enough to be so fully exposed to the outdoor life. But to me then, and now, it just seemed the natural way to be. I started rock climbing in earnest when I was fourteen and this effectively meant I went my own separate way.

That way was always to wild places: the high Black Cuillin of Skye, the stark slate hills of Wales, quiet Northumberland, the dark Peak and the sea cliffs of Cornwall. As my climbing developed I travelled further afield to Europe (both East and West), the USA, and Japan. During these travels I've seen many fine sights, climbed many spectacular mountains and met many wonderful people; yet it is pertinent to say that the experiences to be enjoyed doing these classic British walks will stand with the best I have enjoyed anywhere.

When the opportunity came along for me to write and photograph CLASSIC WALKS IN GREAT BRITAIN I grasped it with eager anticipation. I took to the road in my faithful caravanette and to do it justice I walked (and often rewalked) the different routes making notes and taking photographs. On the rainy days when the wind raged, and the caravanette rocked, I hit the keys of my portable word processor. To give the book balance and other informed opinion I asked four friends, well known in the writing and climbing world, to write up the classic walk, or walks, which fall under their specialist knowledge.

To choose thirty-one walks from the entire length and breadth of Britain requires careful consideration. I discussed the selection with many people and listened to their opinions but in the end the selection is a purely personal one. It is a choice designed not only to give a series of outstanding individual walks but also to portray the essence of all that makes Britain great. In some instances it is the grandeur of the scenery that makes the walk classic. In other cases it may be the history of the area through which you are travelling that gives it its fascination.

The body is designed to walk and in today's tremendously stressful world it is both healthy and therapeutic to do so. It is a pastime for all those who are prepared to make the effort of putting one foot in front of the other. The reward for so doing is to discover the wonders of the natural world and the powers of your own body. Walking is something that can be enjoyed in good company, perhaps with the family, or it can be a solitary experience; the choice is yours.

The walks in this book span a wide range of difficulty and commitment; it is up to you to select a walk that matches your capabilities. They range in difficulty from the mild-mannered and delightful Wordsworth's Way to the savage magnificence of the Black Cuillin Pass via the Harta and Lota Corries. They can be successfully completed in anything from a comfortable three hours on the Betws-y-Coed River Walk to three weeks along the Cornish Coastal Path (although many will tackle these long-distance paths in day or two-day sections, completing the route through a season). Really it is sound practice to start with a route well within your expected capabilities and then with this successfully completed push a little further; take heart and remember that even the journey of a thousand miles begins with a single step.

We are now in an age of great mobility, and with Britain's excellent road and motorway network, even the remotest and farthest of these walks can be reached within a day's drive whatever your starting point. But respect the environment through which you pass for it is extremely delicate and very precious. You are responsible for this environment and you must look after it or it will be destroyed. If this means guiding others to this end then that also is your responsibility. Follow the country code and be courteous to your fellow man. Take only photographs and leave only footprints.

Walking is about fun and freedom and if you derive as much pleasure from reading and using this book of *Classic Walks in Great Britain,* as I have in preparing it, then you will have a time to remember.

Using This Book

For ease of use this book is split geographically into five areas:

Southern England covering an area from Cornwall to Oxfordshire (5 long-distance walks).

Wales from Pembroke to Snowdonia (1 long distance walk, 4 day walks and 1 centre described).

English Lake District the central and southern Lakes (1 long distance walk that extends to the east coast), 4 day walks and 1 centre described.

Northern England from the southern Peak District to Northumberland (2 long distance walks, 3 day walks and 2 centres).

Scotland the Cairngorms in the east and from Glasgow to the far north west including the Isle of Skye (3 long distance walks, 8 day walks and 2 centres).

For each walk there is an introductory list of information a concise route description and a

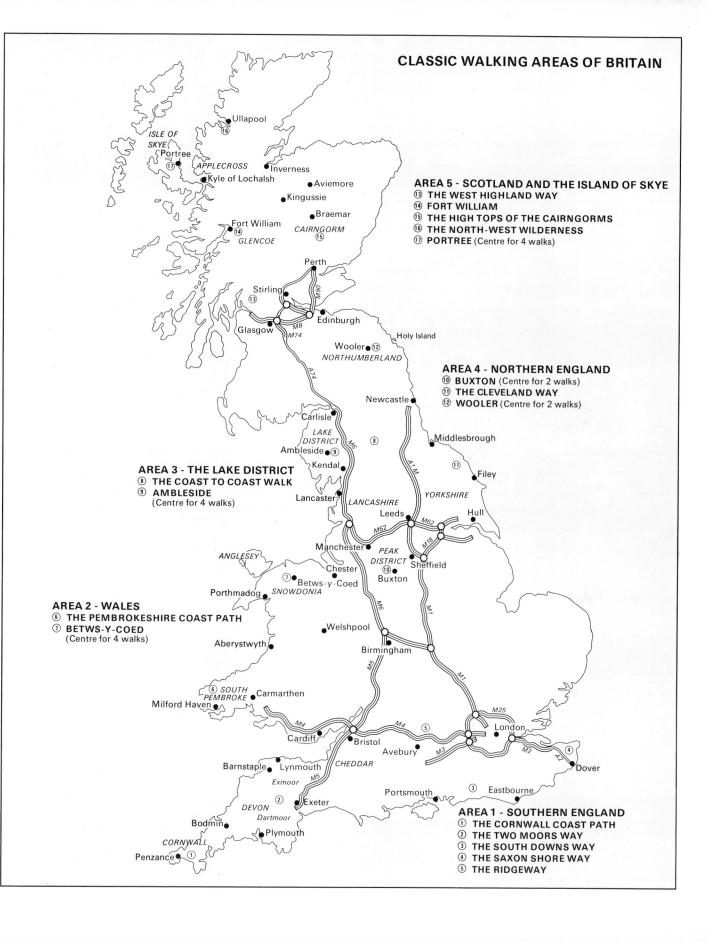

CLASSIC WALKING AREAS OF BRITAIN

AREA 5 - SCOTLAND AND THE ISLAND OF SKYE
⑬ THE WEST HIGHLAND WAY
⑭ FORT WILLIAM
⑮ THE HIGH TOPS OF THE CAIRNGORMS
⑯ THE NORTH-WEST WILDERNESS
⑰ PORTREE (Centre for 4 walks)

AREA 4 - NORTHERN ENGLAND
⑩ BUXTON (Centre for 2 walks)
⑪ THE CLEVELAND WAY
⑫ WOOLER (Centre for 2 walks)

AREA 3 - THE LAKE DISTRICT
⑧ THE COAST TO COAST WALK
⑨ AMBLESIDE
(Centre for 4 walks)

AREA 2 - WALES
⑥ THE PEMBROKESHIRE COAST PATH
⑦ BETWS-Y-COED
(Centre for 4 walks)

AREA 1 - SOUTHERN ENGLAND
① THE CORNWALL COAST PATH
② THE TWO MOORS WAY
③ THE SOUTH DOWNS WAY
④ THE SAXON SHORE WAY
⑤ THE RIDGEWAY

map. The layout is mainly self explanatory but the following comments should be noted.

Maps: I have listed the Ordnance Survey maps that MUST be used to undertake these walks. The maps provided within the text are to locate and plan the walk only; they are NOT sufficiently detailed to be used as a navigational aid whilst on the walk.

The maps are as follows: **OD** the Outdoor Leisure Map series with 2.5 inches to 1 mile or 4 cm to 1 km, 1:25000 scale; **L** the Landranger Maps with 1.25 inches to 1 mile or 2cm to 1km, 1:50000 scale; **T** the Tourist Maps with 1 inch to 1 mile or 1 cm to 0.63 km, 1:63360 scale.

For all the walks in this book I recommend the **L** series maps.

Approx Time: This should be treated as a guideline only and it is the time which I consider that an averagely fit walker will reasonably take. It is based on the time I took on the walk but is modified to the above because I walk faster than most. It takes into account lunch breaks and rest stops. Mainly I have aimed for consistency and if you find your own personal pace is at variance with the above then the correction factor you obtain for one should equally apply to the other walks of similar nature.

Difficulty: This should be considered along with the approx time, the footage of ascent and descent (on hill walks), and the distance, to obtain an overall impression of just what you are about to undertake. I have used the term 'technical difficulty' and if I state that there is 'technical difficulty' to be found on a walk then you can expect to use both your hands and feet to aid progress at some point during the walk. When I have said that there is no technical difficulty it does not mean there is no danger or exposure or difficult route finding to be encountered, it simply means you can accomplish the route without resorting to scrambling (using your hands to assist progress). High mountain walks can be serious undertakings and everyone attempting these walks must be competent, suitably fit, correctly equipped and possess suitable map reading and navigational skills. This is not an instruction manual and it is assumed that by paying due regard to the notes on difficulty the walker will be assisted in choosing a route within his/her capabilities. These comments on difficulty are only applicable to walks in good weather during the season indicated. Carefully note that both the prevailing weather and the forecasted weather must be carefully assessed before commencing any particular walk.

Seasons: This information is a guide only and is inclusive of the months stated. Obviously there will be seasonal variation and full discretion must be used. However to tackle the mountain walks outside the times stated will mean that one can expect winter conditions — anyone then tackling these walks must be proficient in winter mountaineering and survival skills.

The Route: is a concise description to enable you to follow the walk. By necessity it is limited on the long-distance footpaths which are anyhow, generally, depicted on the 'L' series OS maps and by Waymakers en route.

Photography

The photography in this book, unless otherwise stated, is my own. It is 35mm and is reproduced from colour transparencies and black and white prints.

SOUTHERN ENGLAND: The Cornwall Coast Path by John White

The Route

It is not practical, because of the length of this route, to split it into day sections. There is ample accommodation to be found at almost any point and there are few people who will actually complete this route in one outing.

The Walk

Few readers will not be able to reflect on childhood holidays when they braved the icy chill of the North Sea or the dirty grey swell of the Irish Sea and enjoyed the seaside pleasures of ice creams, sand castles, yellow spades, crazy golf and occasional hot sunshine; of amusement arcades, deckchairs, fishing boats and voracious gulls; of massive seas thunder-

ing against solid sea walls, or the swish and gurgle of gentle waves on pebbly beaches.

We are of course, only a tiny island compared to the great continents of the world and the waters that surround us have been vitally important in our development providing food, raw materials, a means of transport, protection and, sad to say more recently, a dumping ground for all manner of society's waste. Even so, for most of us the coast remains a place for recreation.

There are some stretches of coast which combine many of the best features in a relatively short length and the coast of Cornwall is one such stretch. As more active forms of recreation became popular and the concept

Old mine workings looking north from Carn Kendijack. (Photo: John White.)

9

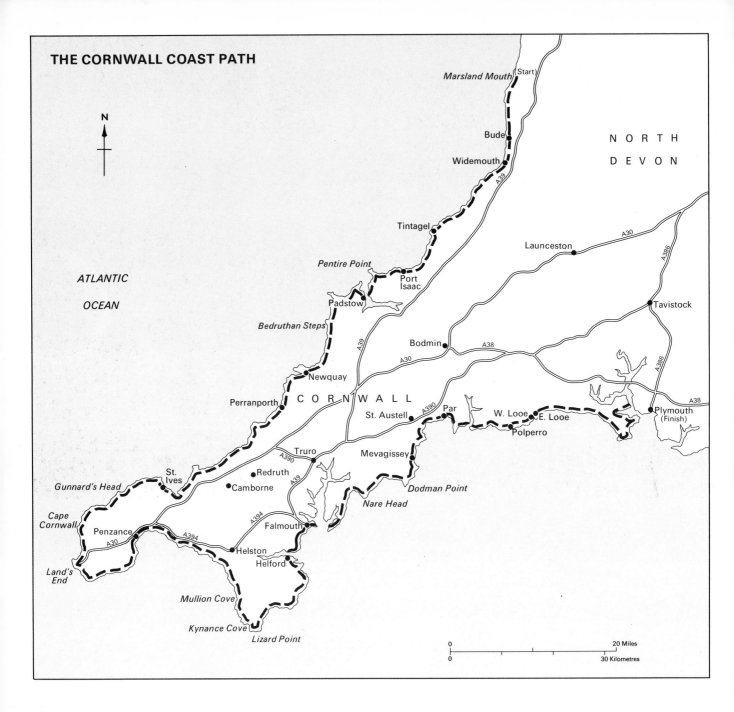

THE CORNWALL COAST PATH

N

ATLANTIC

OCEAN

NORTH
DEVON

Marsland Mouth (Start)

Bude
Widemouth

Launceston

Tintagel

Tavistock

Pentire Point
Port
Isaac

Padstow

Bedruthan Steps

Bodmin

CORNWALL

Newquay

Perranporth

St. Austell
Par
W. Looe
E. Looe
Polperro
Plymouth
(Finish)

Truro
Mevagissey

St.
Ives
Redruth
Camborne

Gunnard's Head

Dodman Point

Nare Head

Falmouth

Cape
Cornwall
Penzance

Helston
Helford

Land's
End

Mullion Cove

Kynance Cove
Lizard Point

0   20 Miles

0   30 Kilometres

The Walk: A long traverse of one of Britain's most spectacular coastlines from Marsland Mouth on the Cornwall/Devon border, rounding the granite headland of Lands End, and on to Plymouth and Cornwall (South-West England).
Maps: OS L180, L190, L200, L201, L203, L204.
Start: Marsland Mouth (map ref: SS 212174).
Finish: Plymouth (map ref: SX 454535).
Waymarks: Mostly wooden fingerposts (some in a poor state) with the long distance acorn symbol.
Length: 268mls (430km).
Approx Time: 14–21 days.
Difficulty: An arduous walk in places with

many ins and outs and ups and downs although the route is easy to follow.
Access: Car. Good access, but at peak holiday times be prepared for a slow road journey.
Seasons: All year.
Observations: The walk can be backpacked or there's accommodation en route. A route of great variety. The cliff scenery is often magnificent and the flora and fauna without comparison. An agreeable climate and first class local hospitality complete an attractive walk.
Accommodation: All types available.
Guidebooks: *Long Distance Paths of England and Wales* by T.G. Millar, *The Cornwall Coast Path* by Edward C. Pyatt. (HMSO).

of Long Distance Paths became attractive, here was one region where a continuous coastal route could link existing paths and popular tourist haunts with more remote headlands and bays, to produce a walk of the highest quality and kaleidoscopic variety. After much negotiation and work, the 265-mile (426km) long Cornwall Coast Path was officially opened in 1973.

The traverse of the Cornish coastline is a much more arduous walk than some would imagine, combining as it does, the ups and downs of steep wooded valleys with the ins and

outs of headlands and coves. On the other hand, habitation is normally within easy reach, a road of some sort not normally being more than a mile from the path. Route-finding is normally easy — waymarking together with the use of the appropriate 1:50 000 map usually being sufficient — though new housing or cliff-top disintegration, for example, may alter things slightly.

There are numerous places where, at low tide, beaches may be used as an alternative to the cliff-top paths, and as an extension to this, scrambling along the base of the cliffs can provide some exciting moments for those with the appropriate skills and experience.

The route is walkable at all times of year — it all depends on what you want to get out of it. Early summer provides carpets of flowers; winter a rugged desolation, while autumn and spring often exhibit sharp colours with impressive seas. Always there is something of interest. Each of the seven sections of the coast described is between about 35 and 40 miles (56–64km) long. Most people will wish to take a minimum of two days per section, depending on speed and proposed accommodation.

Marsland Mouth to Port Isaac

One glance at the OS map for this part of the coast will immediately reveal the terrain. Flat cliff tops are cleaved at regular intervals by steep and narrow valleys, whose sides are often smothered by dense and ancient oak woodland. Boulder-strewn beaches sport ragged pinnacles and bow-breaking reefs, a paradise for the wrecker (the person interested in shipwrecks) and walker alike, though hopefully the latter now well outnumbers the former.

As you move west, you pass Bude, the largest town on this stretch of the walk, and Tintagel, the other main tourist area, whose legendary association with King Arthur will always ensure its popularity. Otherwise, there are many quiet and lonely stretches where you can slow down to taste the salt in the air, feel the wind in your hair and come to terms with the natural forces that have created such a magnificent coastline.

North Devon becomes Cornwall, the journey begins — and what a beginning it is. Climbing out of Marsland Mouth, the beaches

Polperro with its sheltered harbour, jumbled houses and old inns, is a typical Cornish village. (Photo: John White.)

The overlapping rocks of the Culm coast near Bude.
(Photo: John White.)

bare their rocky teeth to our impatient backward glances and we soon appreciate the terrain to come as the first of many slim valleys has to be descended and then re-ascended. At Cornakey Cliff, you can look back on dozens of huge slabs, overlapping and beautifully juxtapositioned. The highest of them, Wrecker's Slab, sports one of the longest rock climbs in North Devon.

If you feel an attraction — a desire to descend and explore these exciting places — your feelings might well be the same as many others, for as the late Tom Patey, first ascentionist of Wrecker's Slab, wrote:

Man despite all his noble standing still bears the indelible stamp of his hairy arboreal ancestors.

If you do descend here, take care, for the ground is steep, but watch for the small wooden look-out hut, a relic of World War II, complete with drawings of aeroplane outlines and someone's now antique leather gaiters. The distant views are superb — to Bodmin Moor, Hartland Point, Lundy and the far-off hills of Wales.

Further west, Lower Sharpnose produces one of the most impressive cliff formations in Cornwall. Three enormous rectangular sheets of rock point out to sea, like huge playing cards standing on edge; beaches of giant-size circular pebbles and rocky pools separate these fins — altogether an impressive and primaeval atmosphere, which contrasts strongly with the huge radar installation seen inland. The path hereabouts offers easy walking among stringy gorse and close cropped grass and you walk easily to the holiday village of Bude, where high tidal range means impressive surfing. Easy paths close to the coastal road lead away from the climbing slabs at Compass Point to the sands of Widemouth. After dipping down into Millock, you climb out to cliff tops suffering seriously from landslip, necessitating some slight detours.

More ground of similar character leads past Crackington Haven to the headland of Cambeak, 700ft (213m) above the beach, definitely not the place for those suffering from vertigo. Some 6 miles (10km) of varied and interesting walking leads to King Arthur's Castle Hotel, a conspicuous and somewhat ugly landmark.

The site of the castle, probably first occupied

by the Romans, and subsequently with its links to King Arthur, is a major tourist attraction, and the village above the cove capitalises on these medieval links with King Arthur's this and Merlin's that. Despite this, the scenery is superb.

Whether you're an Arthur fan or not, the castle is worthy of a look round and the views are excellent.

Once away from here you can walk a much quieter section of coast, descending gentle valleys and rising onto low headlands which lead via a minor road to Port Isaac.

Port Isaac to Newquay

These 33 miles (53km) offer scenery and walking far gentler than either the savage coastline just passed or the mine-scarred cliffs and granite fortresses that lie ahead.

There are many more wide, sandy beaches. Colourful surfers skit over and in front of refreshing Atlantic rollers, the experts balancing easily — part of the board moving with the powerful flow of the water beneath them — whilst the beginners stop and start, board tips flipping skywards, outflung arms signalling exasperation and another big splash.

Lots of opportunities exist here for the walker to descend to the sands and splash barefoot in the sea to soothe aching feet. Relax for a while. Shut your eyes and savour the sounds of the same Atlantic swell that has washed the beaches and scoured the cliffs for a length of time we cannot begin to appreciate in our insignificant span.

You climb typically abruptly out of Port Isaac to Lobber Point, descending again before following the cliff edge to Port Quin. Despite a history of access problems, the way forward is now clear, passing a few pleasant coves to National Trust land at Pentire Point. The spectacular cliffs here provide some difficult modern rock climbs which combine technical difficulty with extreme seriousness and commitment.

Pentireglaze and Polzeath are excellent surfing centres and have attracted the attendant development. Perhaps the only good views here are backwards, so hurry on to the ferry at Rock, whose history goes right back to

Cliffs near Cornwall's most well-known landmark: Land's End. (Photo: John White.)

the 14th century.

The old fishing port of Padstow is now a popular resort and a good watering hole before continuing easily to Stepper Point. For a mile westwards from the 40-ft (12m) high white daymark, the cliffs are vertigo-steep and only by boat can one investigate the mysteries of the Butter, Pepper and Seal Holes.

You continue on past the natural arches of Porthmissen Bridge and on to the sands of Trevone. From the lighthouse at Trevose Head, excellent views of the far ends of the two great bays on this northern coast can be seen in clear weather — Hartland Point to the north east and the cliffs and hills of West Penwith to the south west. From here to Newquay are a succession of sandy beaches — invariably busy during the summer months. Though the path usually follows the cliff top, plenty of sea level alternatives can be found, where access and tidal conditions permit. Bedruthan Steps is one of the more well known areas hereabouts, whose rocky islets were said to have been used as stepping stones by the Cornish giant Bedruthan. Newquay has some fine beaches nearby and also provides all the amenities required for revitalising tired walkers.

Newquay to St Ives

Beyond Newquay, one of the most noticeable features is the appearance of the first mining relics of any scale. Cliff faces are often streaked with the characteristic colours of mineral deposits and specimens of ore and crystal can be found in many places.

The Gannel is crossed by ferry or bridge and

two small headlands are circumnavigated to Holywell Beach which sprouts two impressive beach pinnacles.

After the military range in Penhale, the sands of the same name contain dunes of Saharan proportions, and what may be the oldest Christain building in Britain — the church of St Piran — has been periodically lost and found amongst these drifting sands. The site is now protected by concrete walls. A buried city — Langarrow — is also said to lie here, gradually overwhelmed and finally smothered by storm and sand.

Nearby Perranporth has suffered no such fate and is another small but seasonally hectic resort.

At Cligga Head there was once a dynamite works, ironically belonging to Nobel, of Peace Prize fame. At the turn of the century this was described as 'tall chimneys, large buildings and insulating sheds of this great manufactory of high explosives . . . suspicious-looking boilers, evil-looking tanks, sinister little black sheds . . .' Little remains of these works, but the next few miles display countless relics spanning the hard years of mining. In all directions the land is studded with chimneys and other workings. Some may find strange beauty here, perhaps in mist, at dawn or dusk, but most will hurry on. The going along this stretch is easy and you should make better time than on some of the more arduous sections. The path changes direction at St Agnes Head and leads easily past yet more mines to the beach at Chapel Porth and low-tide sands to Porthtowan.

We now pass a beach islet, the Tobban Horse, before the path is defined by fencing for a good distance before Portreath Harbour. More easy going on a flat cliff top follows, with the coast road close by. Good cliff scenery exists at Hell's Mouth, one of those places close enough to a car park to allow tourists to stroll across and peer down into the void. The path crosses the Red River, whose name predictably results from coloured mining spoil from Camborne and leads onto the dune area of Upton Towans, whose backcloth of chalets and caravans may lead to neckache as you try to look west and retain some feeling of isolation. Through to St Ives is urbanisation unworthy of description.

St Ives to Penzance

More than anywhere else on the Cornish coast, here the mountains have come to the sea. Boulder-strewn, ankle-breaking moors defy their diminutive height and sweep bleakly down towards the sea, providing an often mist-shrouded and wild environment. On those grey, drizzly days when a steady Atlantic

Forceful Atlantic winds form strange tree shapes. (Photo: John White.)

The prominent mine chimney at Cape Cornwall.

wind shapes horror-story trees and the crows and gulls hover high above before wheeling away on a stiff south-westerley, this high land seems as remote and uninviting as anywhere in the country. Yet the next day could herald such a marvellous contrast: clear blue skies, heat haze rising, the skylark's melody — heaven and hell — the land of contrasts.

Down at the Atlantic, the mountain atmosphere continues. A unique combination of towering bastions of iron-hard orange granite, of sombre black-streaked greenstone, of white sun-scorched beaches, of crashing seas and barren, heather-clad cliff tops, together produce an exciting and primaeval climbing atmosphere with a dash of holiday spirit.

In front of us a cliff we would not climb
and to our right, America, sea and night.
When time and tide were flowing much too fast
and each escape seemed trickier than the last.

This quote, from A.W. Andrews, the undoubted father of British sea cliff climbing and inventor of the sea-level traverse, captures effectively the romance and sense of commitment that help make Cornish climbing so

great. Problems with tides and freak waves, with loose finishes and angry gulls somehow add to, rather than detract from, the overall climbing experience. Add to this the abundance of wildlife, from cliff top flowers to seals, puffins and falcons and the result is a melange guaranteed to excite and enthuse anyone who revels in the feel of rough rock beneath exploring fingers and toes — rock climbing in Cornwall is addictive.

This stretch of coast is also bountiful in its supply of antiquities. Iron Age hill-top promontory forts, village sites, standing stones and circles combine with more recent remnants of a once prosperous mining industry to provide many fascinating diversions for the cliff top visitor.

The names encountered here are from another age, another language — Zennor, Porthmoina, Geevor, Carn Galver, Pendeen, Morvah — these words are synonymous with the strong visual landscape conjured up by our mind's eye. They combine an image with a sense of mystique and romance from another era. Much of Cornwall, and this part in particular, seems truly to be another country.

15

Rock pinnacles at Land's End.
(Photo: John White.)

How sad then that recent closures in the local mining industry and the inevitable job losses have probably heralded the end of an era in Cornish history and the termination of a way of life for so many. The other alternative industry — tourism — merely relies on the wealth of others, it does not create wealth, and the future for many of these north-coast villages with their sombre granite block houses seems as bleak as the wind-blasted moor tops.

Let's stretch our legs. Out of St Ives, it is uphill and over the Greenstone Cliffs to Wicca Pool, where a 60-ft (18m) granite intrusion forms the impressive Wicca Pillar. The path continues, past Zennor and Gunnard's Head, the site of an Iron Age promontory fort. At Gunnard's Head, the cliffs form a mighty corner whose bottom drops away into a black, Atlantic-scoured cave. Climbers call the route up this corner Right Angle — look out for it — you won't mistake its stark cuboid presence.

The next impressive headland is at Bosigran, perhaps the most popular climbing area along the north coast, although much of it is not strictly a sea cliff, as its base is way above sea level. Just west of the main cliff, a long jagged ridge — Commando Ridge — runs down into the foam. The name gives away its past as one of the popular training climbs for commandoes in years gone by. Just beyond this is Great Zawn. This is an impressive place: vertical walls, a grand scale and that continuous booming as the great Atlantic swell continues its utterly timeless motion. Near the road here is another remnant of the mining industry — the Count House (now a climbing hut), said to be haunted by a woman's screaming voice, and at least one completely rational and previously disbelieving climber has elected to camp outside rather than spend another night in its barren rooms.

This spectacular coast continues to impress. In the distance is Pendeen Lighthouse, while above Morvah stands a superb Iron Age fort — Chûn Castle — whose ramparts and ditches have a diameter of 280ft (85m).

The next stretch of coastline is real mining country. Copper, tin, arsenic and tungsten have all been extracted from these steep, slaty cliffs. The resulting landscape is a combination of nature's proud architecture and man's equally proud, but destructive domination and exploitation of her riches. Folliott-Stoke wrote this about his visit, years ago:

Descending the valley, we climb the opposite hill, past mud and miners, arsenic fumes and tramlines, till we reach the top. But the face of the land is still marred and rendered hideous by mining operations. The path winds bravely westwards, but no longer through flowers and ferns, but over a stunted and blasted heath or common, almost denuded of vegetation, and punctuated with little dynamite sheds, whose lightning conductors clatter in the breeze, and unsightly refuse heaps of rock and clay.

The evidence is there and you will judge for yourself the resulting landscape, but for me it is strangely compelling, dramatically impressive in places, yet at the same time soberingly dismal.

The path continues past the prominent mine chimney at Cape Cornwall. Inland is the town of St Just — a good stopping point if that is required, with plenty of good pubs and adequate shopping facilities.

Soon, the huge Whitesand Bay of Sennen is revealed. If the tide allows, it's about time some beachwalking was done — though in high summer you'll have to pick a way through scantily clad bodies and surf boards. Sennen village is attractive, featuring typical stoutly constructed granite cottages and an interesting round building.

Past Sennen, a good path leads to the most popular pilgrimage in Cornwall — Land's End with its perpendicular cliffs, jutting and ragged promontories and islands ringed white with angry water. A magnificent finish (or start) to any country. Perhaps it is as well to hurry past, or at least turn one's back to the cliff top developments here, inevitable though they are, and turn this south-westward tip of England, following now south-eastwards along one of our finest stretches of coastline.

The cliff tops are often sparsely vegetated, only scrubby gorse, and tough salt and wind-resistant species standing up to the extreme climate. Fine headlands alternate with superb sunny coves and tiny villages. This is a place for some 'coasteering' if your experience and skills allow it. Get off the path. Hop skip and jump along the cliff bottom, between crystal pools and orange boulders. Taste adventure, find some solitude, but — be careful. On the south coast of West Penwith, Porthgwarra and Porthcurno are two of the most popular places, and rightly so, but they may be very busy during the summer.

Continuing east, the landscape becomes quieter and more secluded with one of the warmest micro-climates in Britain. Gradually everything becomes gentler and less stark, until the towns of Newlyn and Penzance are reached. There's no doubt in my mind that you'll have just walked one of the finest stretches of coastline in Britain.

Penzance to Helford River

Beyond Penzance, you leave behind the granite which you have followed around the most westerly tip of England and encounter a new series of igneous and metamorphosed rocks — horneblende schist, serpentine, gabbro — each rock type producing a characteristic landscape. This part of the coast is both varied and attractive with at least one site — Kynance Cove — among the most popular in the area. One worthwhile diversion from Penzance is a boat trip to the Isles of Scilly, or for the more affluent, a helicopter trip. These islands offer wonderfully varied cliff top walks similar to, but perhaps better than, their mainland counterparts.

The beaches east of Penzance offer a gentle start to the day with views out across the bay past St Michael's Mount towards the Lizard. Unfortunately, if you are getting a good view, the chances are that you will end up getting wet, for as the local saying goes: 'When the Lizard is clear, rain is near'. So, hopefully the view will be good, but fall just short of the Lizard and you can expect a good day!

The going remains easy: low cliffs (notorious smuggler's retreats) at Cudden Point separate beaches at Perran and Praa Sands and we pass the last granite crags at Trewavas Head. Beyond the fishing village of Porthleven the path overlooks extensive sands for quite a way, passing the shingle banks at Loe Bar. A few more miles bring you to the start of a particularly fine stretch of coastal scenery. Mullion Cove is well visited and justifiably so. The cliffs nearby are torn and contorted, streaked with lichen and exhibit fine arches, gloomy caves and soaring ridges.

The cliff tops are carpeted in May and June with a colourful mosaic which fades to sparse heathland, increasingly black as the year proceeds. The headlands are higher here and receive the full blast of the Atlantic southerlies, indeed a wild day when salt-laden spray whips across the scrubby gorse and heather, is the right day to continue past the dramatic precipices at Pigeon Ogo, and to marvel at the severity and power of nature's forces.

Our next point of note is Kynance Cove; both spectacular in an aggressive way and yet gently beautiful. It is desperately popular and walkers should come here early or late to find any peace and quiet. Soon, you turn the Lizard, passing the lighthouse and then turn north on heavily used paths.

At Cadgwith is the Devil's Frying Pan, a mighty funnel hole, and the cliff has other caves, usually invisible to the cliff top walker. Across the bay is Black Head, where you turn north again and eventually come to the last headland before Helford River which provides a quieter and more vegetated end to some impressive scenery.

Helford River to Par

One outstanding feature of this part of the south coast is the ria-named Carrick Roads at Falmouth. Its tributaries forge bluntly inland like the knotted branches of an old oak, and it shelters the town of Falmouth. A regular ferry operates here, but at Helford River and Portcuil River, swimsuits might be useful out of season. There is only one cliff of any height, at Nare Head, and this section ends at Par, where huge factories and works associated with the china-clay operations spoil the land-scape and produce one of the few eyesores along the south coast.

Once across the river at Helford, a few miles of good path, passing fine views at Rosemull-ion Head, lead along Falmouth Bay and into the town. On both sides of the river mouth are ancient fortifications (Pendennis Castle and St Mawes Castle), built to command strategic artillery positions over the port entrance. A pleasant and regular ferry journey takes us across to St Mawes where the next crossing to Place Manor can take place if the ferry is running.

The path almost completes a circle here at Zone Point (one of the many National Trust holdings near here), and continues along the coast edge, easily to Portscatho. A lazy, sandy bay lies ahead, reached over some mediocre cliffs, and providing a pleasant lunching venue with views out to Nare Head. This curving shark's tooth promontory is over 300ft (90m) high, and offshore, its fine lines are comple-mented by the ridges and towers of Gull Rock. A couple of miles of distinctive views from the lofty headland path leads to the tiny village of Portloe, and a similar distance to beaches and sparse habitation of West and East Portholland.

A straightforward, but meandering cliff top route leads slowly to the second great point of this area, Dodman Point. A tall granite cross tops the 370-ft (113m) cliffs — a conspicuous landmark — and traces of ancient banks and ditches, the tell-tale marks of forgotten defences can be seen across its neck. On a clear day, the views are wide, from Bodmin Moor to the china-clay workings known as the Cornish Alps, to Eddystone Lighthouse and Black

Head on the Lizard.

Turning north-west you pass two more prominent points before reaching the fishing village of Mevagissey, which doubles as a popular tourist resort — the only one of its type on this part of the walk. Despite its popularity, it is still worth looking around, especially just out of season.

There are some minor cliffs in this region, a few shallow caves, and much of the rock is dark, creating a gloomy atmosphere in anything but bright weather. A mile and a half out of Mevagissey you take a slight detour by road before crossing St Austell River, which has a rather grubby reputation, as it has been subjected to pollution for over a hundred years.

Beyond the river is another of those quieter, more remote sections, a fitting contrast to the coming intrusions of holiday camps, hotels, and china-clay works. Put your blinkers on and stride purposefully — somewhere ahead is another stretch of beautiful coast — honestly!

Par to Plymouth

This may well be the last part of the coast you will walk. As such, it is a gentle wind-down to an arduous journey, but equally, as a start, it provides a good warm-up, toning the legs and easing the body into that steady rhythm that makes the going pleasurable and easy. Much of the scenery is less dramatic than the north coast, but it has its compensations: much of this walk is secluded, with interesting flora and good views.

Once away from Par, things improve rapidly. A small fishing village at Polkerris has a handy if somewhat cluttered pub, and we now walk due south to Gribbin Head, which thrusts out ahead of the eastern cliff line and provides an excellent vantage point. This is a sheltered coast with a calm and balmy climate. At Fowey, a regular ferry takes us to Polruan. The few miles that follow to Polperro are quiet. The cliffs are high, but often without that dramatic verticality of other areas. Wildlife is abundant. Sea birds of many types are in evidence and the spring and summer flora is both plentiful and varied, due to a sunny aspect and reasonably rich soil.

The closer we get to Polperro, the more heavily used the paths, inevitably, due to the status of this exemplary Cornish fishing vil-lage. Full of tourists, gift shops, Cornish pasties and piskies of course, it is still charmingly attractive, with its sheltered har-bour, jumbled houses and old, old inns. Perhaps mid-November or mid-February would be the ideal time to visit here, but at any time of year it is easy to head east and leave the

Facing page, top: **Kynance Cove is both spectacular in an aggressive way and yet also gently beautiful.** (Photo: John White.)

Facing page, bottom: **Cape Cornwall.**

18

bustle behind.

A well-signed and well-used path continues the journey towards Looe, which is still a viable and busy fishing village, with shark fishing as a speciality. A short detour at the east end of the town leads back to the cliff tops. The scenery is distinctive. There are more trees. Bracken and other luxuriant growth smothers the cliff tops, altogether a more overgrown and jumbled aspect than many of the wind-blasted cliff tops with their stunted vegetation further west.

High tide means taking the coast road here, but past Downderry we ease off the highway to Battern Cliff, the highest on the south coast at over 450ft (617m). Past Portwrinkle, a detour is in order to avoid rifle ranges, and you rejoin the cliff edge at Tregantle Down.

As you move east, you will become aware of an increase in habitation. Plymouth makes itself known: holiday homes and chalets, caravans and tents. It's easy if this is the end of the walk, to feel it is an anti-climax. Best, perhaps to dwell on the many pleasures you have enjoyed along the way, than the immediate scenery, for this is an extremely pleasurable walk, and although, when you finish you will be tired, you will be tired but satisfied. The Cornish coast has something for everyone; I hope like me, you found that something.

SOUTHERN ENGLAND: The Two Moors Way by Bill Birkett

The Route

Day 1: Ivybridge to Scoriton (12mls, 19km) via Ugborough Moor, Quickbeam Hill, Hickaton Hill.

Day 2: Scoriton to Teigncombe (19mls, 13km) via Holne, Spitchwick Manor, Ponsworthy, Jordan, Hameldown Beacon, Hookney Tor, Chagford Common, Frenchbeer.

Day 3: Teigncombe to Morchard Bishop (21mls, 34km) via Drewsteignton, Hittisleigh Cross, Newbury, Whelmstone Barton.

Day 4: Morchard Bishop to Knowstone (13mls, 21km) via Washford Pyne, Witheridge, North Backstone.

Day 5: Knowstone to Withypool (12mls, 19km) via Anstey, Hawkridge, Tarr Steps.

Day 6: Withypool to Lynmouth (16mls, 26km) via Wintershead Farm, Barcombe, Exe Head, Cheriton Ridge.

The Walk

The most popular image of the two moors, Dartmoor and Exmoor, is one of windswept desolation, of driving snow and lonely stranded farmhouses, of swirling mists and ghoulish hounds. The reality is somewhat more pleasant and these two high moors, stretching through Devon from the English to the Bristol Channel, have a lot to offer the rambler. Dartmoor is the most southerly of the two and contains the greater area of high ground with the highest point being Yes Tor at about 2230ft

Ponies grazing on Dartmoor.

Left: **On a grassy path, surrounded by ferns, my companion John Hargreaves, pauses to admire the view.**

Top: **The engraved stone which marks the beginning of The Two Moors Way.**

Above: **A red admiral butterfly alights on some cow parsley.**

Facing page, top: **John Hargreaves carefully closes the gate as he approaches the moors.**

Facing page, bottom: **Crossing some stepping stones below Butterdon Hill on Dartmoor.**

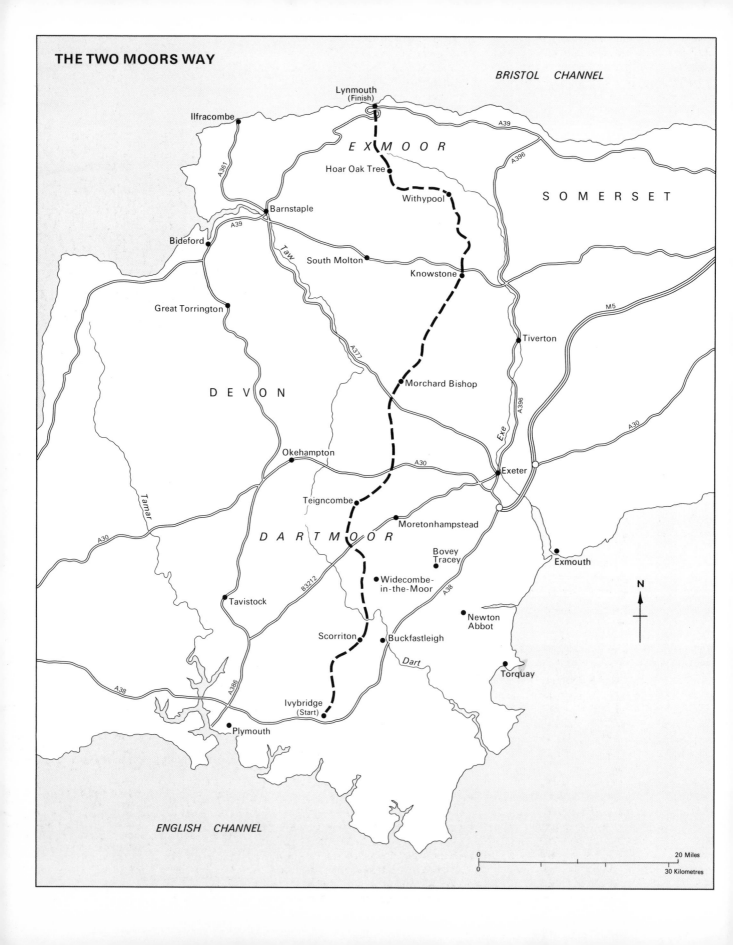

THE TWO MOORS WAY

BRISTOL CHANNEL

Lynmouth (Finish)

Ilfracombe

E X M O O R

Hoar Oak Tree

Withypool

S O M E R S E T

A39

A396

Barnstaple

Bideford

A39

Taw

South Molton

Knowstone

M5

Great Torrington

Tiverton

D E V O N

A377

Exe

A396

A30

Okehampton

A30

Morchard Bishop

Exeter

Teigncombe

Moretonhampstead

Tamar

A30

D A R T M O O R

Bovey Tracey

Exmouth

B3212

Widecombe-in-the-Moor

A38

Newton Abbot

Tavistock

Scorriton

Buckfastleigh

Dart

Torquay

A38

A386

Ivybridge (Start)

Plymouth

ENGLISH CHANNEL

N

0   20 Miles
0   30 Kilometres

(680m). Exmoor is more agricultural but there is still much high ground, the highest point being Dunkery Hill at 1704ft (519m).

Despite the presence of modern roads and our advanced communications these two moors of the south west remain essentially undiscovered. They also remain two separate and very different entities, the character of one being quite different to that of the other. To illustrate this we need look no further than the wild Exmoor and Dartmoor ponies: both are hardy and adapted to their particular environment yet they are genealogically two different animals, originating from different global locations.

The lanes of Devon are narrow and wooded and for those who remain on them, much will be hidden. On the heights, and generally remaining unseen by the average tourist, the rock is granite which forms the twisted and rugged tors. Its slabs span the streams to form the clapper bridges and man has used them to construct an endless quantity of circles and avenues of pre-history. The best, indeed the only real way to explore this fascinating hidden world is to walk through it.

The Two Moors Way guides you over the high ground and through ivy-clad trees; past mysterious crosses, over clapper bridges and finally it drops you down to a charming little fishing village all but hidden at the bottom of a deep-cut gorge. I have suggested a period of six days to walk from Ivybridge to Lynmouth, to feel the wind in your hair, smell the honeysuckle and pass the quaint thatched cob cottages. Six days during which to discover the freedom of the real Devon.

Day 1: Ivybridge to Scoriton

I couldn't really find anything attractive about Ivybridge — it was too big and industrialized for my taste. But as you pull rapidly up to gain the high ground of Ugborough Moor your world changes. A leafy lane with a healthy preponderance of mature oak gives way to open moorland, a fresh breeze and a tremendous sense of freedom.

We aimed for Western Beacon and from it can be seen Plymouth Sound and the rolling patchwork of friendly English countryside below. As you move up and along to Butterdon Hill only the watchfulness of the standing stones breaks the solitude. These stones in straight lines and circles abound, and have a sense of omnipotence about them. What purpose did they serve? Why are there so many? The moors are full of mystery even on the sunniest and most attractive days.

Along the stone avenue to Piles Hill you pass on the left the curiously named Hangershell

Rock and as likely as not you will encounter the wild Dartmoor ponies. Gentle and rolling, the moor is enjoyable in the sunshine, and an exhilarating place to be in the cold and wind.

On this journey you will pass many stone crosses and the first one is Hobajon's Cross. I was just waiting for the sun to move a fraction for the maximum photographic effect when a healthy looking gentleman with white hair and a stout stick walked passed. With a thick Devonian accent he enquired if we knew the whereabouts of Spurrell's Cross. It transpired that he was looking for a letterbox.

The original Dartmoor letterbox was at Cranmere Pool. It was founded in 1850, the idea being that anyone not wanting to take a letter or message the long trek to an official posting box would leave it at this special letterbox, and the next person who passed by would pick it up and post it for them. Today there are over two thousand of these letterboxes around the moor and each box has its own unique stamp. The idea is that you search for and discover these boxes and stamp your own book. When you have collected a hundred different stamps you can join the One Hundred Letterbox Club, and you are allowed to use your own personal stamp. So you not only mark your own record book but also get to stamp the book that is left in the letterbox.

With our enthusiastic friend we searched for and found the Hobajon Letterbox (a plastic container hidden in the rocks) and he stamped the book. His stamp was a cartoon face with eyes and big nose looking over the top of a brick wall. Other amusing stamps included Tamerton Treacle Mines, Baskervilles Hound, The Radon Sniffers, The Saltash Stampers, The Exeter Heather Hackers and the Wide Mouth Toad.

Days 2–3: Scoriton to Morchard Bishop

This is quite a strenuous day and there are many hills to climb and descend. Many will drop down to visit Widdecombe-in-the-Moor because of the famous happenings the day the devil called. One Sunday when the village was at church a thunderbolt struck the spire and it crashed through the roof. There were a number of fatalities and the local population are still convinced it was the work of the devil himself. So take care on those deserted and lonely moors!

You follow a short section of the original Mariner's Way which in the times of sail, took seafarers in search of a berth, overland from Dartmouth to Bideford. On the second day most of the route lies in the valley of the river Teign and it is necessary to follow lanes as far

Hobajon's Cross, one of the many stone crosses you will encounter on the Two Moors Way.

The Walk: A long distance walk over Dartmoor and Exmoor, Devon, (South-West England).
Maps: OS L202, L191, L181, L180, T1-Dartmoor, T5-Exmoor.
Start: Ivybridge on A38 (map ref: SX 636563).
Finish: Lynmouth (map ref: SS 724494).
Length: 93mls (150km).
Approx Time: 6 days.
Difficulty: The high moorland sections are mildly strenuous.
Access: Car.
Seasons: April to December.
Observations: A walk through England's two most famous high moors to discover secret Devon. The moors are notoriously dangerous in poor visibility and inclement weather — they should never be underestimated.
Accommodation: Inns and bed and breakfast accommodation.
Guidebooks: *Two Moors Way* by H. Rowett (Devon Ramblers Association).

25

Hangershell Rock is passed en route to Piles Hill.

as Chagford Bridge. You also pass the last castle to be built in England: Castle Drogo which was constructed between 1911 and 1920.

The A30 just north of Drewsteignton marks the boundary of the Dartmoor National Park. Now you discover the undulating agricultural land, networked with narrow lanes and footpaths, of mid-Devon. The house at Whelmstone Barton is typical of the area, dating back to the 17th century. It has a thatched roof, brick chimneys and a host of features that make this style of building so attractive — more so than today's buildings which so often seem to lack this degree of 'homeliness'. From the churchyard at Morchard Bishop there are views of both Dartmoor and Exmoor.

Days 3–6: Morchard Bishop to Lynmouth

Fairly dull going to start with, this part of the walk gives views to the horizons of Dartmoor and Exmoor. The boundary of the Exmoor National Park runs just north of West Anstey. Before this, at Washford Pyne the church of St Peter has a richly carved screen but outside there are many muddy paths and lanes. The centre of Witheridge is a Conservation Area and a number of scheduled buildings border the picturesque square. They consist of plastered rubble and cob (a mixture of mud and straw) and have either slate roofs or are thatched.

Once the boundary is passed the scenery and countryside become somewhat more inter-

esting. Dane's Brook at Slade separates Somerset from Devon and, interestingly north of this, bulls are allowed alongside public rights of way as long as they are with cows. In my experience bulls, with cows or without cows should be avoided at all costs.

The upland area is liberally splashed with heather, bracken and gorse and with the tree cover provided makes a very good area for the red deer. The section across the Tarr Steps and along the Barle valley is heavily wooded and delightful. The Tarr Steps is the largest clapper bridge on this walk and is a famous beauty spot — best avoided on a summer weekend!

The last day covers ground that is somewhat wilder and higher than the preceding section of Exmoor. You pass the Exe Head which is the very start of the river Exe. It seems strange that it should be only a short distance from the Bristol Channel, when it actually drains into the English Channel almost a hundred miles away. Shortly after this stands Hoar Oak Tree on the east bank of the Hoar Oak Water, which acts as a marker of the present day boundary between Somerset and Devon and was once the limit of the ancient Exmoor Forest. Today it is protected from grazing by a fence and replaces a similar tree known to be 200 years of age which was blown over in 1916.

Cheriton Ridge is the high ground between the valleys that are now Hoar Oak Water and Farley Water. There are a number of hut circles and cairns, but for most, thoughts will lie ahead to Lynmouth and completion of this little trip of discovery. The descent to Lynmouth is steep but despite its popularity with tourists, it is a village of great character. You will stroll onto the sea front past the huddle of attractive little sailing craft, and view the large cliffs of the coast. Maybe you will be in time to see the sun dipping in a pool of gold below the distant horizon. In the rapidly gathering dark as you turn to seek shelter, perhaps you will notice that even the pubs are thatched here in North Devon.

SOUTHERN ENGLAND: The South Downs Way by Bill Birkett

Looking east from Ditchling Beacon.

The Route

Day 1: Eastbourne to Rodmell, 19mls (30km).

Day 2: Rodmell to Castle Town, 21mls (34km).

Day 3: Castle Town to Houghton, 17mls (27km).

Day 4: Houghton to Buriton, 25mls (40km).

The Walk

Officially sanctioned in 1972 this was the first long distance path to be also classed a bridleway along its entire length. It takes the long chalk ridge that starts with the large white cliffs of Beachy Head and the Seven Sisters, and follows the northern escarpment of the chalk downs. This track gives an exposed, and often breezy walk with extensive views across the rounded hills and dry valleys to the sea looking south, and across the Weald to the north. The way I recommend here is to go over Beachy Head and the Seven Sisters rather than taking the inland route.

There are a number of energetic ascents chiefly when crossing the valleys of the river. Cuckmere at Alfriston, the Ouse at Southease, the Adur south of Bramber and the Arun at Amberley. Otherwise, apart from the hard and occasionally sharp flints, the walking is straightforward. Care must be exercised along the coastal tops.

The Way is an ancient track and was

certainly used by Stone Age Man; their worked and shaped flints have been found along the path and it is not an impossibility that you may find one also. The Romans and the Saxons cultivated the rich farming lands near the downs and evidence of their passing can also be seen. Today the crops of barley, oats, wheat and maize abound.

After Alfriston you climb up onto what are known as the whalebacks of the Downs and these continue to Southease. Heading north and inland the Way now crosses the A27 Brighton road and then the A23 near Pyecombe. Then you climb Devil's Dyke, Edburton Hill and Truleigh Hill before dropping down into the Alder Valley.

The next landmark of some significance is Chanctonbury Ring before the rises of Bury Hill, Bignor Hill, Burton Down, Woolavington Down, Graffham Down lead to the A286 south of Cocking. Finally you cross Linch Down, Philliswood Down and Beacon Hill and on to the finish.

Days 1–4: Eastbourne to Buriton

Beachy Head and the Seven Sisters are spectacularly high cliffs and in many respects this first section is the highlight of the walk. Ironically for this famous English landmark, the word Beachy is said to derive from the French *beau chef* and means beautiful headland. As you look from the top, the solitary lighthouse beneath looks very small indeed; the cliffs here are over 500ft high (160m) and are sheer.

Be careful because the chalk road is extremely crumbly and I would advise you to keep well clear of the edge. A little further along, the Seven Sisters present a magnificent sight and are aesthetically pleasing as they roll along, pure white, above the English Channel.

Although not strictly on the recommended route, there is a famous and mysterious sight that only requires a slight deviation backtracking from the Cuckmere valley: the Long Man of Wilmington. He stands on the northern slopes of Windover Hill, a prehistoric figure of some distinction. He doesn't actually appear to be very ancient, holding his ski poles upright in each hand, but they say his 240-ft (73m) high frame is thousands of years old. Incidentally it is also thought that he is the largest representation of a human being in the world.

As you start along the whalebacks and climb

Looking from Birling Gap along the chalk cliffs of the Seven Sisters.

Above: **Looking west across the valley of the Ouse to the ridge beyond.**

Facing page, top: **The Long Man at Wilmington.**

Facing, page, bottom: **Looking north from Ditchling Beacon.**

up from Alfriston there are a few potential hazards which should be pondered upon. Firstly there are snakes to be found on these chalklands; grass snakes, slow-worms (strictly speaking not actually a snake) and adders. Although only the adder is venomous you would have to be extremely unlucky to be bitten by one as they prefer to stay well clear of the much more dangerous species known as Homo sapien. However despite the well publicised guidelines, that adders have a V on the head and zigzags running down the back and mature grass snakes are the larger of the two species, I find it in practice extremely difficult to distinguish between the two. The rule is be vigilant and if you are lucky enough to see a snake then leave it alone.

Totally innocuous to look at, but deadly to eat, is the round black and shiny berry of deadly nightshade. This spindly plant, growing to a metre in height with purple bell flowers, is all poisonous, and in reality is a much more serious hazard than that of a chance encounter with an adder.

Two real problems that you will most likely encounter are generated by the physical prop-

erties of these chalk uplands. Firstly there is an acute shortage of water and secondly, even on a sunny day, there may well be blowing a chilly wind. Carry water and ensure you have a windproof with you as there is little shelter to be found in the ensuing miles.

After the cornfields the path cuts straight across the grasslands and then, after passing Jerry's Bottom, a stony path climbs Bostal Hill; bostal apparently being an original Sussex name meaning hill path. As witness to the difficulty in obtaining water on these heights you also pass New Pond — a dew pond and one of many to be seen on this walk.

The third highest point of the downs, and an exposed and windy hill, is Ditchling Beacon, reaching an altitude of 814 ft (248m). Breached by a road there is a large car park which usually sports an ice-cream van. Who can resist its decadent charm? The trig point has a plaque naming the features to be seen over the Weald; Crowborough Beacon 15 miles, the Caburn 5 miles, Firle Beacon 11 miles and Chanctonbury Ring 12 miles.

Near Clayton Mills there are two windmills known as Jack and Jill. Interestingly Jill, the

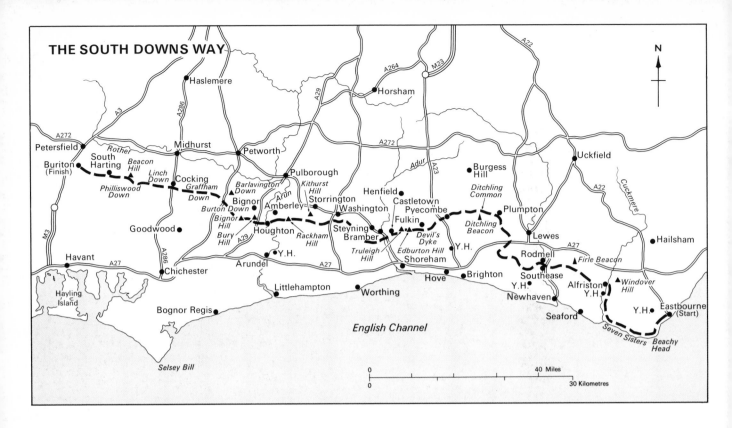

THE SOUTH DOWNS WAY

The Walk: A long distance footpath taking the chalk ridge that begins at Beachy Head and continues along through the South Downs.

Maps: OS L199, L198, L197.

Start: Eastbourne (map ref: TV 598983).

Finish: Buriton, Hants/Sussex border (map ref: SU 740200).

Waymarks: Signposts and concrete plinths with acorn plaques.

Length: 82mls (132km).

Approx Time: 4 days (only the fittest walkers will achieve this schedule).

Difficulty: No particular difficulty.

Access: Car.

Seasons: All year.

Observations: A route, that may be backpacked, following the northern escarpments of the chalk downs. The flinty paths can be hard on the feet and there is no shelter from the wind.

Accommodation: Inns, bed and breakfast establishments and rough camping en route.

Guidebooks: *Along the South Downs Way to Winchester* by Eastbourne Rambling Club, *South Downs Way* by Sean Jennett (HMSO), *The South Downs Way* by H.D. Westacott and M. Richards (Penguin), *The South Downs Way* by Y.H.A., *South Downs Way Public Transport Guide* by West Sussex CC.

white wooden one, was built in Patcham near Brighton in 1821 and was moved across the downs (pulled by a team of oxen) to occupy its present position. Jack, made of brick, is a mere youngster and was constructed in 1876.

After Saddlescombe the Devil's Dyke provides one of the most striking natural features to be found on this South Downs Way. Deep and dry, the story is that it was dug by the Devil to let the sea enter and drown all the Christian churches on the Weald.

Rising from the valley formed by the river Adur we pass the Horsham stone roof of the ancient Annington Farm and the Georgian fronted Annington Manor. A Saxon spearhead was found on Coombe head in 1847 and now it bears a clump of trees. But it is the great Chanctonbury Ring, a prehistoric oval earthwork with a Romano-Celtic temple in the centre, that sports the largest circle of trees for which it is justifiably famed. The beeches, ash, sycamore and pines can be seen from some 38 miles (61km) distance and were planted by Charles Goring in 1760. He lived to an old age and saw his trees grow from seedlings. At eighty-five he penned the following:

> How oft around thy Ring, sweet Hill,
> A Boy, I used to play,
> And form my plans to plant thy top
> On some auspicious day.

Bignor Hill belongs to the National Trust and as we leave it we cross the Roman Stane Street. This was an important Roman road and linked London to Chichester. On the map it can be seen to follow the shortest route to Chichester in the typically dead straight line of the Romans. Down in Bignor there is a Roman villa with mosaic floors proving the Romans did have some aspirations for the ornate; they just liked to keep their walks as short as possible!

Above Littleton Farm you climb to the highest point of the downs. Crown Tegleaze is wooded and its height is 837ft (255m) above sea level. Some fine blackberries can be had not far from here in late September.

Nearing the end of the walk at Treyford Hill you pass the south end of a line of five Bronze Age bell barrows and these are named the Devil's Jumps. Afterwards we find some tall beech trees. The going is as it has been for many a mile — chalky and stony. But at the end of it all you drop down to Buriton by the Maple Inn, where if you've timed it right refreshment is available.

SOUTHERN ENGLAND: The Saxon Shore Way by Bill Birkett

The Route

Day 1: Gravesend to Strood (19mls, 31km) via Shornmead Fort, Cliffe, Cooling, Northward Hill (heronry), Fenn Street, Hoo and Upnor.

Day 2: Strood to Kingsferry (18mls, 29km) via Rochester, Chatham, Gillingham, Motney Hill, Ham Green and Lower Halstow.

Day 3: Kingsferry to Faversham (20mls, 32km) via Sittingbourne, Conyer and Oare.

Day 4: Faversham to Herne Bay (14mls, 23km) via Nagden Marsh, Cleve Marsh, Seasalter, Whitstable and Swalecliffe.

Day 5: Herne Bay to Sandwich (18mls, 29km) via Reculver, Marshside, Stourmouth, Plucks Gutter and Richborough.

Day 6: Sandwich to Dover (15mls, 24km) via Deal, Kingsdown and St Margaret's Bay.

Day 7: Dover to Hythe (13mls, 21km) via Folkestone and Sandgate.

Day 8: Hythe to Ham Street (12mls, 19km) via West Hythe, Court-At-Street, Aldington and Horton Green.

Day 9: Ham Street to Rye (12mls, 19km) via Warehorne, Appledore, Isle of Oxney, Iden Lock and Walland Marsh.

The Walk

At the foot of Britain and heel shaped, the south east has anchored England in times of both peace and war. In peace its ports provide

Fishing boats at Rye greet you at the end of The Saxon Shore Way.

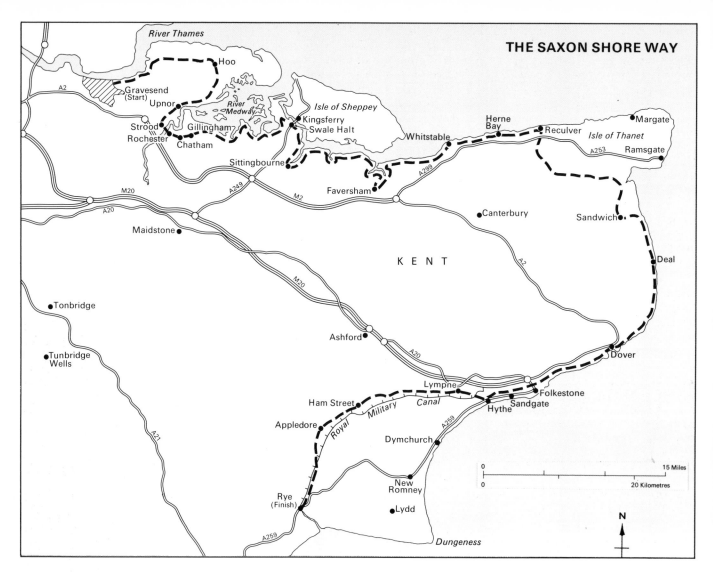

THE SAXON SHORE WAY

The Walk: The Saxon Shore Way is a long distance walk following the coastline of south-east England as it was in Roman times. It lies mainly in Kent, starting on the south bank of the river Thames — 26 miles (42km) downstream of London Bridge — and ends in Sussex. The route follows the chain of coastal defences erected against the Saxons and includes the Roman forts of Reculver, Richborough, Dover and Lympne.
Maps: OS L177, L178, L179, L189.
Start: Gravesend (map ref: TQ 646740).
Finish: Rye (map ref: TQ 918205).
Waymarks: Red-horned Viking helmets on concrete and wooden posts and on gates.
Length: 140mls (225km).
Approx Time: 9 days.
Difficulty: Level walking on reasonable paths, tracks and roads. Route finding requires attention in places.
Access: Rail, bus or car.
Seasons: All year.
Observations: A route of some variety and contrast following and crossing sea walls, marshes, woods, fields, large chalk cliffs, towns and industrialized areas. It is a walk rich in history and, for many, this will be its predominant interest.
Accommodation: Plentiful — grand hotels, pubs, bed and breakfast establishments and youth hostels.
Guidebooks: *Saxon Shore Way* by Kent Area Ramblers Association.

the vital trading link between Britain and the nearby continent. In war its fortifications and fighting men have formed a resilient buffer zone to protect London, the heart and capital of the great country.

This walk follows the coastline from Gravesend, on the south shore of the Thames Estuary, to traverse the line of the defiant Saxon Shore. It takes in the Medway Towns, skirts the Isle of Thanet along the Wantsum, and continues through Dover and Folkestone eventually to touch the edge of Romney Marsh before it moves along to Rye. It's hard to accurately assess the character of this walk in a single word or even a sentence. It starts and lies mainly in Kent, the garden of England, but finishes at Rye in Sussex, both towns having the distinction of being razed to the ground by the French in 1377.

It is a walk of contrasts: parts are coastal and parts are rural; sometimes it is forlorn and desolate and sometimes a hive of activity; parts are historical with forts and castles; parts are industrial, of grime and abandonment but sometimes clean and efficient; parts are urban old and new. Without doubt it is predominantly a walk of humanisation.

Before the Roman came to Rye or out to Severn Strode,
The rolling English drunkard made the rolling English road,
A reeling road, a rolling road, that rambles round the shire,
And after him the parson ran, the Sexton and the Squire;
A merry road, a mazy road, and such as we did tread
The night we went to Birmingham by way of Beachy Head.*

Don't start this walk expecting breathtaking scenery. Rather, treat it as a rich voyage through history. Look for what has been and, before you set out, learn a little about the areas through which you are ready to travel. There is a rich tapestry to be seen and its interpretation is up to you. Areas of quiet and frail beauty will be revealed — enhanced by their unexpectedness.

For those of us who originate in the north there are a number of surprises in store. Firstly, the air temperature is noticeably more equitable than the norm experienced elsewhere, and secondly, the crops and rich fields of fruit are bountiful, equalling those of foreign lands.

Geologically the land is chalk and we pass flat flint beaches and towering white chalk cliffs. For those who like to potter along the beach note that, mixed with the plastic bric-a-brac, fossils, marcasite and amber can be found.

This walk can be tackled in nine days (although many will wish to take longer), and I have divided up the stages accordingly. Of course there are no hard and fast rules and on such a walk, which is never far from civilisation, you can really tackle it how you please. Accommodation and transport are frequently to hand but you must still walk and be prepared for all the little hardships and practicalities of this fact.

Day 1: Gravesend to Strood

A long and fairly arduous day; take care not to get blisters! Throughout you will experience many different sights and sounds and gain, on this premier day, an appreciation of the remarkable contrasts of this Saxon Way.

I wasn't in the best of spirits at Gravesend; cities do not agree with me, and I was more than a little apprehensive as I neared Father Thames. Then the sun came out and I arrived at the start to find tugs and barges chugging cheerily up and down, and I felt better. It was a stirring sight and, as I proceeded along, the industry generated by the great river predominated. Even the power station, half a mile away, on the northern banks seems to have a majestic bearing. It is 26 miles (41km) from here to London Bridge and traditionally this is where the many ships take on a pilot before proceeding up river.

For there is good yet to hear and fine things to be seen,
Before we go to Paradise by way of Kensal Green.*

Cliffe Fort comes and goes and you're now in quite a different world: lowland marshes and open spaces, fields and crops. Shornmead Fort is surrounded by trees and over on the far side of the river is Tilbury where the mutiny of the Nore was instigated in 1797. The reason for the mutiny was the conditions aboard the ship.

The sailors protested about their conditions but the mutiny was unsuccessful and inevitably the leaders and trouble makers were whipped or hanged and the men resumed their duties.

Cooling Castle has an impressive turreted entrance, and around the sides, through the foliage, the solid walls continue. It was the subject of a determined attack by Sir Thomas Wyatt in 1554, who was rather upset with Mary and her Catholic connections. The castle held good and Sir Thomas was eventually disposed of, but not before he had helped Queen Elizabeth.

In many ways an even more powerful image is the sight of the graves in Cooling churchyard. As Dickens describes those of Pip's brothers and sisters in *Great Expectations*, so you can see the sad reality in those miniature stone graves.

The graves at Cooling churchyard which reminded me of those described in Dickens' *Great Expectations*.

Fruit trees — pears and apples in particular — are in abundance. Enjoy the sunshine and let your mind drift towards thoughts of nature and away from the follies of man. Kent truly is the garden of England and it's possible to see why W.P. Haskett Smith, the father of British rock climbing and explorer of the world's high places, regarded it as his favourite English county. At High Halstow the R.S.P.B. maintain the largest heronry in Europe, and if you are lucky you might see one of these huge birds flying off to enjoy his fishing.

At last you sight the Medway and note the pleasant nature of the boating village of Upnor where the steep street falls into the river. You can either stop in Strood or go over the river to the Roman-influenced town of Rochester, depending on your pocket or your taste.

Overleaf, top: **Cooling Castle and its impressive turreted entrance.**

Overleaf, bottom: **The wood and plaster houses in Sandwich step out in overhangs above the narrow streets.**

Days 2–4: Strood to Herne Bay

Rochester is attractive, very Dickensian, and its cathedral and castle deserve to be looked over. Now our route becomes marshy, with tidal mud flats and creeks, as it weaves its way through tangled industrial quays and wharves, all with the accompanying smell of sea salt and sewage. Halstow has a 12th-century lead-fronted church, which was a surprise discovery during the bombing of the Second World War. The coastal features around Chetney Hill are charmingly named Deadmans Island, Slaughterhouse Point, Slayhills Marsh and such like — a throwback to the quarantine ships used to isolate the bubonic plague victims, and prison hulks that used to anchor hereabouts. Interestingly the civil rebellions of 1381 and 1450 took place not too far away from these parts. Neither should the agricultural riots of the 1830s be forgotten.

Outside Sittingbourne lies a Saxon burial mound and within the industrial sprawl, amongst the weedling inland creeks, there is the Dolphin Yard Sailing Barge Museum. Old barges lay in various stages of restoration and energetic noises emitted from a large shed. On one of the moored barges a lass hung out her washing.

Kent grows the best hops in the world and Faversham has two breweries along with many pubs. The marshes were once the home of both sheep and gunpowder manufacture. Only the sheep remain; in 1916 over a hundred people were blown up on Gunpowder Marsh.

From Faversham to Herne Bay there exists the brash tourist world of chalets, bathing huts, caravans, bungalows and car parks. The sea appears to become cleaner and at Whitstable a huge oyster bed is farmed. From here in Roman times, this delicacy was sent to Nero's Golden House and Domitian's Alban Villa. At Herne Bay the second pier, constructed in 1896, has mainly fallen down. The first pier, Telford's of 1832, was eaten by the teredo worm. Although it is called Herne Bay, there is no bay!

Day 5: Herne Bay to Sandwich

The two towers of Reculver are prominent to the east and Reculver church itself is built on the site of the Roman fort Regulbium. This was the fort that, in the third century, guarded the northern entrance of the straits dividing the Isle of Thanet from the mainland. It was one of the strategic defences against the Saxons. King Egbert of Kent founded a monastery here in 669.

They say that a Roman city lies under the water and that the sea bites off two feet a year,

but not to worry for we now turn to follow the channel, the Wantsum, between Thanet and Kent. Although there's no shore left it was a waterway in Saxon times which is why it is still very much a legitimate part of the Saxon Shore Way.

Richborough was the fort at the southern end; today there is a huge power station. Once this flat cultivated area was all marsh, but now it has been extensively drained and leads to salt marshes between Sandwich and Pegwell Bay. In fact, in Roman days Richborough castle was on an island in the mouth of the Wantsum. Aulus Plautius established it and went on to use it as a base to supply the Roman conquest of Britain. The Romans held out until the 5th century.

The salt marshes, created by a channel cut across a bend in the Stour, as any civil engineer will tell you, was the site for the construction of the Mulberry Harbour. The Normandy landings required some kind of harbour, and as there wasn't one there, with typical British engineering ingenuity, we built one here and took it over with us.

Sandwich is a delightful little town at which to rest. Its wood and plaster houses step out in overhangs above the narrow streets and you don't have to know the details to feel the sense of history. It has a Shakespearian feel about it.

Day 6: Sandwich to Dover

As you leave Sandwich beware of golfers. Perhaps it was the breeze blowing across the channel from France but, for me, the walk livened up from here, and I found its physical character changed and more enjoyable. Of course the historical interest does not wane and walking along I noted a number of local ladies with long red hair — living witness to the Dane's rout of the Saxons. There are also many fine castles situated along the Cinque Ports which are worth visiting.

Deal and Walmer have fine squat castles and a quick trip round either will impress on one something of the genius of Henry VIII's engineers. The castles were built to resist the latest technology of the time — cannon fire. Their circular crenellated shape gives an immediate visual impression of strength and inside, the arches and intricate stonework are, to the discerning eye, quite amazing.

On Deal beach you will find a pier, a small-boat fishing fleet, holiday makers in reasonable moderation and a sloping bank of pebbles. The pebbles, grey, brown, black and white are rounded flints from nearby chalk cliffs. On closer examination it is found they are often holed and fit on kids' fingers

wonderfully well. Getting them off is another matter! Across on the other side of the seafront there can be found a rather fine ice-cream parlour and on a Saturday the market offers further variety.

It is strange, on a peaceful summer's day, to stroll along here and think that on occasion storms have been so violent as to bury the road in pebbles and smash the shopfronts; and that once Hitler's army stood, almost within eyeshot, poised to invade. Four miles out and clearly visible are the masts, and sometimes the hulls of some wrecks poking out from the notorious shifting Goodwin Sands. The recorded loss of life in these sands is around 50,000! Julius Caesar however was luckier and landed here on the 25th August 55 BC.

A drop into St Margarets Bay, this time a real bay, is worthwhile. Never crowded, always bearing an air of desertion, it is flanked on either side by large ghostly white cliffs of chalk. Sitting here eating my sandwiches, listening to the rolling waves and tinkling pebbles, watching the ships come and go, and the seagulls reeling and swooping in the breeze, I think it was the most relaxing section of the walk so far.

After a storm I once found marcasite nodules the size and appearance of small cannon balls below the cliffs here — not that I recommend you collect them as they are heavy and there is still some way to go. Looking around, cut into the cliffs you will see the blocked entrances to war-time defences tunnelled into the chalk. One, stopped with concrete, resembles a disfigured face where the chalk has been eroded by the sea leaving the concrete plug sticking out proud.

Up and on to Dover, the European gateway to Britain. Cross channel traffic is heavy and many boats come and go yet the busy port appears clean and attractive. The castle is distinctly the largest and the most impressive on the walk, its flint walls illuminated at night.

Days 7–9: Dover to Rye

Before dropping down to Folkestone, you can see the Romney Marshes. The walk doesn't actually take in this desolate area but, after Hythe, skirts above and across higher ground. Folkestone is perfectly acceptable as seaside resorts go and was once a much favoured holiday town. Charles Dickens referred to it as 'one of the prettiest watering places on the south-east coast'.

After Hythe the nature of the walk changes and as it is frequently wooded, route-finding does become tricky. Hythe is I believe Roman in origin, the name meaning haven, although two hundred French soldiers did not find it so when they landed in 1293; they were set upon by the townspeople and all were killed. The Royal Military Canal, of which we will see much in the next two days, starts in Hythe and runs 23 miles (37km) to the Isle of Oxney where it joins the modified River Rother running to the sea at Rye. It was built in two years from 1805 to discourage Napoleon from invading.

I knew no harm of Bonaparte and plenty of the Squire,
And for to fight the Frenchman I did not much desire;
But I did bash their baggonets because they came arrayed
To straighten out the crooked road an English drunkard made,
Where you and I went down the lane with ale-mugs in our hands,
The night we went to Glastonbury by way of Goodwin Sands.*

From our walk none of the lonely beauty of the Romney Marsh can be fully appreciated and I was a little disappointed not to get closer. Always inhospitable it abounds with legend, and was a haunt for smugglers. The Saxons used to give it a wide berth. In those days, after a few glasses of mead perhaps, the marsh gas phenomena of 'Jack O' Lantern/Will o' the Wisp' must have been quite unnerving. I remember crossing it on the night train from Paris, just as daylight broke. Mist hung thickly in all the hollows and it seemed, even from the warmth and comfort of the train, to be hostile and have unnatural powers.

At Appledore the sun was hot and cows waded in the meadows to eat the luxuriantly green growth. Earlier I had sampled some watercress from a little spring by the path and was now wondering whether this had been entirely wise. But no matter, it was too late now and really nothing should stop you at this point for there is, relatively, not far to go.

Rye is brilliant. The town caps a little hill and is a delight of Elizabethan construction and cobbled streets. Below, at the point of arrival, fishing boats pose stylishly. I crossed the bridge and bought some seafood from a little wooden shop. The proprietress was friendly and to my questioning she answered that the seafood had originated in Scotland. After 140 miles (225km) of sea shore I couldn't help but smile wryly as I set off to explore the little Sussex town poised above.

*'Before The Roman Came to Rye.' By G.K. Chesterton.

Previous page, top: **Walmer Castle, with its crenellated shape gives an immediate visual impression of strength.**

Previous page, bottom: **Cows drink along the banks of the Military Canal at Appledore.**

SOUTHERN ENGLAND: The Ridgeway by Bill Birkett

The Route

(The distances given are along the Ridgeway itself and a further allowance must be made to seek accommodation off the path and if one walks from Avebury.)

Day 1: Overton Hill to A338 (near Wantage), 24mls (38km).

Day 2: A338 to Wallingford, 19mls (31km).

Day 3: Wallingford to Princes Risborough, 21mls (34km).

Day 4: Princes Risborough to Ivinghoe Beacon, 21mls (34km).

The Walk

In nature there are certain features which instinctively appeal to man: fords offer safe routes across rivers, passes lead through the mountains, valleys are places to live in and cultivate. These features often inspire a certain emotional, primaeval if you like, response. In times past they would have been treated as sacred and were thought to have been given to man by divine providence; gifts from the gods.

The Wessex Ridgeway is a long chalk ridge that rises from the plains like the spine of an animal. As a geological feature its gesture to the surrounding flatlands is simple and basic. To the mind of man it is a symbol that immediately says 'highway'.

Between this great highway to the west, and the Chilterns to the east, flows Father Thames. The eastern lands are traversed by another ancient route known as the Icknield Way. In

Recently harvested fields stretch as far as the eye can see along the Ridgeway.

The standing stones of Avebury's great circle at sunrise.

1973 these two routes were joined to form the official long distance path now named The Ridgeway Path. It is a path of some distinction: 85 miles (137km) in length, it passes through the five English counties of Wiltshire, Berkshire, Oxfordshire, Buckinghamshire and Hertfordshire.

Do not set off on this walk with the expectation of experiencing spectacular scenery or being enraptured by the beauty of the scene. This would only lead to disappointment. Rather treat this walk as a journey back through time, a voyage that discovers the standing stones of Avebury's great circle and the stylized art of Uffington's White Horse. The fascination of this walk is its association with the past. The Ridgeway so obviously had tremendous importance in prehistory that the evidence can still be seen in the magnitude and scale of the many mysterious remains that abound on this high chalk ridge. Treated in this fashion the ancient highway still holds its primaeval power.

Days 1–2: Avebury to the A338

First of all I will point out that although the official path starts a couple of miles up the road at Overton Hill, you will probably feel obliged to visit the great stone circle at Avebury. It is the largest such structure in Europe and is some four times the size of Stonehenge. Within the outer ring of standing stones there are two smaller rings *and* the little town of Avebury. The stones are known as sarsens and are hard lumps of sandstone that were left lying on the surface of the chalk when the softer cap of sandstone into which they intruded was eroded away.

As the faithful turn to Mecca so the Ridgeway walker should first watch the sunrise over Avebury; sample the expectant atmosphere amidst the silent sentinel sarsens awaiting the new day. I was lucky, or perhaps it was fate, but my timing was such that I first witnessed the full moon rise over the circle then, as dawn broke I watched a perfect red sun rise over those ancient stones. The sarsens

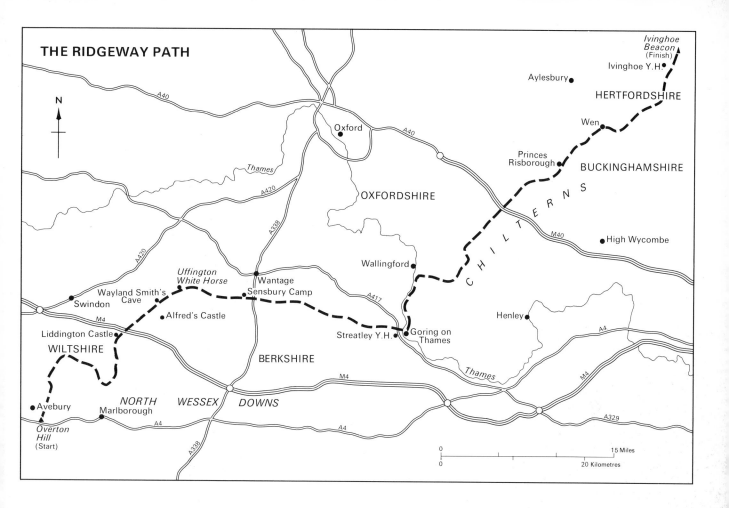

THE RIDGEWAY PATH

looked like rumpled grey men ready to awake.

As you proceed along the flinty chalk track, often rutted and pot-holed, you are amidst the food of life. In season the tall corn waves on either side and red poppies line the edge of the track. In spring the predominant colour is white, when the blossom of the sloe followed by the hawthorn and elder are most noticeable. Later the colour yellow becomes more obvious as the many hawkbits raise their heads, and this is followed by the purple of the thistle. Between June and August look out for the orchids; the bee orchid and possibly the even rarer military orchid can be spotted. Try to avoid picking the flowers so they can live on in their natural surroundings and seed.

Another feature of these chalk lands is the variety and numbers of butterflies you will see. If like me, you know little about these delicate creatures it doesn't matter a great deal, for the joy is simply in observing as they skip colourfully through the air from plant to plant: the milk chocolate meadow brown, the tortoiseshells, the marbled white, the fritillaries, and the most spectacular and beautiful of all, the red admirals, and the peacocks. Although

not the most striking, the chalkhill blue is certainly the rarest, and with 85 miles (136km) to go you stand a better chance than most of seeing one.

There are many prehistoric features along and beneath the ridge but the one that most fascinated me was the White Horse at Uffington. The earthwork of Uffington Castle on the top of the hill is interesting yet this pales into insignificance when compared with the White Horse. This is not just another chalk figure cut from the turf, but is, however primitive, a symbol of power — of a horse in movement. It is as much a work of art as Landseer's 'Monarch of the Glen'.

The most intriguing thing of all about this ancient work is that, try as you might (and I was trying to photograph it), it cannot be fully seen from any point on the ground; its head curls over the brow of the hill making it impossible. Indeed the only place from which this splendid horse can be fully viewed, is the air which is odd when you consider how long ago it was created.

Below there is the flat-topped conical mound of Dragon Hill and below this, and

The Walk: A long distance track of prehistoric origin following a distinct chalk ridge through the North Wessex Downs then down to the Thames before rising up again to traverse along the Chiltern Hills.
Maps: OS L173, L174, L175, L165.
Start: Overton Hill on the A4 near Avebury, Wiltshire (map ref: SU 118681).
Finish: Ivinghoe Beacon, Buckinghamshire (map ref: SP 961168).
Waymarks: Signposts and concrete plinths then acorn plaques and painted white arrows and acorns in the Chilterns.
Length: 85mls (137km).
Approx Time: 4 days.
Difficulty: No particular difficulty.
Access: Car.
Seasons: All year.
Observations: This walk passes through some of the most impressive prehistoric sites in Britain. The route can be backpacked. Ensure an adequate amount of liquid is carried as the ridge is dry. Watch out for trail bikes!
Accommodation: Hotels and bed and breakfast accommodation; some camping en route.
Guidebooks: *The Ridgeway Path* by Sean Jennett (HMSO), *The Ridgeway Path* by H.D. Westacott and M. Richards (Penguin), *Ridgeway Information and Accommodation* by D. Venner (Oxfordshire CC), *The Ridgeway Path* by Alan Charles (Frederick Warne).

Uffington Hill, is a large scalloped hollow named the Manger. I was convinced looking with a civil engineer's eye at the shape and folds in this valley that both it and the Dragon's Table were man-made. For what purpose and how long ago I wouldn't care to speculate but there's certainly 'some muck been shifted'. These works on such a large scale and the presence of the horse up above leave a lot of questions to be answered as you proceed.

Dropping down to the muddy waters of the Thames at Goring provides a pleasant contrast to the high chalk ridge. The river bifurcates here and you cross the trestled bridge, first to an island and then over the second leg of the river with a weir and lock gates above. This gives an excellent view of the lock gates and if you are lucky you will see them in action as the pleasure craft move up and down the river. The rushing of the water over the weir and the long flowing branches of the weeping willows makes this a most attractive place to linger.

From here you join another ancient track, the Icknield Way and the character of the walk changes with it. The Chilterns are more wooded and overgrown. Houses with walls of flint nodules tend to take over from the thatched cottages of red brick that are found beneath the Wessex Ridgeway. The presence of modern man, his roads and industry, is much more prevalent here but the walk still has its attractions.

As you pass through the grounds of Chequers, the Prime Minister's famous country house, it may seem surprising that only a few 'Private' notices protect it. This large sixteenth-century house, with its attractive mullioned and transomed windows was given to the nation specifically as a country residence for Prime Ministers, by Lord Lee in 1921.

Ivinghoe Beacon is a fitting high point to finish this ancient and elevated highway and you will enjoy looking back along the chalk edge of the Chilterns and the route you have just followed, across the flat, now relatively industrialised plains below. You most probably won't be alone, the place generally abounds with day trippers and model gliding buffs; nevertheless you will feel aloof from all these distractions as you remember the many delights you have experienced along the ancient Ridgeway path.

Above: **Ivinghoe Beacon is a fitting high point at which to finish this ancient and elevated highway.**

Facing page, top left: **Red poppies nod and wave as you pass by on the Ridgeway.**

Facing page, top right: **Beyond the windmill lies Ivinghoe Beacon and the end of the walk.**

Facing page, bottom: **The riverside scenery by the Thames at Goring provides a pleasant contrast to the high chalk ridge.**

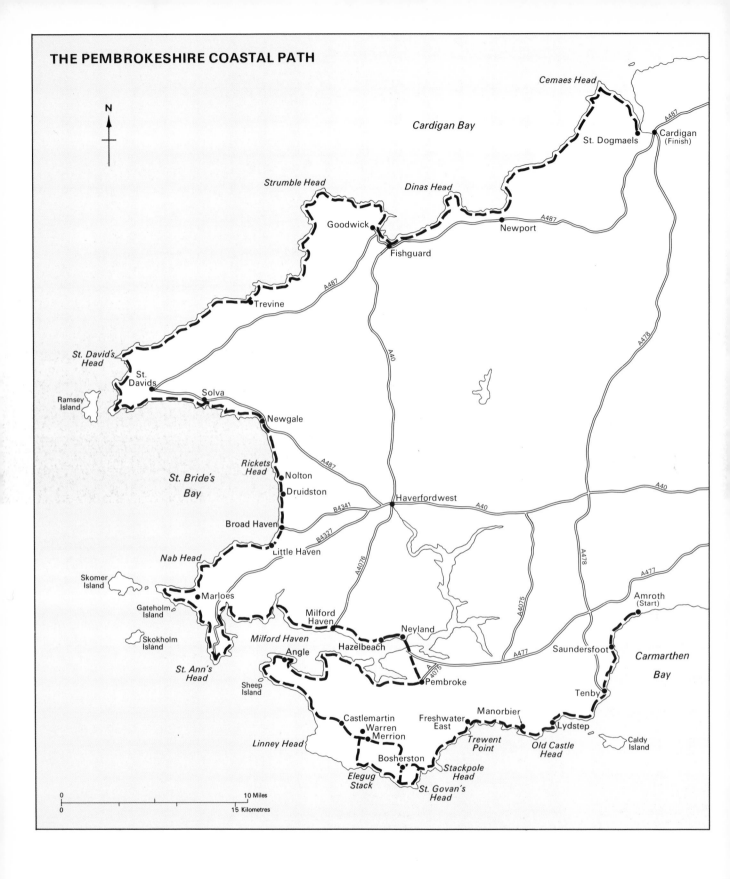

THE PEMBROKESHIRE COASTAL PATH

N

Cardigan Bay

Cemaes Head

Cardigan (Finish)

St. Dogmaels

Strumble Head

Dinas Head

Goodwick

Newport

Fishguard

Trevine

St. David's Head

St. Davids

Ramsey Island

Solva

Newgale

St. Bride's Bay

Rickets Head

Nolton

Druidston

Broad Haven

Little Haven

Nab Head

Haverfordwest

Skomer Island

Marloes

Gateholm Island

Milford Haven

Neyland

Skokholm Island

Milford Haven

Hazelbeach

Angle

St. Ann's Head

Pembroke

Sheep Island

Amroth (Start)

Saundersfoot

Carmarthen Bay

Tenby

Castlemartin

Warren

Merrion

Freshwater East

Manorbier

Lydstep

Linney Head

Bosherston

Trewent Point

Old Castle Head

Caldy Island

Elegug Stack

Stackpole Head

St. Govan's Head

0   10 Miles

0   15 Kilometres

44

WALES: The Pembrokeshire Coastal Path by Bill Birkett

The Walk: A long distance coastal walk from Amroth to St Dogmaels (Pembrokeshire, South Wales).
Maps: OS L158, L157, L145.
Start: Amroth (map ref: SN 172072).
Finish: St Dogmaels, near Cardigan (map ref: SN 163469).
Waymarks: Signposts and acorn symbols.
Length: 172mls (278km).
Approx time: 11 days.
Difficulty: Paths are well marked and clear to follow. The going is not particularly arduous although the route does undulate from cliff top to bay.
Access: Car or bus.
Seasons: All year.
Observations: Despite the modern day intrusions of the M.O.D. artillery ranges and the oil refineries the overall theme is one of great natural beauty and solitude. The path is rich in flora and fauna and travels through cliff and land scenery that spans a geological time period from 250 to 3000 million years and encompasses nine different major rock types. Man's influence and history is marked, from pre-history to the present day, including Stone Age burial chambers and quaint and perfectly proportioned Norman chapels. Of course the greatest natural feature is the ever present sea, the great provider, and man has shaped his environment to accommodate this fact: harbours, ports, fishing villages and castles all add a particular flavour to this great long distance walk. On Day 2 Castlemartin Artillery Range East may be closed but this is unlikely at weekends or during holidays. (This can be checked in advance by telephoning Castlemartin 286 and requesting the firing programme). Range West is permanently closed to the public.
Accommodation: Bed and breakfast establishments and pubs can be sought at the staging points suggested but many will prefer to remain independent and back pack.
Guidebooks: *Walking the Pembrokeshire Coast Path* by Patrick Stark, *Pembrokeshire Coast Path* by John Barrett (HMSO).

Looking to Ramsey Island from St David's Head.

45

Above: **Waves break against the cliffs and rocks of St Govan's Head.**

Facing page, top: **Looking across the snow-covered cliff tops to Chapel Point.**

Facing page, bottom: **A sandy path leads you to St David's Head.**

The Route

Day 1: Amroth to Freshwater East (18mls, 29km) via Saundersfoot, Tenby, Lydstep and Manorbier.

Day 2: Freshwater East to Warren (12¹/₂mls, 20km via Barfundle Bay, Stackpole Head, Broad Haven. **Alternative 1** (if Range East is open): St. Govan's Head, Flimston Bay. **Alternative 2** (if Range East is closed): Bosherston, Merrion.

Day 3: Warren to Pembroke (19mls, 30km) via Castlemartin, Broomhill Burrows, Castles Bay, West Angle Bay, Angle, Bullwell Bay, and Brownslate.

Day 4: Pembroke to Milford Haven (9¹/₂mls, 15km) via The Haven Bridge, Neyland and Hazelbeach.

Day 5: Milford Haven to Marloes (17¹/₂mls, 28km) via Sandy Haven, Great Castle Head, Musselwick, Dale and Hoopers Point.

Day 6: Marloes to Broad Haven (14mls, 22km) via Gateholm, Wooltack Point, The Nab Head, Borough Head and Little Haven.

Day 7: Broad Haven to St. David's (16mls, 26km) via Nolton Haven, Newgale and Solva.

Day 8: St David's to Trevine (19¹/₂mls, 31km) via St. Justinian, St. David's Head and Abereiddy.

Day 9: Trevine to Fishguard (20mls, 32km) via Strumble Head and Goodwick.

Day 10: Fishguard to Newport (11mls, 17km) via Dinas Head.

Day 11: Newport to St. Dogmaels (16mls, 26km) via Ceibwr Bay and Cemaes Head.

The Walk

Soon after the Pembroke Coast became Britain's fifth National Park the concept of this walk was born. It became a reality on its official opening in 1970 and was the third long distance path to be so designated. Despite the presence of the M.O.D. and some oil refineries around Milford Haven the vast majority of this walk remains unhindered and true to the coastline.

The Pembroke coast, despite one or two intrusions, remains a place of exceptional natural beauty. Whether it be the spectacular form of 'The Green Bridge Of Wales' or the

subtleties of the orange and red sands of Broad Haven, the resonating shrieks of the peregrine or the silent glowering glide of the fulmar, the vivid yellow broom or the washed sea-pinks, whatever the season this walk is always an incredible voyage of discovery. And always too there is variety and change influenced by the moods of the sea and her tides.

Stone Age burial mounds, Iron Age forts and Norman castles are just a few of the historical remains to be seen and enjoyed. The Christian influence has always been strong and can be seen in the splendid village churches and towers that are scattered frequently, and heard in names such as St David's and St Ann's Head. On Caldy Island a sect of Trappist Cistercian monks who arrived from Belgium in 1928 remain in residence.

The geological make-up of this coastline is remarkably varied. The technicalities may escape most but the physical differences can be seen by all, a typical example being the marked change from the blood reds of the old red sandstone to the brilliant whites of the carboniferous limestone. Some of the youngest rocks, the coal measures, can be seen at the beginning of the walk at Amroth. Indeed, coal from her beach was once exported. You then pass through millstone grit to arrive on the white carboniferous limestone at Tenby. Alternating now are bands of sandstone and limestone and Caldy Island, off Giltar Point, is half sandstone and half limestone. The view east from Freshwater East is red, and to the west it is white, but the rock on the ground is dark and slate-like, of the Silurian era. And this is just the first day! By the time the dramatic folds of the Ordovician sediments are exposed to you at the end of the walk, much more will have been revealed.

Look for brightly clad rock climbers on the cliffs of St Govan's, the yachtsmen in the hidden sanctuary of Solva, the fishermen out at sea, the monks on Caldy Island and through the fields and crops, talk if you can with the locals, who so much form the backbone of the character of this unique land — this 'Little England beyond Wales'. Enjoy all this, but I hope you will also make discoveries of your own so lace up your boots and off you go!

Day 1: Amroth to Freshwater East

Amroth castle is founded on a Norman site and marks the beginning of your journey. Out on the beach, at low tide, can be found the fossilised remains of a drowned forest. But by Saundersfoot the overall influence can be seen to be that of coal extraction. Because of coal, Saundersfoot grew from two houses in 1764 to a town that exported 11,500 tons of anthracite in 1833. After Wiseman's Bridge you follow along the defunct line of the Saundersfoot-to-Stepaside colliery tramway.

Approaching Tenby look out for the wild Tenby daffodils and examine the proliferation of sea shells to be found on the shore. In the 8th century the town was Viking controlled, in the 9th the Welsh held it, calling it 'the little fort of the fishes', and in the 12th century it was Norman. Once a Victorian seaside resort, Tenby remains popular with holiday makers today though, thankfully, the National Park planning board keep tourist development to an acceptable proportion.

As you proceed westwards enjoy the clean sands and desert-like dunes. The dunes are a precious part of the natural environment but their stability is precarious and dependent on the natural binding of the vegetation. Think of their delicate ecology as you walk over them: how the first plant to usually take hold is marram grass which is followed by ragwort thistle and sand sedge, followed by silverweed and creeping buttercup which add colour to the scene. Overtramping cuts through this protective layer of vegetation which causes the sand particles to be blown away, so denuding the dunes and changing the environment.

Trips run out to Caldy Island (not that you have time to visit in the 11-day schedule I have suggested), to see the strict order of Trappist Cistercian monks. Originally the monastery was used by the Benedictines and it was only when they left to live at Prinknash that the Cistercians took it over.

Lydstep Point gives good views and the rocks below are of brilliant white limestone. Despite the M.O.D. occupation which forces you to retreat to Lydstep, it is worth a trip round if you have the time and the energy. Mind you, the proliferation of brambles and prickly juniper make it hard work should you stray from the paths. Down below, when the tide is in, you can see the seething cauldron of Mother Carey's Kitchen.

Our first Neolithic burial chamber (3000 BC) can be found on Priest's Nose just outside the French-sounding village of Manorbier. Hidden bays and limestone blow holes lead to sandstone cliffs, then down to the sandy bay and dark rocks of the strategically sounding Freshwater East.

Day 2: Freshwater East to Warren

This is my favourite section of the walk because I know it well from repeated acquaintance with the steep limestone cliffs which provide magnificent rock climbing. But for those who will never venture onto the rocks this is still an absolutely superb section to walk. Depending on whether Range East is open or shut there are two ways to tackle this section. Infuriatingly Range West remains closed to the public at all times and the Linney Head area cannot be seen — rather a thorn in the side of those who believe in freedom of access in our National Parks.

The loneliness of the clifftops is scarcely broken by man's intrusion all the way to Stackpole Quay where the presence of tree and leaf is welcome. Along again to Barfundle Bay, the discerning sunbathers' paradise, you rise up through stunted and wind-blown woodland to again reach the solitude of the heights. Across Barfundle Bay, best seen deserted when its sands lie perfectly smooth, harder bands of rock plunge headlong into the sea. Caved and holed by the sea, the limestone eyes wink at you as you pass by.

Broad Haven, with its Stack Rock out to sea, is another remarkable little bay between the heights. I have been there when it is so serene even the sea doesn't seem to have the energy to move and at other times when, shrieking with fury, the wind has driven huge Atlantic rollers in from the south. In either event, tides permitting, note the unique blend of colour contained in the sands of the beach. Depending on which route you take there is a freshwater stream issuing from the large ponds beyond. If you go straight across, tempted to reach the sands as quickly as possible, you will inevitably get wet. If you walk upstream a little way you will find the stream is bridged and you will cross dry.

If Range East is open you can rise up to continue along the cliffs to St Govan's Head (Alternative 1) and if not you will follow along the delightful lily ponds to Bosherston and its quaint little church (Alternative 2). The coastal route is of course the first choice but for those not in a hurry I would recommend a trip along the ponds and into Bosherston and then along the road to return to the coast at St Govan's. The view from the head across Broad Haven and Stack Rock, to the distant cliffs of Stackpole Head is quite superb. Down the highly polished steps (below the car park) is a chapel mysteriously built into and between the cliffs, while towards the sea lies a little well, which is now dry.

Along through the guarded Range East (only if it's open of course) is first revealed a long narrow zawn coming in from a slit to expand into a deep little bay. As you look down into the dizzy depths, that paradoxical feeling of fear and fascination enables you to understand the origin of its name 'Huntsmen's Leap'. Don't try it for you still have far to go and much to see!

In many respects the cliffscapes, and the alternating heads and zawns, along this section are the finest on the whole walk. They reach a crescendo with the Elegug Stacks and a climax with the great rock archway known as 'The Green Bridge of Wales'. This is best viewed by proceeding fully along to the boundary fenceline of Range West and then looking down, back east, from the wooden observation platform provided. Having seen it, the brave (or foolish), may wish to walk out along its narrow back. If you do, take great care for it is really climbers' terrain.

The fine cliffscapes of this walk climax into the great rock archway known as The Green Bridge of Wales.

Be careful also, if you stray from the path (particularly around the Bullslaughter Bay area), not to fall down one of the many blowholes that lead directly into the sea which pounds in subterranean caverns far below your feet.

What a pity you are stopped by Range West and forced to detour inland.

Days 3 – 5: Warren to Marloes

Out of Gravel Bay a small stack of coarse conglomerate can be seen and this marks the return to the red sandstone. I was interested to note that a public house over on Thorn Island was a fort in 1854. The name of the next little port, Angle, is Norse for turning, and as you proceed on towards Pembroke the significance of the name is very apparent. Now as you turn into the Haven the presence of the modern world hits you: the deepwater of the Haven enables huge oil tankers to deliver their wares. But here, and on the far side of the Haven there are many forts and gun batteries to be seen as a testimony to the historical importance of this sea inlet.

Pembroke Castle is very fine and you see it from its most advantageous position on this path down by the river. Henry Tudor was born here in 1457 although its building was begun by Arnulph of Montgomery in 1090. As one would expect, Cromwell gave it a hammering. The rest of this section through the oil refineries and related industrial conurbations at least serves to provide vivid contrast with most other sections of this coastline.

A dry crossing of Sandy Haven can only be achieved 3 hours either side of low tide and the bridge between Musselwick and Dale is impassable at high water. St Ann's Head gives good views and below lies impressive rock scenery. Wooltack Point lies across from here and the heads form, on the map, the shape of a fish's tail fin. At the other end of the dale from Dale (Norse for valley), Westdale Bay lies between the cliffs (actually a fault line) and beneath the aerodrome.

The Viking-sounding Skokholm and Skomer Islands are both important bird sanctuaries. In fact the former was the site of Britain's first bird observatory. The latter is separated from Wooltack Point by Jack Sound and then Little Sound, both forming noteable tidal rushes. Skomer Island is a National Nature Reserve and provides a home for many wild flowers and a breeding ground for kittiwakes, fulmars, puffins, razorbills, guillemots, shearwaters and many more birds. Day visits are possible from Martin's Haven. In October seal pups can be seen on the rocks. It all seems a million miles away from Milford Haven.

Days 6 – 7: Marloes to St David's

The Nab Head holds a Mesolithic chipping floor where 10,000 years ago flint was worked to produce cutting tools. Although fragments can still be found, they should not be removed. From the cliffs north of St Brides, small stone coffins, thought to be 6th to 10th century, are occasionally unearthed by wave erosion. Looking across to Mill Haven observe the hard irregular Pre-Cambrian rocks rising high above the flat-topped sandstone. A little further on we pass an impressive Iron Age fort whose northern end marks the junction of the Pre-Cambrian and Old Red Sandstone rocks. The colour change is distinct.

After Broad Haven the 'Harold Stones' mark the legendary sites of victories by Harold over the Welsh — but in fact they are thought to be much older. On Newgale beach you return to the coal-bearing measures. Before you arrive in Newgale, at Brandy Brook, you cross over the west end of the 'landsker'. This was a defensive and fortified line built by the Normans with castles from Roch, through Haverfordwest and on to Tenby. It is thought that this line separated the Anglo/Normans in the south, from the warring Welsh to the north. The existing change in place nomenclature supports this theory.

The drop down into Solva provides a pleasant interlude and this sea inlet, with its pleasure yachts, bears more resemblance to some Mediterranean anchorage than to a Welsh one. At low tide oyster catchers and dunlin can be observed. From 1536 it was recorded as a 'creek for ballingers and fishing boats'. It boomed in 1851 with nine warehouses and a population of 1252, but now it is relatively quiet.

Days 8 – 9: St David's to Fishguard

A very beautiful section of the walk and quite different to anything experienced so far. The reason for the difference is that now the rocks are mainly volcanic, giving attractive fine grained rocks of a reddy-pink hue. Correspondingly the vegetation pattern changes and the overall feeling walking this section is more akin to walking in a mountain region. The approach to St David's Head can be along the superb beach of Whitesands Bay and even in midsummer, when the place is full of holidaymakers, it still retains an air of tranquillity.

From the head itself there is a great view to the 'Eight Peril' rocks and across the bay, to Ramsey Island. But there is much of interest all round and I will talk a little of this. As you approached, from the opposite side of Porthmelgan Bay you will have noticed the precariously supported capstone of a Neolithic burial chamber and its position should be noted for a further inspection. To walk out onto the headland you cross a thick and powerful-looking wall reputedly from the Iron Age. Directly in line with the wall but beneath it, on the cliffs of Ogof Coetan (crystal cliff), is a cave cut into an obvious band of quartz running through the volcanic rocks.

It is situated above a narrow sea inlet and can only be reached by climbing, but on closer inspection it leads first to an extremely narrow tunnel which opens almost immediately to a wider and more roomy chamber. It is certainly man-made and, equipped with a geologist's hammer and torch, I discovered why: under debris in the floor of the chamber I extracted chunks of optically perfect quartz about one inch long: they were just like pieces of broken ice. Obviously at some time, in some civilisation, this had been a valuable commodity.

Along from here there are a number of notable man-made features, particularly the Iron Age forts and burial chambers (look at Carreg Samson outside Trevine), but it is the natural world that takes precedence. The rare red-legged choughs and the even rarer swooping peregrine falcon can be seen if luck is with you. Fulmars breed on the cliffs and seals on the rocks below.

Before you arrive at Strumble Head lighthouse you will have been seduced by the blueness of the sea in the numerous inlets secreted among the precipitous cliffs. There are many seals to be spotted in the clear waters hereabouts and much to interest the naturalist. Even so, should it be open, the lighthouse is worth a look around — it cost £40,000 to build in 1908.

Not many people know that the French did actually invade Britain but it's true and, of all places, it happened here. They landed at Carregwastad Point and little good it did them. A French division, timed to coincide with a rebellion in Ireland, landed an unruly mob of 1200 'rag-a-muffins' under an American by the name of Tate, at 5 pm on 22 February 1797. The plan was to march to Chester and Liverpool but the Pembroke Company of Gentlemen and Yeomanry Cavalry, under Lord Cawdor of Stackpole leapt into action and by 4 pm on 24 February the French surrendered on Goodwick Sands. The tally was 8 Frenchmen drowned, 12 killed, but the only British casualty was one Welsh woman killed in a pub — due, it is said, to the accidental discharge of a pistol.

In Goodwick Bay today you will most probably see only the ferry to Rosslare in Ireland. The boat looks massive and one assumes there must be much coming and going over the 54-mile (87km) stretch of water. Fishguard is still very much a fishing port and provides an interesting contrast between the old and the new.

The precariously supported capstone of a Neolithic burial chamber at St David's Head.

Days 10 – 11: Fishguard to St Dogmaels

The rocks of Dinas Head are well frequented with nesting sea birds and a good view of these can be had looking across to the Needle Rock. Over in the distance across Newport Bay the sands beckon. Newport is an attractive resort and is well populated with holidaymakers; it is particularly noted for its surfing. Its Welsh name of Trefdraeth means 'town of the shore'. In 1191 Norman William Martin, lord of Cemais, founded Newport castle.

The cliff scenery becomes again the dominant interest of the walk and Ceibwr Bay is a fault in the folding of the rocks here. It is at Pen yr Afr that the folding is displayed to its best. This is a much publicised feature of the National Park and for many it is representative of the whole of the wonderful Pembroke coastline.

As you make those last few steps past Poppit Sands, the moored boats and the graceful swans gliding before the tide, where salt and fresh water meet, you will have your own recollections of the last 170 miles (274km). Maybe it will be a cliff feature or a remarkable bird sighting or a chat with someone interesting on the way, but most likely it will be a colourful collage of many things. One thing for certain is that the memory will be rich and live forever.

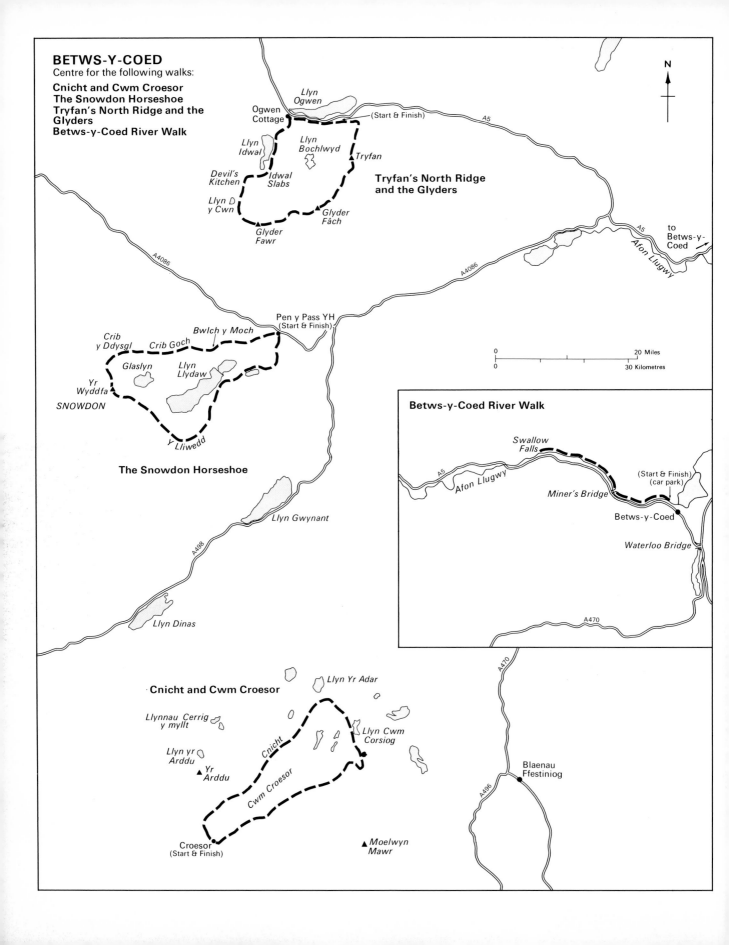

BETWS-Y-COED
Centre for the following walks:

Cnicht and Cwm Croesor
The Snowdon Horseshoe
Tryfan's North Ridge and the Glyders
Betws-y-Coed River Walk

N

Llyn Ogwen

Ogwen Cottage

(Start & Finish)

A5

Llyn Idwal

Llyn Bochlwyd

Tryfan

Devil's Kitchen

Idwal Slabs

Tryfan's North Ridge and the Glyders

Llyn y Cwn

Glyder Fâch

A5

to Betws-y-Coed

Afon Llugwy

Glyder Fawr

A4086

A4086

Pen y Pass YH
(Start & Finish)

Crib y Ddysgl

Crib Goch

Bwlch y Moch

0   20 Miles

0   30 Kilometres

Glaslyn

Llyn Llydaw

Yr Wyddfa

SNOWDON

Betws-y-Coed River Walk

Y Lliwedd

Swallow Falls

The Snowdon Horseshoe

A5

Afon Llugwy

(Start & Finish)
(car park)

Miner's Bridge

Betws-y-Coed

Llyn Gwynant

A498

Waterloo Bridge

Llyn Dinas

A470

Llyn Yr Adar

Cnicht and Cwm Croesor

Llynnau Cerrig y myllt

Llyn Cwm Corsiog

A470

Cnicht

Llyn yr Arddu

Yr Arddu

Cwm Croesor

Blaenau Ffestiniog

A496

Croesor
(Start & Finish)

Moelwyn Mawr

BETWS-Y-COED – Wales

Betws-y-Coed: Centre for the following 4 walks: Cnicht and Cwm Croesor; The Snowdon Horseshoe: Tryfan's North Ridge and The Glyders; Betws-y-Coed River Walk.

Map Ref: SH 795565.

Location: Situated on the A5, Snowdonia, North Wales.

Distances to Walks: 23$\frac{1}{2}$mls (38km) along A5, A4086, A498, A405 to Cnicht and Cwm Croesor 10$\frac{1}{2}$mls (17km) along A5, A4086 to The Snowdon Horseshoe. 9mls (15km) along A5 to Tryfan's North Ridge and The Glyders. No distance to the Betws-y-Coed River Walk.

Accommodation: Every type including camping.

Population: 658.

The Town: Betws-y-Coed is a very pleasant Welsh town where the predominant influence in the buildings is Welsh slate. Although situated near to the hills it retains an air of openness, unlike many Welsh towns, and the surrounding countryside is attractively wooded. A number of short walks can be undertaken in and from the town. Shopping and restaurant facilities are perfectly adequate. It is situated between two swift flowing mountain streams: Afon Lledr and Afon Llugwy. Two bridges are of particular interest: Pont-y-pair (Bridge of the Cauldron) which with its five slate arches is 400 years old, and Waterloo bridge, which is elegantly arched in cast iron and was designed by Telford for his great London to Holyhead road. Cast proudly on the arch are the words 'This arch was constructed in the same year the battle of Waterloo was fought' (1815).

Waterloo Bridge, designed by Telford and built in 1815.

WALES: Cnicht and Cwm Croesor by Bill Birkett

The Walk: Cnicht and Cwm Croesor (South Snowdonia, North Wales).
Accommodation Base: Betws-y-Coed.
Maps: OS L115 Snowdon and Surrounding Area, L124 Dolgellau (only showing village of Croesor and the outlook south, possible to do walk without).
Start and Finish: Croesor village (map ref: 632447).
Length: 7mls (11km).
Approx Time: 4¹/₂hrs.
Ascent and Descent: 3642ft (1110m).
Difficulty: A straightforward mountain walk with little technical difficulty.
Access: Car to the village of Croesor (car park).
Seasons: April to October
Observations: Cnicht is an impressive looking mountain that is often called the 'Matterhorn of Wales'; it gives a straightforward walk with super views, particularly of Snowdon.
Summit: Cnicht: 2264ft (690m).

The Route

From the car park in the little slate village of Croesor cross the bridge and follow the road up past the chapel. Where the surfaced road ends, continue up a delightfully wooded track until the open hill is gained. Go right along a path and on up, passing a little quarry tunnel and then abandoned buildings, until the back of the ridge itself is gained (views of the Moelwyns). Continue along until a stile leads under a little crag and then onto the angular 'Matterhorn' itself. A steep walk up by a well-defined path takes you to a level plateau (fine views of Snowdon) a little way under the summit. Traverse right under this then up to a rocky runnel after which slabby rock steps lead

to the summit (2264ft/690m, 1³/4hrs). Continue along the ridge and tops to eventually descend a broadening ridge. Keep left to drop down adjacent to Llyn yr Adar (³/4 hr. even better views of Snowdon). A cairn (positioned centrally relative to the Llyn) marks the way to the right. Follow the straggling path (sometimes indistinct) contouring round to descend past Llyn Cwm Corsiog. When the dam is reached at the foot of the Llyn break immediately right (do not cross the dam), to move on down to the slate embankment of the ruined quarry. Across to the right the line of an old railway takes you back to the head of Cwm Croesor. Before the line curves right (prior to the large masonry embankment) break off sharply left down a little path. This leads to a well-defined track cleaving diagonally down across the hillside below Moelwyn Mawr to reach the road leading into Cwm Croesor at Croesor-Fawr. Continue down the road to Croesor (2 hrs, total: 4¹/₂hrs).

The Walk

It was down below the rock climber's cliffs at Tremadog, in Eric Jones' cafe, that I enquired as to the English meaning of the name Cnicht. The proprietor stopped his sweeping up and lent on his broom. I had expected that he would give me the standard reply and simply say that it was the Welsh Matterhorn; indeed it was this striking similarity that first compelled me to climb it.

Only the steel in the eyes and the athletic frame gave any indication to this man's mountain authority. So for those of you who don't know I should say that I was talking to Britain's greatest solo mountaineer. Eric Jones was the first Briton to solo climb not only the north face of the Matterhorn but also the notorious north face of the Eiger — the Alpine face that still sends a shudder of respect down every mountaineer's spine.

Shouting for assistance from one of his girls, a staccato, quick conversation in Welsh followed until he said 'Come on Sarah don't be shy, the man's writing a book.' She said she would give me two meanings. The first was that 'the English' had named the peak first, calling it 'The Knight', but the Welsh had been unable to get their tongue round the name and so simply pronounced it 'kh-nekt'. The second she said was that in the white frosts of winter, when this apparently symmetrically angular peak shimmers in the sunshine, it resembles a stalagmite which in Welsh is 'Cnicht'. 'So you can please yourself as to which you want,' she said with a smile.

Thanking them both I set off for Cnicht which may not be too impressive to a man of Eric Jones' calibre but is in fact one of the most pleasant mountain walks to be had in Wales.

Despite its fearsome appearance, the ascent of Cnicht is in fact rather gentle. It has its own peculiarly Welsh character and gives superb views of Snowdon. Once the exposed, but safe, summit has been reached it conjures up a hidden ridge which takes you along to Llyn yr Adar, and then down through slate workings, so much an important part of the history and character of Wales, to eventually lead you back to your starting point.

It was Monday and a fine washing day as we set off past the chapel and up the track leading out of the little slate village of Croesor. After a gate the track becomes shrouded by trees but the wood is soon quitted for open hillside, soft green grass and the company of the white Welsh mountain sheep with their rumps streaked blue for identification. Immediately the hillside is gained the distant Moel Hebog (behind) becomes a dominant feature of the available panorama, but as your height increases its importance diminishes.

As you make upward progress, passing a little slate trail tunnelled into the hillside and a few derelict stone buildings, the perspective of Cnicht becomes increasingly akin to its Alpine namesake and I would forgive you for imagining that there was going to be a tricky climb ahead. Cresting the ridge leading to that symmetrically sculpted peak your attention is held by the impressive form of the Moelwyns on your right. The end of the broad ridge is marked by a stone wall, crossed by a stile below a little rock cliff, and beyond this lies the true summit cone of the 'Welsh Matterhorn'. Despite those nagging doubts as to the difficulties ahead, you still can't fail to notice the old slate workings and buildings down to your left and across these look to the frequently white-streaked, quartz-vein ridge of Yr Arddu, soon to display its secretive and glass-like lakes — Llyn yr Arddu and Llynnau Cerrig y myllt. After this little cliff the going steepens and there is no doubting that you are tackling the Welsh Matterhorn.

The path is distinct, there are no problems, and you soon arrive at a tiny level plateau before the steepest top-most section; a useful place to rest and gather yourself together before the final pull. Magnificent views of Snowdon are framed by the white quartz-seamed rocks on the edge. Above, a little rock face halts direct progress and this should be avoided by traversing to the right. A steep rock runnel is gained (perhaps difficult for children under 10 who may need some assistance), and you must scramble up this for a way to reach easier slaty steps that will take you to the summit. It's no disappointment and the rocky pinnacled top of Cnicht is a summit fitting of its outlook from below. (It had taken us just over the hour at a steady pace.)

The exposure looking down the ridge you have just climbed and down Cnicht's steep mountainous flanks to the valley of Cwm Croesor far below is exhilarating. To your left the Snowdon range looks massive even if its head remains lost in the billowing clouds that constantly roll over into Glaslyn. In fact the panorama from the high mountains of Wales right across Porthmadog to the sea is quite breathtaking and is only interrupted to the south east by the Moelwyns. But what an interruption, for the Moelwyn Mawr itself

Facing page: **The ruins of the slate quarry near Moelwyn Mawr.**

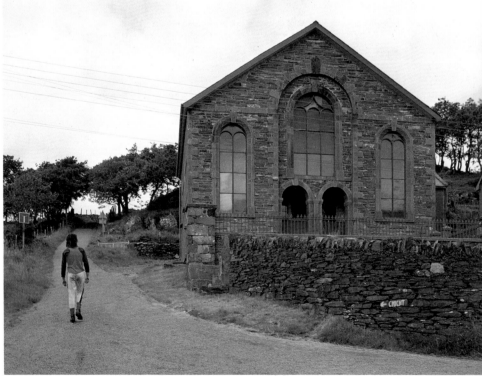

stands some 2256ft (770m) high and Moelwyn Bach is a remarkably featured mountain.

It is useful to note here the green track cutting down diagonally across the slopes of Moelwyn Mawr beneath the distinct scar of the road leading to the large slate quarry. The recently defunct quarry forms a great circular embankment of slate, like a fungi growth on the hillside, supporting a ghost town of disused skeletal slate buildings. Somehow I always feel a sadness in witnessing these relics of times past, once so much an important economic facet of a more industrial Wales (and Britain), perhaps because I was brought up myself amongst the Lakeland slate quarries. The latter part of the walk takes this track and is dominated by the surrounding industrial archaeology. You shouldn't really be depressed for there is much of interest to see and admire in man's industry and ingenuity.

From here you cross to another small peak then follow the path down to gain a broad grassy ridge. When I was there the prevailing atmospheric conditions highlighted the razor sharp edge of Lliwedd and beyond this, behind Glyder Fach, the black pimple, that is Tryfan. As you drop down, although it does not feel quite right, you bear over to the left to observe the serene Llyn Yr Adar with its single, centrally placed island. The raucous calling of the black-headed gulls broke the solitude, reminding us that we weren't that far from the sea. The view to Snowdon remains unimpaired and as we turned right by the cairn situated mid way along the length of the Llyn, I overheard a fellow walker remark that this was the finest aspect of Snowdon he had ever seen.

Although the path is well defined it is fairly circuitous here and you must concentrate to keep in the right direction to pass the shores of Llyn Cwm Corsiog. Although dammed, this is not an unattractive little llyn and for us the waters shone alternately black and silver as the wind rose and fell. In the far corner the cotton grass fluttered and in the centre a gaggle of local boys, talking excitedly in their native tongue, aimed their worms into the depths beyond the weeds. Walk to the dam and turn immediately right (do not cross it) to follow an indistinct path down to the old slate embankment and ruined buildings.

Proceed rightwards across the musical slate rivings tinkling beneath your feet, past the derelict walls, arches and gravestone-like vertical slabs to follow the route of the old railway level out to the head of Cwm Croesor. Just before the level curves rightwards, forming a high masonry retaining wall, a tiny path sneaks down off leftwards. This is the start of the diagonal track, the way the quarrymen would

walk to work each morning, and it leads gently back down to Croesor.

' The valley is now silent except for the bleating of the Welsh mountain sheep, but it is worth looking around to admire man's works of the past. Abandoned inclines emanate from the numerous sources of slate extraction and production. Here the slate, in dressed form, was carried down the hillside in iron trolleys. The weight of the laden trolleys, connected by a steel chain round a revolving wheel, dragged the empty tubs back to the top. Nothing was wasted, energy was precious and expensive; it cost jobs. Rusting in obscure corners, you can still see these trolleys lying disused and unwanted — sometimes just their axle and wheels, sometimes their rusting bodies — the disembowelled remnants of a once thriving industry.

Over on the far hillside, running across the face of Cnicht, a battered and broken pipeline races to a now defunct turbine house on the valley flow. As you drop down you will pass underneath the power lines that were once the lifeblood of the great quarry you observed from the summit of Cnicht.

Of course, the mountains will always remain and so it is with Cnicht. Standing impressive and proud as we again near the car park in Croesor, it looms magnificently over the lines of washing that are drying in the sunshine. A satisfying sight to end your walk on this delightfully Welsh Washday Monday.

Top: **My companion, Greg Cornforth, temporarily supports a falling slate slab underneath the raised path.**

Above: **Rusting bogey wheels are all that is left of one of the iron trolleys that used to carry the slate away from the quarry.**

Facing page, top: **Looking to the sea from the summit of Cnicht.**

Facing page, bottom left: **Cnicht: The Welsh Matterhorn.**

Facing page, bottom right: **The way to Cnicht is clearly signed near the chapel at Croesor.**

WALES: The Snowdon Horseshoe by Bill Birkett

The Walk: The Snowdon Horseshoe, Snowdonia National Park, North Wales.
Accommodation Base: Betws-y-Coed (see p53).
Maps: OS OD17 Snowdonia National Park, L115 Snowdon, T10 Snowdonia and Anglesey.
Start and Finish: Pen y Pass (map ref: 647557).
Length: 7 1/2 mls (12km)
Approx Time: 6 hrs.
Ascent and Descent: 6500ft (1981m).
Difficulty: A long and potentially serious mountain walk involving a small section of scrambling and a high degree of exposure.
Access: Car to Pen y Pass.
Seasons: This is a walk in summer conditions only. Walkers strictly note, in winter or inclement conditions it becomes a mountaineering expedition.
Summits: Crib Goch: 3022ft (921m), Crib-y-Ddysgl: 3494ft (1065m), Snowdon: 3560ft (1085m), Y Lliwedd: 2946ft (898m).

The Route

Pen y Pass (1168ft, 356m) to the col of Bwlch y Moch (1706ft, 520m) via a miner's track. (The Pyg track goes left from here.) Rise steeply with a little easy scrambling to the summit of Crib Goch (3022ft, 921m). Traverse the knife-edge ridge (very exposed but not technically difficult), to rocky pinnacles which are negotiated to the left. Scramble up rightwards from a gap and continue to the col of Bwlch Coch. Rise up from here to the trig point of Crib-y-Ddysgl (3494ft, 1065m). Note: there is no easy or safe escape from the path between the col of Bwlch y Moch and the summit of Crib-y-Ddysgl. Amble down to the stone monolith, marking the arrival of the Pyg track from the left, and continue to the railway tracks which are followed to the summit of Snowdon (3560ft, 1085m). A long drop down gains a constructed level path which leads to a cairn (2592ft, 790m). The left path takes you up alongside the great cliff of Lliwedd to gain its west then east summits (2946ft, 898m). Drop to Lliwedd Bach and continue descending to a cairn marking the obvious break down and left to the shore of Llyn Llydaw (1430ft, 436m). Follow the wide track winding back down to Pen y Pass.

The Walk

As we drove up Llanberis Pass we were impressed by two things: the brilliant blue sky and the incredible amount of snow still lying on the heights. It was almost the end of April and yet the snow was obviously still thick and deep up on Snowdon. We pulled into the car park at Pen y Pass to find it almost empty. Sometimes you get the feeling that the day is going to be one to remember and this was just such a day.

Cameron McNeish recalled in a recent magazine article that the Snowdon Horseshoe was often described as the greatest mountain walk in Britain. Being a loyal Scotsman, he confided to me that he thought the accuracy of the description extremely unlikely because of the wealth of mountains north of the border, 'but we'll give it a fair trial,' he concluded.

So we set off, Cameron well equipped with full winter kit and protective gaiters that sealed leg and boot from all that the snows of Snowdon could throw at him, and me not so well equipped; when I unpacked my sac and took out my climbing hardware and rubber boots there didn't seem to be much left. So I slung my camera bag over my shoulder and set off.

The first section of path has a primaeval feel about it as you pass along the miner's track through black-blue slaty rocks that mark the head of Llanberis Pass. Great slabs bridge the streamlets and rectangular blocks create the steps that take you rapidly up from the valley head and onto the heights. You have to hand it to those lads, they certainly knew how to build and use the natural materials around them.

Cameron had set a cracking pace and we burst onto the notch of Bwlch y Moch conveniently situated underneath the steep ridge that marks the start of the Horseshoe proper. Simultaneously we stopped in our tracks. Opposite, the black cliffs of Lliwedd reared vertically from the pure white snows, a dramatic and awesome sweep of rock, while below, nestling at our feet was the wonderfully calm Llyn Llydaw, still sporting a skin of ice as yet untouched by the rapidly rising morning sunshine. The lake contrasted with the cliffs as

Facing page: **Cameron McNeish looks along the knife edge ridge of Crib Goch to the summit of Snowdon beyond.**

Below left: **Along the track from Pen y Pass with Crib Goch above.**

Below right: **Steep scrambling is necessary in places to climb Crib Goch.**

a lamb would stand against a lion. It was a breathtaking and soberly impressive sight.

Up above you now lies the first challenge of the walk, an ever steepening ridge that seemingly terminates in unscalable bastions of rock. It is a pull and you need to be fit to tackle it but in practice it gives straightforward scrambling; you definitely need both hands and must weigh the situation up before you commit yourself to any particular section but it is a straightforward scramble to the summit of Crib Goch.

The situation rapidly becomes impressive with a plunging landscape of verticality on either side. When we were there, there was deep snow even at this lowly height through which only the steepest sections of rock protruded. A large party in front were now beginning to show signs of nervousness as they grappled with the vaguaries of the rocky buttresses and steps. I guided a boot here and coaxed a little there and soon they were moving up with renewed confidence. What they would make of the ridge beyond the summit of Crib Goch I didn't dare to think.

Once the rocky bastions relented there followed a perfectly defined ridge created from the effects of wind-blown snow. Fortunately its consistency was soft enough to make easy footholds and yet supportive enough to safely bear the weight: a few degrees variance in temperature during the night would make this happy condition an extremely different prospect. If the snow had been hard and icy this would have been a tough and precarious climb. Had the temperature been higher, the mass of snow would have been simply downright dangerous and prone to avalanche.

Throughout this steep pull from the col there is always a good excuse to rest, for the views become increasingly more magnificent as the Glyders unfold to your right and Lliwedd beckons to your left. When you eventually reach the summit of Crib Goch you have climbed around a 1000ft (305m) from Bwlch y Moch.

In front of us now the spectacle wasn't Welsh, or British even; it was purely Alpine. A thin razor-edged arete led across to a cirque of rock pinnacles and buttresses; the tip of it was rock liberated by the sun, but the rest was snow. Down to the right the blackness and appalling steepnesss made you wince and to the left the ground appeared only marginally less steep.

In line with the ridge, but much further beyond, now reared the mighty head of Snowdon (Yr Wyddfa) watching in anticipation. Under these conditions it honestly took on the appearance of some Himalayan giant. The fascination of reaching its summit,

the highest peak in either England or Wales, beckons you along the knife edge that separates you from it.

The traverse of this ridge is mentally, because of the extreme exposure, a tough proposition and demands a cool approach. Fortunately it is not technically difficult and remains a walk as distinct from a climb, but under winter conditions it is a mountaineering undertaking. Even in the most perfect of summer conditions the position and consequences of a fall should not be brushed aside lightly. After the initial section it is usual to follow the left side until the crest can be regained from a little gap. After about $1/4$ mile the (usually grassy) col of Bwlch Coch marks the end of the most technically difficult section.

The elegance of form of the snow ridges remained with us right up to the concrete OS trig point on the summit of Crib y Ddysgl. We passed a father and son team on this section accompanied by their dog. While the dog kept to the true crest of the ridge the others, when they found the going a bit too much, followed the path below and to the right. Despite the deep, ever-softening snow the dog was obviously enjoying the adventure tremendously.

So were we, and as we dipped down to the col of Bwlch Glas, where the Pyg track joins the Horseshoe (marked by a considerable monolith of rock); we were strengthened by that feeling of elation knowing the summit was within reach. Pretty soon we were scuttling along the tracks of the steam railway, the lines buried under the snow, to reach the summit in just under three hours from leaving the Pen y Pass.

A lot has been said of the squalor and crowding of this famous summit but on our day the crowds were elsewhere and the only sound to dampen the audibility of our words of appreciation was the lonesome croaking of a raven. Sitting on the leeward side of the summit cairn we took in the spectacle of Cwm Dyli, I changed films, shared Cameron's final Mars Bar, and we set off again for the final leg of this tremendous Horseshoe.

We plunged directly down in thigh-deep snow aiming for the obvious continuation which leads onto the very edge of the Lliwedd precipice. In summer conditions the path is rather vague and you must pick a line through and over slabs of rock covered in loose scree. It's a long descent but on reaching the col of Bwlch-y-Saethau the angle eases back almost to the horizontal and a comfortable, well-engineered path is followed for just over half a mile (1km). This section is like a little haven. Sheltered from the wind and basking in the strong afternoon sunshine, it provides pleasant

relaxation before the ground rises steeply to skirt across the top of the great cliffs of Lliwedd.

These cliffs fall sheer for a full 1000ft (305m) and were, in the early days of rock climbing, the most important in the whole of Wales. Such names as Thompson, Eckstein and the Abraham brothers who were the pioneer rock climbing photographers (their photograph of the great O.G. Jones hangs in the Pen-y-Pas cafeteria today), and Mallory (of Everest fame) all made their mark on the north face of Lliwedd.

The way here, again becomes rapidly spectacular. Rising from a cairn, scrambling takes you up and along the very edge of the cliff where concentration must be maintained throughout. At this stage it would be all too easy to be complacent but this must be resisted for you are again in a potentially dangerous situation. We crossed the west summit to complete the traverse to the east 1 hour after reaching the summit of Snowdon now towering aloofly above.

Continue to rapidly lose height by first gaining the lower heights of Lliwedd Bach then descending quickly to reach a prominent cairn at a grassy area where the path falls down to the miner's track along the side of Llyn Llydaw. One feature that struck me as we descended was the completely different colours of the two llyns. Divided artificially by a causeway, the larger most westerly one was typically black-blue reflecting the surrounding slates and derelict mine buildings, but the smaller most westerly one was the colour of copper green and shone like a jewel.

The walk takes you through high exposure and true mountain grandeur; it offers excitement and wonderment and now, down by the shore of Llyn Llydaw, with tired muscles and worn feet, you can only feel contentment at so perfect an ending. The stroll back down to Pen y Pas is pleasant and easy. Following a miner's track wide enough to resume conversation, I asked the Scotsman for his verdict: 'Aye it's a great walk right enough, but ah'll no' say it's the greatest, if you ken what I mean'. For a Scotsman to comment thus on a Welsh walk is, I think, revealing enough.

Looking across Llyn Llydaw back onto the Horseshoe.

The Walk: Tryfan by its North Ridge and then a traverse along Glyder Fach and Glyder Fawr to drop down, through the Devil's Kitchen to Cwm Idwal, Snowdonia, North Wales.
Accommodation Base: Betws-y-Coed (see p53).
Maps: L115 Snowdon and Surrounding Area. T10 Snowdonia and Anglesey.
Start and Finish: Car park by Llyn Ogwen beneath Tryfan (map ref: SH 662603).
Length: 5mls (8km)
Approx Time: 7hrs.
Descent and Ascent: 6490ft (1978m).
Difficulty: Technically the scramble up Tryfan's North Ridge is quite difficult: it involves short sections of very easy climbing but is steep and strenuous. However, despite its appearance, it is not particularly exposed and there is generally a good ledge beneath you. (It is often walked by children.) The remainder of this high mountain walk is straightforward.
Access: Car.
Seasons: April to October.
Observations: The rugged stark grandeur of the Welsh mountains is fully revealed on this walk. It includes a number of rock features synonymous with the Welsh hills including Tryfan's North Ridge, Tryfan's Adam and Eve, Glyder Fach's Cantilever, Glyder Fawr's Castle of the Winds, and Cwm Idwal's Devil's Kitchen.
Summits: Tryfan: 3010ft (917m), Glyder Fach: 3262ft (994m), Glyder Fawr 3279ft (999m).

WALES: Tryfan's North Ridge and The Glyders by Bill Birkett

The Route

From the car park pass through a little gate and traverse up and left underneath the Milestone Buttress to take a wooden stile over the wall. Continue up to gain the shoulder then go straight up the centre of the ridge above. There are a number of scrambling sections before the top of Tryfan is reached, (2¹/₂hrs, 3010ft/917m). From the summit drop down to the gap separating it from the Glyders then cross the broken wall on the left and take the path up steep scree to the left of the buttress above. Make your way over to the summit of Glyder Fach (3262ft, 994m) then take the long easy ridge to the top knoll of Glyder Fawr (2¹/₂hrs, 3279ft/999m). Drop down the shoul-

der until opposite Llyn y Cwn. A path on the right leads on steeply down through the Devil's Kitchen into Cwm Idwal. Continue on past Llyn Idwal until a further steep descent leads to Ogwen Cottage, and finally along the A5 by Llyn Ogwen to finish (1¹/₂hrs, total: 7hrs).

The Walk

The Welsh mountains generally appear unsophisticated; stark, simple and exhilarating they may be, pretty they are not. Their effect is to challenge, rather than entice; to up the pulse and to create the desire to conquer. Once these hills have aroused that latent and primitive urge within you, they must be taken at their most difficult — anything less is unsatisfactory

— and the walk taking Tryfan's north ridge, and the traverse along the Glyders before descending into the Devil's Kitchen and Cwm Idwal, meets that challenge head on.

The dinosaurian naked rock shoulder of Tryfan plunges from its pinnacled top to the A5 in one leap — the very epitome of a mountain ridge. Our route takes it direct, explores the delights of Adam and Eve, the two stone pillars on the summit (which from the A5 far below appear to be motionless mountaineers), and continues to find the Cantilever Slab and The Castle of the Winds. All in all a grand tour, taking in what are probably the most famous rock features in Wales.

Starting from the nearest of the car parks, go through a small circular iron gate to gain the scree and slaty rocks that will be with you for the rest of the walk. Above is Milestone Buttress, once very popular with climbers, but now a little neglected for the more obvious cliffs of Llanberis Pass — but if anyone should be on the steep walls you will get a better idea of its true scale. A stile and steep scree take you up to the shoulder of the ridge and from here the way is straight up the centre. (If you feel it is a little too much then the Heather Terrace goes off up to the left here, giving a gentle walk across to the south end of Tryfan where our path over the Glyders can be joined again.)

There are fine views down Llyn Ogwen and Paul Cornforth and I stopped to watch an RAF jet thunder down at the same altitude as we were ourselves. Heads down and taking the steep ground as forcibly as we could I frequently noticed quite fine samples of semi faceted quartz, good enough to put on the window ledge, but far too heavy to carry. The scrambling is steep in places, and polished, but is constantly broken by large ledges which hide the drop and give the feeling that a fall may not mean the absolute end. Soon a terrace is reached and on one you will see a finger of rock known as 'The Cannon' — look for it when you eventually get back down to Ogwen Cottage.

The nature of the walk changes a little here — the rocks get steeper — but fortunately the handholds improve and so the overall diffi-

Facing page: **Looking up to the North Ridge and Tryfan's summit.**

Top right: **The rocky outcrop known as The Castle of The Winds looks more difficult to climb than it is.**

Bottom right: **The rocky amphitheatre of the Devil's Kitchen is very atmospheric.**

culty stays about the same. As the ridge slackens and you move towards the summit, sheer clean rock is everywhere and, quite apart from the excellent view, the surroundings are most impressive. As you struggle onto the very top of Adam or Eve you can feel justifiably pleased with your ascent. As for gaining 'The Freedom of Tryfan' by jumping from one to the other — well I didn't!

A bit of scrambling and a steep descent takes you down below the Bristly Ridge. I thought we had had enough scrambling for the day and with one eye on the sky, which was rapidly clouding over, took the wide path up the scree over to the left. As we hit the top, infuriatingly, the clouds swirled in preventing 'clean' photographs of the famous 'Cantilever'.

But if anything it served to heighten the dramatic effect of the bizarre collection of stone that forms this unique plateau. The top of the Bristly Ridge consists of large plates and they resemble the scaled back of a brontosaurus. Huge rock slabs lay scattered like an abandoned pack of playing cards. Then there is the 'Cantilever' itself — a curious sight.

Possibly this feature was first publicised by the photographs of George and Ashley Abraham — two pioneer climber-photographers from Keswick in the Lake District, who carried a colossal wooden and brass camera around the hills with them. Moustachioed George was tall and lanky and Ashley was reputedly, at 20 years of age, a big man of 'wide girth'; both had a riotous sense of humour. They had a lifelong love affair with the hills and, enjoying it to the full, had many an adventure.

They produced a number of excellent early books on climbing and mountaineering, each illustrated with their own superb photographs. George Abraham along with O.G. Jones was the first to climb Milestone Buttress, the cliff that marks the start of this walk, in 1899. They also photographed Adam and Eve on the top of Tryfan; typically they photographed it with a gentleman lying horizontal and spanning the gap, with a lady in long dress standing gamely on his person — suspended between the two rock pinnacles!

I'd always wanted to see and photograph the Cantilever ever since those early Abraham photographs first captured my imagination. There was one photograph with a multitude of people, in Victorian dress of course, all balanced on the very tip of the protruding slab. Today the cast of thousands were markedly absent and I would have to make do with less than perfect visibility. Despite this, Paul shouted 'How do you want me?' and I told him to do a hand stand, which much to my surprise

he did! It's not very easy standing on one's hands up there I can tell you — have a look up and you will see what I mean.

The summit itself, a little further on, is another collection of splintered rocks. It stands above the surrounding ground, like a ruined castle. We had our lunch 'inside the ruins' ruminating over the weather prospects. Tantalisingly the mist came and went hinting at the tremendous view to Snowdon and its satellites. It seemed to get worse and we recommenced our journey with the cloud finally down.

The Castle of Winds, yet another distinguished rock outcrop, can be by-passed but really it should be 'done'. It looks more difficult than it actually is and with a bit of grunting and heaving most will manage to climb to the turrets. The ridge from here to the next and highest summit on this round, Glyder Fawr, is easy going. As we arrived the clouds lifted and at last we could see the fabulous grandeur of the Snowdonia National Park beneath us. Many express the opinion that this walk, between the Glyders, offers the finest perspective in the whole of Wales.

Slumped at the summit rocks was a young chap who looked decidedly the worse for wear. He told us he had bivouacked on the slopes of Pen yr Ole Wen over on the opposite side of the Ogwen valley. He was attempting to traverse all the high summits surrounding the Ogwen Valley in 24 hours. He was thinking of giving up but this didn't seem just after all his effort and I suggested he joined us for a while. We set off together, Paul, in his own inimitable way scree running wildly, and the 'traverser' wobbling along in a manner which suggested that he was indeed correct — he wasn't going to do much more. We left him some way behind but on a last glance back he was still plodding methodically on. After spotting the little Llyn y Cwn we bore right to find the steep descent into a brooding Devil's Kitchen.

Care must be taken here as there is a large amount of loose rock and scree which must not be dislodged onto any parties ascending from below. The name, Devil's Kitchen, says it all and this rocky amphitheatre above steeply falling scree is very atmospheric. From a deep cleft within its walls falls a stream and the noise effectively drowns any other sound. On wild days, presumably something to do with the wind, it is said that strange sounds other than those of falling water emit from this vent in the rock.

The path now becomes a constructed affair and passes under the famous climbing ground of Idwal Slabs. I tarried awhile, watching some climbing teams in action, fancying a solo climb up these attractive rocks. But Paul, a hard rock

Paul Cornforth climbing to the top of Adam and Eve.

climber, was impatient and did not want to wait and did not want to climb — he considered the climbs were too easy. Ah, the impetuousness of youth. So we strolled back along by the shadowed waters of Llyn Idwal.

As we walked I recalled that one of the climbs up the delicate slabs was named 'Hope'. It was first led by a Mrs E.H. Daniells and the year was 1915. Another climber to make a climb here was N.E. Odell in 1919; five years later he was to be the last person to see Mallory and Irvine alive and heading for the summit of Mount Everest. We still don't know for sure if they made it or not.

There is nothing to stop you now, and as you tumble down the last steep section you may, perhaps scorn the made-up paths and increased volume of humanity. You have scaled the heights, climbed the difficult north ridge, seen the sights, and conquered Tryfan and the Glyders. Now you can begin to like the Welsh hills a little, too.

Top: **Paul Cornforth doing a hand stand on the 'Cantilever'.**

Above: **The summit of Glyder Fawr.**

Pont-y-pair Bridge.

WALES: The Betws-y-Coed River Walk by Bill Birkett

The Walk: A scenic walk from Betws-y-Coed along the Llugwy river to Swallow Falls and back (Snowdonia, North Wales).
Accommodation Base: Betws-y-Coed (see p53).
Maps: L115 Snowdon and Surrounding Area, T10 Snowdonia and Anglesey.
Start and Finish: Car park by the Pont-y-pair bridge, Betws-y-Coed (map ref: SH 568792).
Length: 4mls (7km).
Approx Time: 3hrs.
Descent and Ascent: 450ft (140m).
Difficulty: An easy stroll that can be made more difficult by keeping below the surfaced road.
Access: Car or train.
Seasons: All year.
Observations: A relaxing and scenic wooded walk along by the singing waters of Afon Llugwy to the spectacle of the tumbling Swallow Falls.

The Route

From the bridge of Pont-y-pair follow along the north bank of the river to rise up steeply past the Miner's Bridge to gain a road. After a few yards either drop down to follow the undulating little path above the river (slippy and awkward), or continue along the road until a good track breaks off leftwards to the top of the Falls. If you take the path down by the river it should be quitted for the road when a small conifer plantation and a little streamlet are reached. (A continuation can be made along at the lower level but as the falls are neared it becomes dangerously exposed and involves difficult scrambling first to reach and then to leave the base of the Falls. It is NOT recommended.)

The Walk

This is a pleasant and relaxing walk along the north bank of the clear waters of the Afon Llugwy — waters which flow from the high mountains of the Carnedds, Tryfan and the Glyders. Although suitable for a day with the family, or if the weather rules out a day in the mountains, this is still an admirable walk in its own right. A reflection of the softer and gentler qualities of Wales, it starts quietly from the ancient Pont-y-pair bridge and reaches a crescendo with the white tumbling waters of the Swallow Falls. Along the way it takes you through mixed deciduous and conifer woodland which offers excellent cover for the abundant wildlife and birdlife.

Betws-y-Coed is a stopping point for many

tourists to Wales; it is an attractive old town which dates back at least to Roman times and one of the nicest things about it is that after just a few hundred yards you're into the first section of wood and have left the crowds behind. The next section allows you to stroll through green meadows and here the river has widened and become lazier. There are a number of fine oaks of great age along here too.

At the end conifers take over for a while and the path steepens as you rise above the river, now channelled into a rocky gorge down below. The steeply angled bridge is known as the Miner's Bridge and there are, indeed, a number of mineral workings to be found on these wooded slopes. The bridge slopes at an alarming angle and, thinking about it, I cannot recall ever seeing a bridge deck placed at such a steep angle — in this form it can only have been used by animals and pedestrians, no wheeled vehicles would clear it.

Walking down onto the bridge is a worthwhile exercise, for the scene both up and down stream is, in summer, of a deep green-leaved tunnel. It is roofed yet the light streams through; delicate and intricate fingers of light that filter unimaginable nuances of colour. In autumn it is even more magnificent. The river here has sprung back into vivacious life and you can appreciate that in full spate it must be a formidable torrent. The rocks are polished smooth from its influence.

After this you gain the road, but within a hundred yards you have a choice either to keep on the road (which leads to a good track to the top of the Falls), or you can drop down left, nearer the river, onto an undulating little path. This path is muddy, washed away in places, and often blocked by fallen trees. We, Paul Cornforth and myself, followed it with glee. You will return, in any case, by the upper route, so I will describe something of this lower alternative.

As you pass through the large conifers you notice the distinctive pine smell of resin and the river sings, sweeter even than any Welsh choir, not far below. One imagines that if the Welsh pixie is alive and well then he undoubtedly lives hidden here in these idyllic woods. A large-diameter, rotting iron pipe suddenly marks the entrance to a mine shaft. The water flowing from the tunnel is obviously rich in minerals for it has stained the rocks dried blood red. In the river old slate pillars are the only remains of a bridge.

When a little conifer wood and stream is reached it is time to quit the riverside and rejoin the track to the right. To continue along by the river is exposed, dangerous and involves sections of climbing on rotten rocks. It is a pity that this path is unsuitable because it takes you right to the bottom of the Swallow Falls. Seen from this angle the Falls reveal themselves to

Top: **The path along the Afon Llugwy**.

Above: **The woods along the Afon Llugwy give delightful dappled shade.**

67

Above left: **The white tumbling waters of Swallow Falls.**

Above right: **This gentle walk is ideal for the family.**

be a three-tiered affair; three considerable rock slides that break the clear flowing Afon Llugwy into a foaming, writhing mass of turbulent water. Both exciting and beautiful, there is something fascinating when water reveals its potential power.

The track is reasonably well fenced but there is a considerable drop into the gorge and care and discretion should be exercised if a closer view of the Falls is sought. Really this higher path only gives a satisfactory view of the uppermost fall but this alone is a fine and worthwhile sight — the high point of a classic little Welsh walk.

THE LAKE DISTRICT: The Coast To Coast Walk by Tony Greenbank

The Route

Footpaths and roads lead from the St Bees sea cliffs via Cleator to Ennerdale Bridge. Ennerdale Valley is followed to its head beneath the North Face of Great Gable. This is turned to the left, the route going up and over the slopes of Brandreth before descending into Borrowdale via the summit of Honister Pass.

Leaving Borrowdale by Stonethwaite and Greenup Ghyll, the way continues south east over Greenup Edge and down Far Easedale into Grasmere. Grisedale Pass is the next stage, a north-east passage, leading to Patterdale and offering the option of climbing Helvellyn and traversing Striding Edge en route.

From Patterdale the walk heads east across High Street (the high-level Roman Road), descending to the shores of Haweswater Reservoir and leading along paths and roads to Shap.

Continuing east, the route crosses the M6 motorway by footbridge to traverse a limestone plateau (elevation about 1000ft, 305m) to Kirkby Stephen. Then, after an energetic climb, the main Pennine watershed at Nine Standards Rigg (2170ft, 661m) is topped, and high open moors spread to the half way point at Keld in Swaledale.

The section from Keld to Reeth can either be taken by following the banks of the River Swale — or at a higher level using the old lead miner's tracks over the moors. A similar choice

An energetic climb is needed to reach the main Pennine watershed at Nine Standards Rigg, the point where all streams on one side flow to the Irish Sea, whilst on the other they go to the North Sea.

of route exists between Reeth and Richmond, the higher hillside tracks via Marrick Priory now offering increasingly rural and homely countryside.

The walk next spans the Vale of Mowbray from Richmond to Ingleby Cross before regaining the heights of the Cleveland Hills via Beacon Hill, Carlton Moor, Cold Moor and Hasty Bank — not forgetting the magic Wainstones. From Clay Bank Top (on the B1257 Helmsley to Stokesley Road) it is possible to reach accommodation by bus or hitching. Otherwise continue along Car Ridge and over Urra Moor to the old Rosedale Ironstone Railway (its cinder track a walker's freeway) and a bed for the night at the Lion Inn, Blakey (B & B or camping).

The skyline ocean of purple heather continues over Roseland Head, Danby High Moor, Great Fryup Head and Glaisdale Head. After a respite at Glaisdale in lovely Eskdale a final score of miles leads idyllically — via Egton Bridge, Littlebeck, Falling Foss Forest Trail and Hawkser — to cliffs overlooking the North Sea, and finally Robin Hood's Bay.

The Walk

The Coast to Coast Walk is the finest long-distance cross-country walk in the British Isles. In its traverse it takes in a cross section of that distinctive splendour that is unique to the English countryside. In few other countries are areas of natural beauty so easily accessible; in no other are the scenic contrasts so dramatic.

This walk absorbs them all from the sandiest beaches to the highest mountains — and with vast tracts of purple moors plus country lanes and sylvan glades as well. Here are stretches so lonely that the golden eagle soaring overhead can be the only other living thing immediately in sight, while in the same day you will sample the delights of a pub meal by a village green. Here are scenes of wilderness vying with others of rustic splendour, either of which extremes have barely changed through the centuries.

The ritual of dipping one foot in the Irish Sea at St Bees on the fringes of the Lake District and the other in the North Sea at Robin Hood's Bay (bordering the North Yorkshire Moors) must signal 190 miles (306km) of the most satisfying yet at the same time challenging travelling on foot imaginable.

In its span are encountered the phenomena of how natural landscape has been formed and shaped. It also amply demonstrates along the way the part played by man since prehistoric times in moulding it to his purpose — whether it be remnants of the Industrial Revolution, ancient lead mines, the variety of farming landscapes, old pubs, incomparable churches or the rural crafts and skills daily encountered in every mile that are the countryman's inheritance.

The Coast to Coast Walk is the brainchild of Alfred Wainwright. This innovator of today's 'state of the art fell walking guidebook' may need no introduction. How he created this gem possibly does.

Envisaging a cross-county expedition that linked footpaths and bridleways through areas of open access — along with quiet roads and lanes that skirted towns and busy roads — he devised a 'pleasant' route that anybody was free to walk without 'fear of trespass or restriction'. This he finally accomplished in 1972, and he admits in his subsequent guidebook to the route, that he dreamed of it as a possible alternative to the then growing popularity of the Pennine Way.

His scheme has brought about a crossing of England that has no stamp of being 'official'. It has not required the blessing of the Countryside Commission or any other body nor have any special permissions had to be sought. Wainwright's genius can be seen to have worked in this respect by his weaving a golden thread entirely along existing rights of way or over terrain where access is traditionally free to all.

Two thirds of the crossing — were you to place the edge of your cheque book across the map from St Bees to Robin Hood's Bay — straddle the territories of three National Parks. These alone are areas of outstanding natural beauty. Added to the lovely countryside that makes up the rest of the way . . . perfection.

The walk begins on the sea cliffs at St Bees Head, traverses the heart of the Lake District, crosses the Westmorland limestone plateau, takes in the Eden Valley and Pennine watershed and joins up with Swaledale. The next stage is across the Vale of Mowbray to the Cleveland Hills and North Yorkshire Moors before arriving on the sea cliffs of Robin Hood's Bay.

It is generally agreed — indeed Wainwright suggests it — that this is the best direction in which to tackle the walk. It is a tenet of mountain travel that you ascend by the steepest way and descend by gentler slopes rather than vice versa. You will therefore find it pays on this high-level walk to first tackle the heady heights of Cumbria's finest giants, and then bring yourself safely back to earth over the wonderful heather moors of north-east Yorkshire.

Go equipped for the hills. Try to resist planning too far ahead. There are hundreds of beds for the night along this popular way. Popular, yes. But still providing such Big

Country scenarios that you will have all the room you desire. Have a wonderful two weeks!

Day 1: St Bees to Ennerdale Bridge

The Cumbrian coast makes a splendid start for a crossing of England. At St Bees the red sandstone cliffs which soar above the Irish Sea to over 300ft (90m) are a breeding ground for guillemot and puffin, and give a splendid view across the Solway Firth. It is with some reluctance that you finally turn your back on the view but given clear weather the feeling of loss is replaced at once by a sense of mounting excitement as the blue of the Lakeland mountains is seen to stretch out along the eastern horizon in an unbroken and deeply rifted chain. That is the barrier you must eventually breach and how the heart soars!

So to the actual start . . . After the obligatory wetting of a foot in the sea (reached by a path leading down to the beach from the village), the route heads initially west — yes, west! — from St Bees' seawall towards Fleswick Bay, a terrific slot in the coast.

After Fleswick Bay proceed north past the lighthouse (open to the public — tel: Whitehaven 2635). Then at an old quarry crater a turn south is taken by passing between two cottages into a red sandstone-paved lane. A private road (open to walkers) is taken to Sandwith village.

It is from 'Sanith' that the traveller can be said to be launched well and truly along the way.

Though the Lake District has become a key part of the nation's heritage, the industrial strip in the west — a Coronation Street lookalike in the shadow of the hills — is too often looked upon as flat and uninteresting, a judgement no doubt based on the scars left by industry. Yet what character there is in the countryside here — and the people.

In some places the industrial life, which originally grew from Cumberland's coal and other minerals, has now died out. And even where it thrives, the smoking chimneys, flare stacks and cooling towers are so scattered that they rarely obtrude for long on the scenery.

The next section to Cleator is one of the

This aerial photo captures the full drama of the view along Striding Edge to Helvellyn.

71

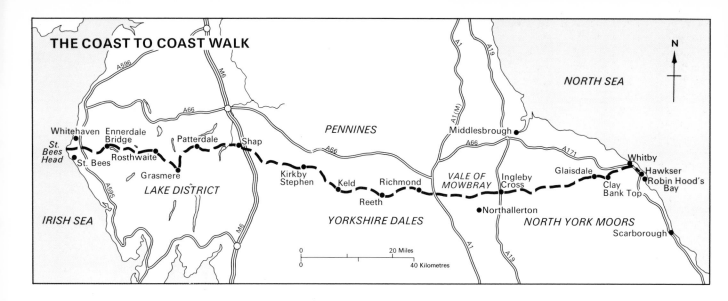

THE COAST TO COAST WALK

The Walk: The traverse of England from the Cumbrian coast to the North Yorkshire coast via the Lake District, Westmorland Limestone Plateau, Eden Valley, Pennine Watershed, Swaledale, Vale of Mowbray, Cleveland Hills and North Yorkshire Moors.

Maps: OS 1:50,000 Sheets 89, 90, 91, 92, 93, 94, 100, 101.

Start and Finish: St Bees Cumbria (map ref: NX 960118), and Robin Hood's Bay, North Yorkshire (map ref: NZ 953049).

Length: 190mls (305km).

Approx Time: 2 weeks.

Difficulty: A beautiful route covering a greatly varied cross section of terrain where the going over mountains and moors predominates. Paths are well defined in general, though several tracts of high ground are sufficiently featureless to prove serious in bad weather. Some skill with a map and compass is necessary if the weather should change. There are low-level alternatives by road and footpath if weather reports sound ominous.

Access: Good rail and bus services to St Bees; bus service from Robin Hood's Bay and trains from nearby Whitby.

Seasons: April to November.

Observations: The walk is possible in winter though the risk of fresh snow on high ground makes the enterprise not so much dangerous as an horrific grind. Given hard frosts the going underfoot becomes a joy. During any dry spell it is worth carrying a drink at all times as streams can prove scarce — especially on the limestone plateau between Shap and Kirkby Stephen. Many variations of route are possible — whether strenuous short cuts or more lengthy detours. Ultimate variant: to walk from east to west, but this could mean facing prevailing winds.

Accommodation: Hotels, inns, bed and breakfast accommodation and youth hostels.

Guidebooks: A Coast to Coast Walk by A. Wainwright (Westmorland Gazette).

exceptions where industrial views do predominate. From the chemical plant of Marchon on the Whitehaven side of St Bees Head, to village streets along the way which still so resemble the Salford that L.S. Lowry occasionally painted, the scenery is all the more dramatic when contrasted with the green hill of Dent ahead. The glorious views in every direction from the summit of Dent puts the industrial belt in its perspective. Predominating is the fact that the Cumbrian coast is essentially a land of pleasant greenness.

Try not to skip Dent (it can be by-passed along the road). It's great. And in its shelter lies the hamlet of Ennerdale Bridge, and a bed for the night.

Day 2: Ennerdale Bridge to Rosthwaite

Ennerdale Bridge lies below a steep hill, and it is from here that a tantalising view is gained of the distant Pillar Rock, one of the finest crags in England. Its profile juts high from the flanks of Pillar Mountain which towers above Ennerdale Water. It is a magnificent prospect and heralds some marvellous country ahead.

Ennerdale Water is the most isolated lake being the only Cumbrian lake without a public road on either side and as such it is ideally suited to the long-distance walker. Recently it has been threatened by a controversial water authority scheme to raise its natural level, but this would be a shame as it is amazing walking country both along its green depths and in the forests of Ennerdale valley beyond.

Taking the right-hand side of the lake — below the bizarre Crag Fell Pinnacles and then under Angler's Crag by an interesting scramble skirting the water — the route eventually joins the main forest road along the valley. The

River Liza flowing down from the head of Ennerdale and into the lake has to be crossed by the bridge.

The rest of the way along Ennerdale is via the forest road. It is idyllic — a magic passage through plantations of rowan, hemlock, larch, spruce and pine. Full of birdlife, flowers, mosses and ferns, it is heady with the scent of fresh pine needles. Towering above up to the right — and glimpsed suddenly through the breaks of fire lanes — towers Pillar Rock.

When the forest ends another famous mountain prospect faces the walker now approaching the valley headwall: the North Face of Great Gable. This great rock face is so redoubtable that even today one of the routes up it is still called Mallory's Climb after its founder, the great Everest mountaineer.

The Coast to Coast Walk, after passing England's remotest youth hostel (Black Sail), now pierces the ring of mountains by contouring along the left flanking hillside to Loft Beck, and up. The scenery is so spellbinding hereabouts that on the top of nearby Haystacks, Mr Wainwright intends his ashes to be scattered after he passes on. And so the way continues up and over the open mountain slopes of Brandreth to the quarries old and new of Honister Pass.

The walkers' signpost to this moonscape of slate is the hulk of the old Drum House which used to operate the tramway cable from the cutting sheds below. And it is by the old tramway sleepers that the route goes steeply down to the roadside.

From the summit of Honister an ancient green toll road provides a welcome alternative route to the hamlet of Seatoller at the bottom of the 1-in-4 road gradients. The remaining short stage of the day to the hamlet of

Rosthwaite is a joy. Here, at the head of Borrowdale, is wonderful countryside: whitewashed cottages clustered in a raggle taggle of rich green fields and thick drystone walls. Raven-haunted cliffs, gurgling waterfalls and rustling woods of birch and oak bring alive the hills on every side.

The wettest place in England lies approximately a mile from Seatoller just off the Coast to Coast route, and it is worth a visit if there is time. The annual rainfall can be more than four times the London average. But don't be deterred! According to shepherd Stanley Edmondson, May, June and September are the driest months, with the scenery at its best in spring and autumn: lush and green in spring, and speckled with yellows and brown from September until its vivid fiery climax of colour in October.

Generations of Edmondsons still live at Seathwaite where one of their addresses is Raingauge Cottage. And Stan will tell you he has no need to go anywhere to see the world. The world and his wife come to Seathwaite. 'This is Paradise,' he said while clipping a ewe, the sound of the waterfalls of Sour Milk Gill above bringing music to our ears.

Day 3: Rosthwaite to Grasmere

The next two days ahead promise further magnificent scenery — a succession of valleys and high passes strung together not necessarily in the shortest sequence but more than compensating for that with their superb mountain grandeur and ever-changing views.

The shorter direct route due east to Patterdale is a beeline fraught with much more uncompromising terrain, and is less rewarding while proving doubly strenuous. A series of skylines running north to south block the way. They present a giant roller coaster of a route where height gained is as quickly lost. The Coast to Coast Walk instead tacks across these obstructions by first zigging south east to Grasmere, then zagging north east back to Patterdale. While the total zig-zag can be done in a day, it is a strenuous undertaking. By far the easier way is to break the leg at Grasmere.

The first objective is the hamlet of Stonethwaite nestling under The Hanging Gardens of Borrowdale in a little Hobbit kingdom of its own. It can be hard to leave such an English heaven from another age and address yourself to the climb up Greenup Gill. This passes beneath Eagle Crag, a 'Giant Grim' of a precipice and from the valley the going looks tough.

Any ordeal likely to be found, however, is not in this fairyland where tiny wild flowers glow from bowling green turf flanking the rough track, but beyond Lining Crag above which signals wild open countryside and rugged terrain. The path becomes less obvious, the ground more peaty and in misty weather the need for careful compass work is a must.

Greenup Edge is the Great Divide between Borrowdale and Grasmere and it arrives next — an old iron fence post marking the spot. It does not mean, however, that Grasmere lies just ahead. On this high wilderness of crags, bogs, valleys, streams and scree slopes the traveller must literally pick his way by the faint track (and sometimes there seem so many) before reaching the head of Far Easdale (marked by the remnants of another old wire fence plus iron stile).

Instead of following this valley's track (now without fear of complication) to Grasmere, a detour can be made to the left at the fence and over Calf Crag, then down its east ridge to Gibson Knott — a fun skyline of ups and downs. This leads to a grassy col and a final steep little climb to the top of Grasmere's pride, Helm Crag.

Helm Crag is better known locally as The Lion and The Lamb on account of the shape of the summit rocks. The view from here, and of Grasmere in particular, is out of this world. And just across the way is the most popular of all the Lakeland peaks — Helvellyn — a treat it is possible to include in the next day's walk. Meanwhile a steep track leads down towards Grasmere.

Day 4: Grasmere to Patterdale

An advantage of splitting the route at Grasmere is that the summit of Helvellyn (3118ft, 950m), one of Lakeland's finest, can be taken in more conveniently and safely along the way east. Although it is not directly on the main route, it is within easy range.

Grasmere itself — that natural amphitheatre in the hills and a grand stadium for its famous annual Grasmere Sports (on the Thursday nearest to August 20) — has unrivalled settings. The landscape is virtually unchanged from the days when William Wordsworth explored this very terrain. Fellow writers sometimes accompanying him were Sir Walter Scott, Charles Lamb and Samuel Taylor Coleridge.

Grasmere Sports are England's Highland Games. The games which attract thousands of visitors include Cumberland and Westmorland wrestling, fell racing up and down Butter Crag and hound trailing where hounds follow an artificially laid trail around the hillsides at speeds of up to 25 mph. The main road from Keswick to Ambleside (A591) passes the

Stan Edmondson, hill farmer from Seathwaite. (Photo: Anthony Greenbank.)

73

showfield. And it is by walking north along this busy artery we begin.

Just past the Travellers's Rest Inn at Mill Bridge the Coast to Coast Walk climbs through woods, past waterfalls and on up Tongue Gill by a choice of paths to Grisedale Pass. And just beyond is the wild scenario of Grisedale Tarn in a mountain bowl amid the tops.

Grisedale Tarn lies at 1768ft (539m), and is the place to make the decision whether or not to climb Helvellyn, the third highest peak in the Lake District. The ascent can be safely tackled by any fit and properly equipped walker, but a head for heights is needed along the exciting skyline of Striding Edge.

If weather, fitness or other factors persuade you to by-pass the mountain, then you go down the valley of Grisedale and through a spectacular defile between high mountains which will guide you as surely as if you were on rails.

If the choice is to climb Helvellyn instead, the start is from the outlet of the tarn and up the well-etched path of Dollywaggon Pike. A heady traverse is now taken on over Nethermost Pike, then up to the top of Helvellyn itself. Given good visibility, there is something other than one of the best views in England to consider — and that is tackling Striding Edge. 'This', says Alfred Wainwright, 'is an exhilarating traverse (the best quarter-mile between St Bees and Robin Hood's Bay).' Look for Gough's memorial erected on the edge of the summit above the path down to Striding Edge. A friable path leads down rocky terrain below, but once Striding Edge itself is reached, the route — whether by its very crest or the well-polished footholds on the Red Tarn side — is a joy. What a way to arrive in Patterdale!

Day 5: Patterdale to Shap

A popular tourist village ringed by mountains where St Patrick, the patron saint of Ireland is said to have preached and baptised converts, Patterdale is also the final outpost of civilization before crossing Lakeland's last great barrier to those journeying east: High Street, the lofty Roman Road that stretches for nine unbroken miles from north to south.

The day begins along the main road from Patterdale to Kirkstone Pass. A little way south of the village church at a small lay-by, a track leads to the steep slopes of Place Fell. These are ascended by a gentle rising traverse which aims for the col between Patterdale and Boardale. Not far below this it turns south, kinks beneath the craggy knoll of Angle Tarn Pikes and dips towards Angle Tarn, a Lakeland jewel.

The way now traverses around the flank of Satura Crag, crosses over a peaty depression and ascends on up to The Knott. Endless acres north give refuge to Lakeland's red deer, sometimes golden eagles are seen flying at tremendous heights above and the route has never seemed so lonely — nor lovely.

It continues south east past The Knott to a point on the summit ridge which looks down into the hidden valley of Riggindale. It was here Hugo Holme hid from the vengeance of King John, survived, and so began a succession of The Kings of Mardale.

At Twopenny Crag on the verge of Riggindale the route now turns for Kidsty Pike and a fine vantage point. Then it's down the east ridge (easy) and so on to the path along the left-hand side of Haweswater Reservoir, courtesy of Manchester Corporation.

Submerging the village of Mardale, once at its head, the waters sometimes reveal the ruins of the Dun Bull Inn and also of Mardale's

Holy Trinity church which was demolished in 1936. Nearly 100 bodies from the graveyard were reburied at Shap. And local legend says that when the waters are ruffled by strong winds, the church bells can still be heard.

Soon the Coast to Coast Walk begins to follow footpaths through fields and cultivated valleys, some of them only recently having been brought back to life by the introduction of this walk. Fortunately OS maps and guidebooks — used with due care — cope. And from Haweswater dam to the remnants of 12th-century Shap Abbey via Rosgill Bridge, the transition from fell-going to cross-country walking begins.

Shap Abbey Farm is one of the biggest sheep farms in Cumbria with 6000 acres of rugged hill country. Shepherd Edward Bindloss knows them well. 'As a lad I got lost on the fell at Christmas,' he told me. 'Stars were starting to twinkle, there was ice on the ground. I started roaring and ran downhill until I met someone. Was I relieved! This is big country.'

Day 6: Shap to Kirkby Stephen

Shap lies on the A6. This, the highest main road in the country, peaks at nearly 1400ft (425m) amid desolate moors. And Shap village has a similarly wild ambience. Cut-off in winter time and time again, it is invariably the hardy who live here. In contrast to the communities of Lakeland this is a much more elemental outpost in every sense.

Yet the next stage is delightful. It crosses a limestone plateau nudging the 1000-ft (305m) contour. Underfoot the going can resemble treading on green baize underpinned with marble, and everywhere the white stone is sculptured into the stuff of a rock garden wonderland — and is a haven for wild flowers and ferns.

Directly across the A6 through Shap from the King's Arms Hotel, a road starts travellers on the way via a housing estate, lanes, stiles and — the key thing — a footbridge over the M6 motorway. A series of paths and tracks continue past limestone quarrying to Oddendale, a tranquil hamlet.

Heading on south a track leads past an ancient double stone circle with other archaeological remains en route: a Roman road crossed, a tumulus and an ancient dyke. Eventually the age-old cairn of Robin Hood's grave arrives — and so does Crosby Ravensworth Fell.

A short detour away, in Crosby Ravensworth, is a cameo cathedral ringed by trees — the 12th-century Church of St Lawrence — and one of the finest churches in Cumbria. And so it is across the splendid fells surround-

Facing page, top: **Daffodils bloom at Grasmere, home of Wordworth; Helm Crag can be seen in the distance.**

Facing page, bottom: **Looking across the placid waters of Grasmere Lake to Helm Crag.**

The colourful shelter at Kirkby Stephen.

ing this village — dotted with countless more Iron Age burial mounds, Roman remains and ancient settlements — that this glorious walk continues . . .

There are marvellous views of the Howgill Fells on the way to Great Asby Scar, a backcloth to the upper Lune Valley that resemble giant scatter cushions. The going underfoot needs watching too. Here are the crevassed limestone pavements of Orton Scar and beyond.

And so the good things continue to reveal themselves. Sunbiggin Tarn with waterfowl and botanical life on its sunny limestone banks; Rayseat Pike and barrow (bones galore have been found here, many charred); a mound of rocks on a green hill; heathery acres on Ravenstonedale Moor; and Smardale Bridge among a regular complex of primitive village earthworks and numerous Giants' Graves mounds.

Limekiln Hill is the last major landmark before reaching Kirkby Stephen. Tracts of lovely purple heather and the best limestone terrain with firm green slopes make it a pleasure to approach this busy market town — which is both on the famous scenic Leeds to Carlisle railway line and also a staging post on the A685 for visitors to the Blackpool Lights from the north-east.

Days: 7–8: Kirkby Stephen to Reeth

Kirkby Stephen has the charisma of a frontier town. Those who choose to live here are hardy, moulded by the force of the elements. Around the town, the smoke curling from the chimneys of some of England's loneliest farms hints at the spirit of the people in this wild and rugged land.

It is on neighbouring high ground that the main watershed of the north of England arrives, the point from where all the streams flowing on one side of the hill are destined for the Irish Sea, while on the other side such watercourses are promised to the North Sea. Until now the Coast to Coast Walk has followed the upstream path. But from the hilltop called Nine Standards Rigg (2170ft, 661m) things change, and the rivers then flow in the same direction as Robin Hood's Bay.

Nine Standards Rigg commands great views. It is obvious from here why the elements can seem even harsher than in the Lake District mountains. While the Cumbrian peaks constantly vary in shape and height, so sheltering the deep valleys between, the Pennine country has great aircraft-deck horizons that seem to stretch endlessly.

Such country is streamlined to slipstream the worst weather across its tops and into the valleys. Because of this the wild moorland stretch to Keld is a serious one if there is any hint of bad weather.

Fortunately a high, lonely road from Nateby to Keld (the B6270) provides an alternative route either totally or in part. Start along this on a wet day, find the weather improving and Nine Standards Rigg can still be reached from the road's summit. If, however, the weather breaks while you are on the fell, and you have already ascended the long slog by bridleway towards the giant cairns, steering south will lead you directly to this escape route.

Nobody knows how the stone men of Nine Standards Rigg originated but they signal the end of the really high ground is near. Above Coldbergh Edge the route flicks the 2000-ft (610m) contour for the last time on the walk. And so these upland moors with a score of summits above 2000ft (610m) are left for that deep, sinuous Yorkshire Dale with a secluded grandeur of its own: Swaledale.

The slopes of the valley are a jigsaw of drystone walls — a contrast from the open acres so far walked of cotton grass and heather, speckled with crowberry and bilberry. Keld is the forerunner of villages and hamlets yet to come with its greystone houses and swiftly flowing river. It also marks the half-way point of the walk.

There is a choice of ways to Reeth — both are superb, and both begin the same way. Opposite Keld post office a footpath joins the Pennine Way in a few hundred yards (also the route to Kidson Force) in a momentary meeting of the ways. Then they go their separate ways.

The low-level route follows the ever-snaking Swale, running alongside torrents like Kidson Force, where the water tumbles in a never-ending thunder. Muker (three miles on) is a village gem. The other way is high level. It uses the old lead miner's tracks across the moors. It is interesting, the views wide and the going is splendid.

Swaledale, a pastoral haven today, was very different in the past. Then lead mining was an important industry and relics of this bygone era are still visible today where the moors and gill-flanks were plundered for the mineral. In the 1880s the industry went into decline with the competition from foreign imports. Some families stayed to readjust to the ever-changing fortunes of farming, but many left and the moors went back to being the sole haunt of curlews, lapwings, red grouse and black-faced Swaledale sheep.

And this is how it still is today. Ironically among these workings are the ravines known as 'hushes'. They were bulldozed for the damming of hillside streams thus building up a flashflood to gouge out the minerals below. Hushes! It's a lovely thought as yet another low-flying RAF Tornado jet fighter screams by.

And so past Swinner Gill mines, East Grain smelt mill, Lownathwaite mine, Gunnerside Gill (hushes galore here), Old Gang and then Surrender Bridge smelt mills to Reeth, the heather capital of Upper Swaledale.

Days 9–10: Reeth to Ingleby Cross

Reeth buildings form a square around a green, in all a grand centre for a beautiful dale. The village has a folk museum which is useful for gleaning local information on this section of England's wonder crossing.

Although the banks of the Swale can be followed all the way to Richmond, the higher hillside paths are more rewarding. If you take the latter the road to Marske leads towards the farm road to 12th-century Marrick Priory.

Swaledale recalls the Middle Ages with a number of monastic ruins and castles. Marske Hall and its beautiful grounds was the home of a family producing two Archbishops of York.

And it is in Richmond (pop: 7000) that an 11th-century Norman castle sits on a bluff or rock high over a loop in the lovely River Swale. From its top there is one of northern England's great views, taking in the dales and homing in on to the Vale of York.

The curfew is rung each night at 9pm from the Holy Trinity Church. It's a hint. The next day's tough stretch to Ingleby Cross (Blue Bell Inn and nearby hotel) is a 23-mile (37km) leg. Accommodation is sufficiently scarce along the way for walkers sometimes to have to bus to nearby Northallerton.

This crossing of the Vale of Mowbray is low key, yet it has bucolic charm. It fits.

Day 11: Ingleby Cross to Clay Bank Top

If the 23-mile (37km) walk to Ingleby Cross was the 'col' of the Coast to Coast, and even Everest has its South Col between two summits, the dozen miles on to Clay Bank Top carries the route to the heights again. And — given luck with the weather — a splendid day ahead.

Ingleby Cross is a springboard for this superb leg, a route along the great scarp of the Cleveland Hills and one so good it shares part of its way with those time-established classics, the Lyke Wake Walk AND the Cleveland Way.

It is from the rim of the Vale of Mowbray to

A Force near Keld.

the east coast of Yorkshire — some 30 miles (48km) of rich purple moors — that this marathon across England climaxes towards a brilliant end. The way is a blaze of colour from midsummer into autumn. Out of the wild sandstone plateau, streams flow into the deep

77

valleys with only a greystone village here or there huddled on the banks. And higher still lone farms brave out the winter blizzards.

It is remote, lonely and exciting on these bracing moors. Totally unfenced, the feeling of freedom they give is unique. Yet here too man has, in the past, used this high and barren ground to his own ends, be it the numerous earthworks, cairns and burial mounds to be seen — or where iron and coal, jet and alum has been wrested from the earth.

Basically the day's walk is so good because it crests the edge of space over which gliders fly. This rim consequently commands extensive views of moorland heights and rural vales. It is bracing and airy, delightful in every way.

The top of Beacon Hill is the first objective, reached after a woodland detour and passing en route the OS trig point (no: S4413) that starts the Lyke Wake Walk — an exacting 40-mile (64km) slog with a 24-hour time limit to qualify for membership of the Lyke Wake Club.

The walk through bonny Scugdale is a sylvan refuge before climbing the slopes of Live Moor. This summit plateau at 1025ft (312m) is a joy, while through the heather, the route is now also visible way beyond Holey Moor on the skyline of Carlton Moor.

The updraughts of air on Carlton Moor make this a gliding paradise. Below are the pink spoilheaps of the old jet workings and from the summit is seen Roseberry Topping, Yorkshire's Matterhorn, plus a monument on Eastby Moor to Captain James Cook, the best known of a number of Cleveland's great seafarers.

And so it goes on! Up, along, down. Up, along, down . . . Cringle End . . . Cringle Moor . . . Cold Moor . . . Hasty Bank with the jagged Wainstones outcrop . . . until finally the splendedly airy Hasty Bank traverse to Clay Bank Top brings you momentarily down to earth on the B1257 Helmsley to Stokesley road.

Day 12: Clay Bank Top to Glaisdale

Clay Bank Top is not the place to spend the previous evening unless you are backpacking, but it does mark a stage where accommodation is reasonably near — either at Great Broughton or Stokesley (reached by bus or thumb, the return to Clay Bank Top next morning by bus). It also signals the popular alternative — to press on for another three hours of good going and stay at the Lion Inn at Blakey, directly on the way.

The day's walking really starts on reaching Carr Ridge, peaty and straight, which then climbs easily to Urra Moor. The view back to Hasty Bank is brilliant.

The route presently joins the old Rosedale Ironstone Railway, a mineral line with a significance. The ancient rock from which these hills are shaped has helped stamp the Cleveland character. From the ironstone in this belt of hills have developed the iron and steel industries of Teesside. The waters of streams run red, so rich is the iron ore here.

The cindered track of the former railway continues on over this wilderness topping the 1000ft (305m) contour and giving a motorway of a path to travel. Between Dale Head, Farndale Moor and on to High Blakey Moor, it runs on an embankment.

Around Blakey Gill loop, the line is left for a track. This leads to the Lion Inn at Blakey and a road. More high moorland follows. More rich purple. More standing stones and monuments. Finally — after Roseland Head, Danby High Moor, Great Fryup Head and Glaisdale Head — comes Glaisdale in Arcadian Eskdale.

Days 13–14: Glaisdale to Robin Hood's Bay

Robin Hood's Bay can be reached in a day from Glaisdale. The going is easy underfoot (19 miles, 31km), but such is the beauty and variety of the countryside en route it is more enjoyable when traversed without pressure. Hawkser village gives an ideal opportunity to break the journey and arrive fresh.

Egton Bridge is a hillside village among bountiful rustic scenery that makes England famous. It is a warm, rural landscape, punctuated by buildings of warm mellow stone now beneath the rim of hills and moors, and with luxuriant woodlands as green as watercress.

Littlebeck hamlet is the stuff of nymphs and shepherds. The purple mantle of heathery high ground returns and from the tumulus of Flat Howe you can see — as well as the gigantic golf balls (soon to be replaced with a tall pyramid) of Fylingdales Early Warning System — Whitby Abbey and the glint of ocean.

The route follows the Falling Foss Forest Trail for a mile, then the heather of Greystone Hills to Hawkser. It is possible to make a beeline straight for Robin Hood's Bay. The proper ending of the Coast to Coast Walk, however, takes the longer coastal route along the cliffs overlooking the bay and its rocky reef running in strange concentric patterns.

The narrow main street plunges down giddily into the North Sea between the little shops and houses. And so do you, to complete your walk in the traditional way by putting one foot in the sea.

Facing page, top: **Looking across Upper Swaledale.**

Facing page, bottom: **The splendid view down to Robin Hood's Bay and the end of the Coast to Coast Walk is in sight.**

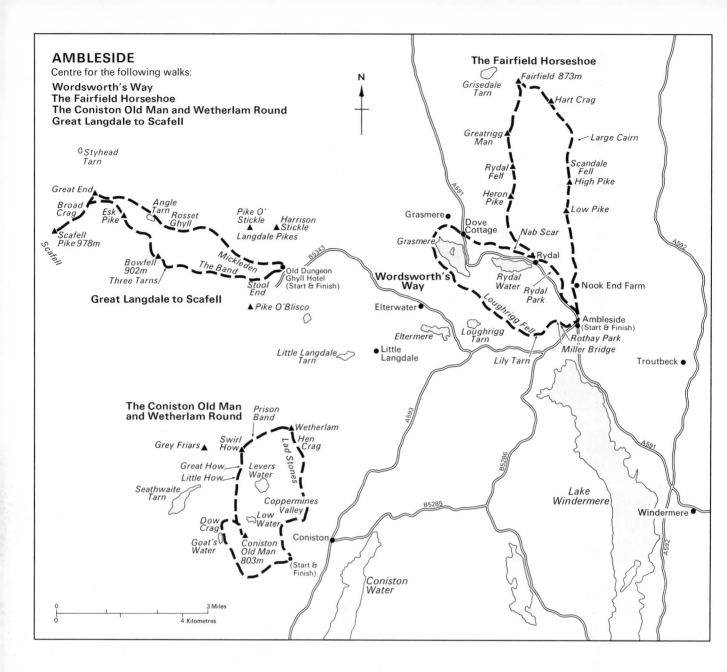

AMBLESIDE

Centre for the following walks:

Wordsworth's Way
The Fairfield Horseshoe
The Coniston Old Man and Wetherlam Round
Great Langdale to Scafell

N

The Fairfield Horseshoe

Grisedale Tarn

Fairfield 873m

Hart Crag

Large Cairn

Greatrigg Man

Scandale Fell
High Pike

Rydal Fell

Styhead Tarn

Heron Pike

Low Pike

Great End

Broad Crag

Angle Tarn

Rosset Ghyll

Esk Pike

Pike O' Stickle

Harrison Stickle

Langdale Pikes

Grasmere

Dove Cottage

Nab Scar

Scafell Pike 978m

Scafell

Bowfell 902m

Three Tarns

Mickleden

The Band

Stool End

Old Dungeon Ghyll Hotel (Start & Finish)

Grasmere

Rydal

Wordsworth's Way

Rydal Water

Nook End Farm

Rydal Park

Great Langdale to Scafell

Pike O'Blisco

Elterwater

Loughrigg Fell

Ambleside (Start & Finish)

Rothay Park
Miller Bridge

Eltermere

Loughrigg Tarn

Little Langdale Tarn

Little Langdale

Lily Tarn

Troutbeck

The Coniston Old Man and Wetherlam Round

Prison Band

Wetherlam

Swirl How

Hen Crag

Grey Friars

Lad Stones

Great How

Levers Water

Little How

A593

Seathwaite Tarn

Coppermines Valley

Lake Windermere

Dow Crag

Low Water

Goat's Water

Coniston Old Man 803m

Coniston

B5285

Windermere

(Start & Finish)

Coniston Water

0   3 Miles
0   4 Kilometres

80

AMBLESIDE – The Lake District

Ambleside: Centre for the following 4 walks: Great Langdale to Scafell; The Coniston Old Man and Wetherlam Round; The Fairfield Horseshoe; Wordsworth's Way.
Map Ref: NY 375045.
Location: Head of Lake Windermere, in the central Lakes, on the A591 (Lake District, North-West England).
Distance to Walks: 0mls to Wordsworth's Way, 0mls to the Fairfield Horseshoe, 7mls (11km) to Great Langdale and the start of The Langdale to Scafell Pike Walk, $8^{1}/_{2}$mls (14km) to Coniston and start of The Coniston Old Man and Wetherlam Round.
Accommodation: Plentiful hotel and bed and breakfast accommodation, a youth hostel and a campsite at Langdale.
Population: 2900.

The Town: Ambleside is an attractive Lakeland town with much traditional building in local slate. Shopping facilities are adequate and there is a cinema/restaurant/art complex for wet days. Attractions include boat hire at Waterhead and the little Bridge House that spans Stock Ghyll. Pronounced 'Amel Sid' locally, the town has a strategic Roman Fort at Waterhead. Walking and climbing interests are well served by the 'Climbers Shop' and 'Rock & Run'. Despite the summer influx of tourists Ambleside retains its individual character and there are probably more authors and artists resident here, per head of populus, than elsewhere in the Lake District. Real beer, brewed in Cumbria (Hartley's and Jenning's), can be found in 'The Golden Rule, 'Stringers' and 'The Unicorn'. (See you there!)

The view over the spire of Ambleside church to the Fairfield Horseshoe.

THE LAKE DISTRICT: Wordsworth's Way by Bill Birkett

The Walk: Through the heart of Wordsworth country starting from and returning to Ambleside via Loughrigg then Grasmere and Rydal (Lake District, North-West England).

Accommodation Base: Ambleside (see p81).

Maps: OS OD7-The English Lakes (South-East sheet), L90-Penrith and Keswick, T3-Lake District.

Start and Finish: Ambleside (map ref: NY 375045).

Length: 8^1/$_2$mls (13.5km).

Approx Time: 5^1/$_2$ hrs.

Ascent and Descent: 2680ft (818m).

Difficulty: An easy stroll involving a little ascent and descent.

Access: Car or bus.

Seasons: All year.

Observations: One of the most beautiful walks in Britain. It takes in the heart of Wordsworth country passing two of his homes — Dove Cottage and Rydal Mount — and provides a mild mannered walk with superlative views of all that makes Lakeland so fine: lakes, woods and hills.

The Route

Pass the spired church of Ambleside to walk through Rothay Park crossing the arched packhorse bridge (Miller's Bridge) to follow the road for a few yards. On the left a side road winds steeply up Loughrigg. After some houses are passed take a small iron stile on the left. Follow the little path through a stone stile to gain the open fell. Keep going up to the left; this way gives the best views down Windermere Lake. Go over the rocky knolls to drop down to Lily Tarn and continue along to the trig point on the top of Loughrigg. Down the shoulder to the woods above Grasmere Lake, turn down right through a gate to follow the track through the woods. When a little stone house with round chimneys is reached double back on the track down to the shore. Follow the shore until you are forced to return to a surfaced road. Follow this into Grasmere. Pass the church and continue to the junction with the main road (A591), go straight across and up the lane passing Dove Cottage on the left. As you rise up, the road forks (above the duck pond), take the left fork and continue steeply up. As the road levels you pass some lily ponds on your left then the surfacing disappears and you are on a track (The Coffin Road). Take this high-level track, contouring beneath Nab Scar, to drop down into Rydal passing Rydal Mount. Take the path past Rydal Hall to follow the track through Rydal Park. At its end continue along the A591 returning to Ambleside.

The Walk

I have named this walk Wordsworth's Way, not only because it passes two of the poet's homes, but because it captures the very essence of the beauty and romance of the English Lakes, about which Wordsworth wrote.

There isn't one thing that makes the Lake District what it is, there are mountains elsewhere that are grander and much more spectacular in form, there are more splendid houses all over Britain; there are moodier lakes, and in New Hampshire, the Japanese Alps or the Forests of Fontainbleau, even the autumnal colour can be more striking. But there is nowhere with the balance and subtlety of form and of colour that compares with the combination of water, tree and fell that can be found here. The walk which I describe takes you into a precious and delicate world — let the spirit roam free but leave only footprints and take only photographs.

In this instance I will describe the walk during a day in spring, but the day you walk it, it will be different. Each season, each moment the Lakeland mood changes; this is part of its romanticism, a quality that was so well understood by, and inspirational to, the Lake's Poets. In summer, above the crowds, the swallows swoop, the house martins dive and the swifts streak like lightning in the free air. Who wouldn't like to join them up there? In autumn, above Ambleside's high church spire the wooded flanks of Loughrigg are a riot of colour. The lime green larch, the golden oaks, the yellow horse chestnut, and the infrequent rich satin reds of the maple, all begin to discard their leaves which the wind carries to fill the lanes. The stubborn green holly and the timeless yew are infrequent sights. Above, the blood red bracken awaits your tread. In winter there is the contrast of the black rock and white snow to catch your eye. On the heights spindrift clouds devil and sweep, and the cold bites. Nearer to you, red gems hang amongst their olive green protectors whilst above, the skaters on Grasmere and Rydal, the snowballers of Ambleside and the rime crystals on Loughrigg await your individual attention.

In spring when life begins to stir, the birds to sing and the first leaves tentatively unroll; when the sun on the face is warm and the air sweet with blossom, then that is my favourite time to be on Loughrigg. This is the season when I did this walk.

The little stone-arched bridge, Miller's Bridge, over the river Rothay (reached after the short stroll through Rothay Park) is typically Lakeland: compact, neat, elegant. You start to feel the pace as you climb steeply up a winding road onto the flanks of Lough-

rigg. After passing through what was once a farm yard you take a little iron ladder stile to follow a shady path beneath great conifers. The open fell is gained by passing through another idiosyncratic feature — a slate-stone squeeze stile. Go over on the left path to climb onto the tops on the edge of Loughrigg. You will scramble over and through some rocky knolls and overlook the confluence of the Rothay and the Brathay to obtain the definitive view of Lake Windermere.

In front of you there will probably be a colourful display of sails on the many yachts, whilst behind, if the weather conditions are right, the classic Fairfield Horseshoe hangs clear as a bell. Beyond the next little rocky bastion the Coniston fells and Wetherlam stretch to Langdale and the distinctive Pikes.

The scene is one of peace, balance and harmony. But be prepared for this to be shattered; when we were there two Tornado jets suddenly appeared over the head of the lake, one turning to streak over Kirkstone Pass, whilst the other passed directly overhead. They may have been the statutory few hundred feet high above the lake but the jet passing directly overhead appeared to be very close indeed. During the course of the walk these monstrous black birds of destruction buzzed us half a dozen times, and they are a frequent source of annoyance to the residents of Ambleside.

It took all the quiet charm of Lily Tarn to restore our sense of calm. Its unruffled waters were broken only by the wispy green fingers of the resident aquatic flora. All around the green shoots of the new bracken vied with the burnt brown of the old. It would only be a matter of time before the new ousted the old. Such is nature — such is life.

You pass a solitary yew to dip down slightly before more undulations take you on and across to the highest point. Prior to reaching the trig point at another cairned rocky bump, we were hit by a sudden, cold and heavy shower of rain. We, Susan Lund and myself, attempted to seek shelter huddled behind the cairn but to no useful effect. (Perhaps if we had brought adequate clothing we would have faired better!)

The sun broke first and then the rain ceased. The silver pools of Loughrigg Tarn, Elterwater and Hawkshead lay sparkling like Tennyson's 'shining levels' before we strode on to the highest point with Silver How stretched out in front and Grasmere Lake down to our right. Easedale, Helm Crag and Dunmail Raise formed a mighty bow above little Grasmere village nestling beneath. In the woods below us and along the top of Red Bank, immature

Facing page: **Grasmere Lake below the end of Loughrigg.**

A jackdaw waits at the riverside cafe with Grasmere church behind.

lemon greens began to dominate the reds of the beech as a fresh breeze turned the leaf edges to reveal their lighter under shading.

We moved down to discover first that the steep descent had been graced with steps and secondly that the flanks of the hillside (along Loughrigg Terrace) were a carpet of bluebells. Looking at the National Trust sign I noted that the delightful woods below Red Bank are named Deerbolts Wood. The track goes through a gate into these woods and in winter there is an excellent view out along Grasmere Lake. Today the canopy of leaves obscured the distant view but no one could object to this loss for the effect is most pleasant and airy.

After a while you arrive at a stone-built Lakeland house with its traditional circular Westmorland chimneys. In the yard outside stood neat rows of timber cut for the fire. How attractive the natural stone is; here tinged red with iron intrusion it was undoubtedly quarried from just below the snout of Helm Crag.

From this location many years ago, they quarried building stone and mined for iron. Of course the Lake District Special Planning Board would not allow such activities today and interestingly they do not require new buildings to be of natural stone. That is why many of the numerous developments you can see around these parts are finished in white 'rendering'. A boon for the developers, for it is cheap, but not so good if you happen to think it rather nasty.

Avoid going out onto the road but descend instead to the shores of the lovely Grasmere. The sunshine, now quite strong brought the scene to life. On the shore before the fine gravel and clear waters grew celandine and bog myrtle and an empty rowing boat dipped in the slight breeze. You could see right through the water to the brown pebbles and darting minnows beneath its rippling surface. After a little stile it is necessary to bend under an enormous bough of a horse chestnut which lies at chest height, horizontally across the path, the shore and the water.

All too soon you are forced to leave the shore and to detour to the road. Take care for it is narrow, particularly through the rock cutting, and inevitably someone will be driving too quickly. But the walk into Grasmere nevertheless, is splendid with a host of fine trees and gardens. The sun brought out the exciting smell of growth and we almost expected the ferns to uncoil their fronds before our very eyes.

Grasmere will most probably be busy with people and you might decide to carry on through, passing the showground without wanting to break the solitude of the walk. But if you should stop then the Tea Rooms perched above the beck provide a splendid place to rest and look over to the churchyard where Wordsworth lies.

Around Dove Cottage there are always many people but not far up the hill it is quieter and in spring you will see the daffodils around the duck pond;

I wandered lonely as a cloud
That floats on high o'er vales and hills,
When all at once I saw a crowd,
A host, of golden daffodils;
Beside the lake, beneath the trees,
Fluttering and dancing in the breeze.
('The Daffodils', William Wordsworth)

The coffin road above Rydal Lake is a scenic and pleasant way to head back to Ambleside. Rydal, with its numerous rhododendron islands is of a quite different temperament to that of Grasmere. Near its end, before you drop down past Rydal Mount, where large oaks mark a little track coming up from below,

Above: **Dove cottage, Wordsworth's home, at Grasmere.**

Left: **Walkers resting by the shores of Grasmere Lake.**

Facing page, top: **My companion, Susan Lund, enjoying a brief rest on Miller's Bridge.**

Facing page, bottom: **Walkers making their way down to the woods at Grasmere Lake.**

above you there is a circular wall of rock — a perfect natural seat to survey and meditate the immense beauty of the scene.

We finished the walk through Rydal Park, where we admired the energy of the spring lambs playing in the fields. Two large ornate wrought iron gates, now rather rusty, mark the end of the park and your arrival at the main road. Not far away is my home, and like Wordsworth, I wouldn't choose to live anywhere else.

THE LAKE DISTRICT: The Fairfield Horseshoe by Bill Birkett

The Walk: A high mountain route taking the scenic Horseshoe that forms the high Rydal valley via Scandale Fell the summit of Fairfield and Rydal Fell (Lake District North-West England).

Accommodation Base: Ambleside (see p81).

Maps: OS OD7 OD5-The English Lakes (SE & NE sheets), L90-Penrith and Keswick, T3-Lake District.

Start and Finish: Ambleside (map ref: NY 375045).

Length: 12mls (19km).

Approx Time: 7hrs.

Ascent and Descent: 5500ft (1680m).

Difficulty: A straightforward mountain walk with no technical difficulty, although the going is sustained.

Access: Car or bus.

Seasons: April to October.

Observations: Considered by many to be the classic Lakeland Horseshoe walk.

Summits: Low Pike: 1667ft (508m), High Pike: 2152ft (656m), Hart Crag 2698ft (822m), Fairfield: 2863ft (873m), Greatrigg Man: 2513ft (766m), Heron Pike: 2008ft (612m).

The Route

Just after the Kirkstone road rises out of Ambleside, Nook Lane goes off to the left. Follow along this through Nook End Farm and over Low Sweden Bridge to gain the fell. Follow the track up Scandale Fell, the way being obvious, with an alternative above High Sweden Bridge; either keep high along the crest passing a little pine wood or follow the lower contouring track. Both lead onto Low Pike (the former with a scramble that can be circumnavigated), and continue along the horseshoe rim to eventually gain the top of Fairfield. From the summit it is necessary to retrace one's footsteps a little way to gain the correct descent ridge down to Greatrigg and

the Rydal Fell (take care in poor visibility that you do not descend the end of Fairfield above Grisedale Tarn!). There are no complications and once Rydal is regained most will return to Ambleside via the track through Rydal park.

The Walk

This a good honest mountain walk, straightforward and obvious, at the end of which you will feel satisfaction. Its shape is perfect, taking you up steadily from Ambleside to the summit of Fairfield (2863ft, 873m) and then gently back down to Rydal, where you link across the open neck of the Horseshoe to return to your starting point. Uncomplicated, no fuss, no communication required to summon distant transport; a classic of its type.

From Ambleside and its environs the semi ring of fell rising to Fairfield at its highest is the most easily identifiable mountain challenge. The east leg is formed by Low Pike and High Pike of the Scandale Fell and these lead to Hart Crag above Rydal Head then the summit. The usual return, and the one described here, is to descend the western leg to Greatrigg Man and the Rydal Fell to Heron Pike and down, passing Rydal Mount.

Little Nook Lane rapidly leaves the houses and tourists of Ambleside behind and the road finishes at Nook End Farm. It is a traditional Lakeland hill farm, and as you pass through it sheep dogs and terriers bark violently from under the doors of barns and outhouses. At certain times of year, at clipping time or when the lambs are being separated, the yard itself and the 'intak' between this and Low Sweden bridge will be full of Herdwicks; the hardy Lakeland sheep that live their lives on the high fells and are said to have been brought here by the Vikings.

Before you reach the bridge notice the large tree stump on the right; it must have been a tremendous tree. The little wooded dell around the stream is just a flash before you start out onto the open fell. A fine ash stands in the field and the views of Ambleside and down Lake Windermere begin to rapidly unfold. Soon there is a choice of ways: to aim up for the crest and walk along the ridge with excellent views along to Rydal, or to keep on the more obvious low trail and enjoy the tranquillity of Scandale below.

The higher route includes a little rocky scramble before it moves along to gain Low Pike. The stone wall which follows the crest of the ridge is of some use here and offers reassurance. Surely if a wall can be built up these rocks they can be climbed! Lakeland stone walls are quite amazing. Their builders must have been absolute Titans and although their lines, snaking up steep hillsides and ringing fields on the heights seem to defy logical explanation they look purposeful. The stone wall is an ingenious design and is constructed to move with the earth as it shifts and settles, without breaking. A good example of all this lies a little further on where the wall bends in the middle but remains intact. This is why, with little maintenance, so many stone walls remain even though their purpose has long been forgotten.

From High Pike views across Rydal Valley show the beck — its rocky pools a favourite swimming place for the lads of Ambleside — and the vegetated Erne Crag which sports a

quarry on its right-hand side. There is one solid white wall of rock and recently a number of rock climbs have been made up this. It is a sign of the times when the cleaner higher rocks of Langdale and the other popular centres are abandoned for the sake of the new. What can I say? I am one of those climbers!

Even before you dip down to make the climb to Hart Crag the windswept nature of these high grounds is apparent and the ground is stripped down to bare rock or scree. The path and the surrounding area appears to have been actually quarried: sharp angular rock protrudes through the finer rock debris. Over to the right, on the shoulder and dropping down to Scandale Head, stands a distinctive cairn. Why out there and just what its purpose was I don't know.

Most of my many trips onto these heights have been made in winter via the large cliffs below to the north, from Dove Crag and Scrubby sited across on the upper slopes of Link Cove. It's exciting up here in winter when it's magnificently wild and desolate but it's a world only for those with the correct equipment and the ability to use it. Great waves of snow build up cornices to the north, especially in the hollows on either side of Hart Crag and around the summit rim of Fairfield itself.

From the summit even in late spring when only the occasional patch of snow remains, the view along to the precipitous ridge to Cofa Pike and St Sunday Crag is dramatic. In full winter garb it's nothing short of Alpine. The mountain scene from Fairfield across Grisedale to the mighty Helvellyn range is one of the finest in England. From here no oasis of humanity can be seen to relieve the seriousness of this totally mountain environment.

But summer days are equally good in their different way, and distinctly warmer and pleasanter to boot. Tremendous views of breathtaking blue down to Windermere are enjoyed all the way down the west ridge. But be careful here after you have walked along to the summit of Fairfield, for it is very easy to descend down the ridge to Grisedale Hause by mistake. If Grisedale Tarn (the keeper of King Dunmail's gold crown) comes into sight in front of you, you are going the wrong way. In poor visibility, declining to use map and compass, I've made this mistake myself and it's a long walk from Grasmere to Ambleside after cresting Fairfield, I can assure you.

Deceptively, for from below it does not appear so, it is a long haul up to Fairfield by Scandale Fell and it's perhaps fortunate that the descent down the west leg of this Horseshoe is straightforward and easy. The richness of colour along Windermere and in

Facing page: **Looking from Flinty Grave across to the summit of Fairfield.**

Below: **Walking down the gap between Hart Crag and the rise to Fairfield.**

the vale of Grasmere offers a welcome contrast to the starkness of the heights and it hastens your descent.

Perhaps if you have tackled this walk in the 'backend' (the Lakeland 'backend' is simply the last few months of the year and starts in mid September) or early spring then you may have heard or seen the Coniston Fox Hounds hill pack in action. Whilst making no comment whatsoever on the ethics of hunting no one can truthfully say that to see and hear the hounds in action on their native ground, is not a stirring experience. Before you see anything you will most probably hear the lead hound 'give mouth' as he takes the scent. This is the signal for the others, and their staccato baying echoes around the horseshoe. To glimpse them

can be difficult but once spotted their white forms move at an amazing speed over wall and crag and along the steep rough terrain. An animal perfectly matched to its task.

But now you are on the last leg of your walk and if you didn't start the day too early you should be treated to the sun setting as it dips out of sight to the west. A red sky with the once grey clouds now edged gold, and Grasmere shining silver in the last remnants of light, is a sight that should be seen by everyone at least once in a lifetime. And as you move on into the gathering dusk and the lights begin to twinkle one by one in the low valley below, you can feel well satisfied with your day out — around this classic mountain horseshoe.

Above left: **The ivy-covered Low Sweden Bridge.**

Above right: **A waterlogged track leading into Rydal beneath the Fairfield Horseshoe.**

Facing page, top: **Storm clouds on Greatrigg Man told us it was time to press on.**

Facing page, bottom: **Approaching Low Pike from the alternative lower route.**

89

LAKE DISTRICT: The Coniston Old Man and Wetherlam Round by Bill Birkett

The Walk: A circuit passing Goatswater to the summit of Coniston Old Man then along the heights to Swirl How descending the Prison Band and along to Wetherlam, returning through Coppermines Valley (Lake District, North-West England).

Accommodation Base: Ambleside (see p81).

Maps: OS OD6-The English Lakes (South-West Sheet), L90 and L96. T3-Lake District.

Start and Finish: End of the surfaced road on the Walna Scar road above Coniston (map ref: SD 289970).

Length: 9 mls (14.5km).

Approx Time: 7^1/2 hrs.

Ascent and Descent: 6200ft (1890m).

Difficulty: A high mountain walk which is strenuous and sustained but without undue technical difficulty.

Access: Car.

Seasons: April to October.

Observations: A very fine mountain walk passing the secretive Goatswater and the imposing Dow Crag to gain the heights and reveal a spectacular Lakeland panorama.

Summits: Coniston Old Man: 2631ft (802m), Brim Fell: 2597ft (792m), Swirl How: 2630ft (802m), Wetherlam: 2499ft (762m), Lad Stones: 2019ft (615m).

The Route

Starting just beyond the gate continue up the Walna Scar road to fork left where the quarry road takes steep zig-zags. After some little way, after two rock cuttings, a path takes off steeply up the grass shoulder to the right. Go up this path eventually to reach Goatswater. Continue along and up to the top of the col. Loop to the summit of Coniston Old Man (3hrs, 2631ft/ 802m) then back along Swirl Ridge to Swirl How. From the cairn drop steeply down the Prison Band then traverse along to the top of Wetherlam (2hrs, 2499ft/762m). Move down along the top of Hen Crag (care: large cliff) to Swallow Scar to drop down the ridge of Lad Stones. Gain and follow the quarry track into the Coppermines Valley and down to Levers Water Beck. Cross this just above the waterfall, by the wall, and over a stile to take the path steeply up to the main quarry track (hidden). If the beck is flooded then take the high path into the head of the Coppermines Valley, past the youth hostel, to gain the quarry track under The Old Man. Follow the track contouring round to the starting point (2^1/2hrs, total: 7^1/2 hours.)

The Walk

If you enter the Lake District from the south, along the A591, as you drop down the hill to Windermere you will see, in the distance, the bulky humps of the Coniston range of fells. Coniston Old Man and Wetherlam rise above Windermere Lake like two black giants.

Sometimes, when their tops are kissed with snow and the mists lie like white clouds over the lake, they could be Himalayan. See them once like this and you won't be able to pass them by.

The south-west Lakeland fells are quite different in character and outlook to those that are perhaps more familiar to you: the Langdales or the Helvellyn range for example. Apart from their obvious differences in physical form, it is not easy to be explicit or to highlight a singular point that illustrates exactly what I mean. They just have a different 'feel' to them and the only true way to know just what I mean is to actually experience them for yourself. The following, then, describes what I consider to be the best possible route of discovery over this high south-west corner of Cumbria.

It's best to park in the ample space just beyond the gate on the Walna Scar road. Although it is possible to drive further, because the road serves a working quarry it isn't advisable. There are so many quarries and mines in and around the 'Old Man' that one could imagine it to be all hollow inside. As you turn right off the track, up a steep grass slope, there are quarries everywhere: below you, above and in front of you on Walna Scar and, as you move along what is itself yet another quarry track, more appear up to your right. On this side of the mountain it is slate that has been extracted, on the far side, copper.

After a level section flecked white with frequent quartz, a little easy scrambling over now polished rocks leads up to Goatswater and, towering above, the lofty Dow Crag. Rather disturbingly for the climbers above, Goatswater is shaped distinctly like a coffin. It is a mountain tarn of infinite mood and expression: I have bathed in its copper blue waters when hardly a ripple disturbed the mirrored surface, yet I have watched the wind lift sheets of water turning them to clouds of spray.

The magnificent rock architecture of Dow makes it one of the best climbing crags in the Lakes. Underneath it you will see a blue object which at first appears to be a tent, but is in fact the Rescue Box containing first aid equipment and stretcher. On the left is 'A' Buttress and moving across rightwards we see the buttresses 'B', 'C', and 'D'. To the right of 'C' there is an obvious slash in the rock and this is a rock climb known as 'Intermediate Gully'. In the early days of climbing it presented a formidable challenge and the following was written of it in the Fell and Rock Climbing Club Guidebook of the day;

There are members of the Club to whom 'Intermediate' is more than a climb; rather its ascent is one of the solemn rites connected with the practice of a cult. To one such disciple did I write, asking for a description of the preparations necessary on the part of those who would attain to this circle. The reply came by wire: 'Train on raw meat and Stout, use Bulldog buttons . . .'

We proceed along the path through the rocks, on the opposite side of the tarn to that of the crag. Then pull steeply upwards to a little col and an excellent view of the distant Scafell range to the north west. Looking back is hardly less impressive as Dow Crag plunges

Facing page: **The view south from the summit cairn of The Old Man.**

Below: **Following the track to Goatswater, mist swirling in the distance.**

Previous pages:

Top left: **Wetherlam seen above Little Langdale.**

Bottom left: **Walkers picking their way carefully along Goatswater.**

Top right: **Coniston Old Man rising above the sleepy village of Coniston.**

Bottom right: **Looking back from Great How along to Coniston Old Man.**

Facing page: **Looking to Great Gable from beneath Broad Crag.**

to Goatswater and beyond Coniston and the Morecambe estuary.

As you take the path along to the head of the Old Man you will probably notice how long and flat the stones are in the cairns. This is because they are of slate, and slate splits into thin yet very strong sheets. Roofs slated with Lakeland stone last hundreds of years without need of replacement. The material is so good that ruined buildings and houses have their old slates removed to be used again to roof modern buildings.

It really is a great view to Coniston and Windermere Lakes and the white houses of Ambleside. As you look at the superb view from the domed bee-hive-like summit cairn spare a thought for the hundreds of quarrymen now almost all gone, who walked from distant Coniston up this mountain to go about their daily work. At night they walked back proud of their day's achievement.

When last I did this walk the wind thundered across Dow Crag sounding like an express train and my hands, exposed to the elements because of taking photographs, were red raw with the cold. I was glad to begin to move back along the long easy ridge between the Old Man and How Crags thinking that this would generate some warmth. In practice I was actually blown off my feet at one stage. The time of year for this extreme weather was midsummer. So be warned and be prepared for the hills.

A little way from the summit you can see the tarns of Blind, Low Water and Levens Water and before you start to climb up Little How, the lonely Seathwaite Tarn comes into view. The top of Seathwaite up to Grey Friar is a lonely and forgotten land. It's worth stepping up to the highest point of Great How for this allows a look at the top of Wetherlam and the line of descent down Lad Stones ridge. The scooped corries either side of High Fell make a wild site and the view to the green Levers Water then on down Coniston offers a scene of some contrast.

Levers Water and the unmistakable rift of Simond's Nick rising through the rocks beyond, seem desolate, savaged by man then abandoned. Coniston appears neat and trim, friendly to the eye. Yet above all this the mountain world remains aloof and uncompromising. Perhaps it is this apparent juxtaposition of man past, man present and the unspoilt beauty of the heights that go some way to explaining the particular feel to this high corner of the Cumbrian fells.

Swirl How sports another rather finely constructed conical cairn (beyond this down Swirl Edge you can find the remains of a crashed aircraft if it's of interest). From here plunge steeply down the Prison Band. In the distance, in the direction of the Langdale Fells, Crinkle Crags and on to Bowfell, Red Tarn is plainly discernable and below lies Greenburn. I mused over the fact that both names spring from the mineral colouring of their waters. Greenburn is the site of extensive copper workings and iron was mined at Red Tarn.

Stickle Tarn, below Pavey Ark and Harrison Stickle, hangs like a silver discus in flight against the blackness of the hillside. But the prime view from the traverse across Black Sails is that into the secluded valley of Little Langdale. It brought back a flood of memories of a happy, misspent youth; from fishing in the Tarn and the River Brathay to scrambling on the little crags of Lingmoor. I remembered how in hard winters at the little school, lessons were simply suspended — the joys of sledging down the fields and snowball fights in the school yard taking priority. Play time seemed to last all day. It seems an awfully long time ago and sadly the school is now closed, but visually time appears to have changed nothing down 'La'al Langal'.

Gain the summit and cairn of Wetherlam after passing through a little rock doorway. The Lakeland mountain writer Harry Griffin wrote that Wetherlam was his favourite mountain — he wishes his ashes to be scattered here. The description of the wonderful panorama and the famous peaks that can be seen would fill a book in itself. Turning full circle could take the discerning eye all day: Coniston Old Man, The Scafell's, Bowfell and Langdale Pikes, Helvellyn and Fairfield and everything between.

The trot down the ridge of Lad Stones is a relatively easy affair and many will be starting to feel that really it is time to be going. As the Old Man range rises above, blackened now the sun has sunk westwards out of sight, it portrays the feeling of indestructability and power. Soon you're within its very clutches, encapsulated in the bowls of the Coppermines Valley. A raped landscape but still retaining a sad grandeur.

Soon, too soon — up a big hill and along the quarry track beneath the east flanks of the mountain — you return to your parked vehicle. The day is over, the Old Man has told his tale, but memories are as yet too personal to be evaluated. Time alone will shape your perspective.

THE LAKE DISTRICT: Great Langdale to Scafell by John White

The Route

From the Old Dungeon Ghyll car park follow the surfaced road to Stool End Farm. Go straight up the long ridge behind the farm (The Band) to the col between Bowfell and Crinkle Crags. Over Bowfell descend to Esk Hause via Esk Pike. Strike off in a semi circular route over Broad Crag to a dip before the steep ascent onto Scafell Pike. Return the same way (then go onto Great End) to Esk Hause and descend via the old pony track first to Angle Tarn then down Rossett Gill. Continue back along the flat valley of Mickleden.

The Walk

Scafell Pike is the highest mountain in England. It lies in the centre of what is arguably one of the most beautiful regions on earth, a perfectly scaled mix of lakes, tarns, crags and scree, whitewashed farms and ancient woodlands.

Its geographical location gives extremes of wet, wind and cold, and winter conditions hereabouts can be as serious as in any comparable mountain range — a formidable and sometimes fatal attraction.

Access routes to the summit are available from all the valleys which radiate from the Scafell massif: short, steep and abrupt from Wasdale via Brown Tongue; long, romantic and wild from Eskdale. From Borrowdale, paths through some of the country's most impressive scenery give access to the same high

The Walk: The ascent of England's highest peak from one of Lakeland's most accessible valleys.

Accommodation Base: Ambleside (see p81).

Maps: OS OD6-English Lakes (South-West Sheet), L90-Penrith and Keswick, T3-Lake District.

Start and Finish: Old Dungeon Ghyll Hotel (map ref: SD 285062).

Length: 12mls (20km).

Approx Time: 8hrs.

Ascent and Descent: 8500ft (2600m).

Difficulty: In summer a long high mountain route but without technical difficulty. In winter a serious expedition only suitable for the experienced.

Access: Car and bus.

Seasons: March to December (all year for the experienced winter walker).

Observations: A route which includes the ascent of several prestigious mountains, including England's highest. A very fine day out in the Lake District's central fells. Easily accessible and with first class views.

Summits: Bowfell: 2960ft (902m), Esk Pike: 2903ft (885), Scafell Pike: 3206ft (978m), Great End: 2984ft (910m).

tract of wilderness. Another important but less frequented route to the summit is from the valley of Great Langdale. 'The Valley' offers the most easily accessible peaks and crags to visitors from the south.

The route I have chosen to the summit from Langdale includes the ascent of Bowfell (2960ft 902m), Esk Pike, and Great End, though the latter is optional. It is quite a strenuous walk, but well within the capabilities of most reasonably fit walkers given favourable weather and underfoot conditions. (Telephone Windermere 5151 for an up-to-date forecast).

Unless you fancy the tortuous drive down Little Langdale and over the Blea Tarn road, there is only one way into Langdale. Out of Ambleside take the familiar turn right at Skelwith Bridge and after the tantalising glimpses through the trees of the Langdale Pikes, soon will be revealed that classic view from the open spaces of Elterwater Common. You'll never see this view too often and you'll never see the same view twice.

The village of the valley, Chapel Stile, has an air of peacefulness about it, especially in winter. A stout grey church peers down on a conglomerate of slate cottages, blemished only by the long row of white, modern and predominantly second homes as you leave the valley. The road twists away past Harry Place, the Achille Ratti hut and then out onto flat, open ground past the New Dungeon Ghyll Hotel to a car park outside the Old Dungeon Ghyll. (If there's no room, go back to the New.)

From this end of the valley, the first goal can be all too clearly seen. Bowfell (locally pronounced Bowf'll), is an impressive mountain. An enormous bulk of land, its top is conspicuously pointed and it always attracts the first cloudy messengers of forthcoming rain. The Mickleden face of the fell rises increasingly steeply past a vast area of dark fellside to the crags protecting the summit plateau. These are, from right to left, Bowfell Buttress, Cambridge Crags, and Flat Crags, or Flat Rock as the local shepherds call it.

A long ridge falls from the south side of the summit, a tortured tentacle of undulating fellside called the Band. This is your route of ascent.

You start by following a tarmac road through hay meadows to Stool End Farm. Its occupant, Keith, is an interesting character with an immense fund of local knowledge, who is also a craftsman with stone; witness the quality of the stonework on the new barn on the left of the yard or the recently repaired wallgaps.

All you can see around you here is the

farmer's shop floor — from the high fell down to the stony meadows. Although picturesque, incredibly, it is heavily abused by visitors. Walls are pushed down, dogs chase sheep, signs are broken, and rubbish is left everywhere; it makes you wonder why some people bother to come to the country when they treat it so badly.

The Band is a notorious slog, but a steady rhythmic pace will soon land you over the fell wall and away up a long, straight, but badly eroded section of path with a rocky step at its top. As the cobwebs clear and your lungs open up, so too do the views. Gimmer Crag and Pike O' Stickle look especially spectacular, catching any sun that's going, whilst to the left Crinkle Crags and Oxendale present an often dark and subdued aspect.

There is a welcome levelling off in the angle of ascent at about 1800ft (549m). Behind the text-book glaciated valley and in front, there is a choice of three routes to the summit. The easiest method of ascent traverses over to the col between Bowfell and Crinkle Crags, known as Three Tarns, before striking off right up a steep, loose path to the top. A steeper, more direct route ascends the ridge to the right, which is a bit of a scramble. A third alternative is to ascend the ridge for a few hundred feet until a slim trod, The Climbers Traverse, leads across to the right under a curtain of steep crags. (It must be noted that this is most definitely not a path for walkers under winter conditions.) If this route is taken, the summit is most conveniently attained by an ascent of the

Above: **Middlefell Place farmhouse sits solidly with a view to The Band and Bowfell.**

Facing page: **Looking across Broad Crag to walkers returning from Scafell Pike.**

97

great rock slab which slants back left after the first large crag is passed. This is known as The Boiler Plate or Flat Rock, and a rough path ascends the right-hand edge, giving access to the rocky plateau.

Most people will prefer the first route. Three Tarns is a good place for a break providing it isn't too windy and the route onto Crinkle Crags can be assessed for another day. The path from here is steep for a short way, but soon eases to a rough area where cairns lead across to the high point, a collection of huge, tilted boulders. I hope the cloud stays high for you because the view is superb: to Ingleborough and the Isle Of Man and to Blackpool Tower and The Solway. Much of the rest of our route can also be seen from here and the panorama of Scafell Pike itself with the upper Esk valley stretching wide below it is particularly eye-catching.

The crags underneath the North Eastern flank of the summit have both summer and winter climbs of great quality, Bowfell Buttress itself being the most popular. A short detour to the corrie edge will reward you with a first-class view of this rock face, which is especially photogenic early in the day. A small shelter lies well hidden among these crags and probably provided a storage place for illicit whisky, and as you look down into the powerful lines of Mickleden, it is interesting to reflect that the upper part of this valley was once well populated, though the climate is thought to have been more favourable than it is now.

Our path leads easily north, then west following cairns to Ore Gap where a path splits north again to Angle Tarn, the first escape route in case of bad weather or premature fatigue. The nature of the rock here may affect a compass in places, but only if it is held close to the ground. You continue north west to Esk Pike, dropping over rocky slopes to Esk Hause (pronounced as in jaws) which might be described as the spaghetti junction of the central fells. Our route leads westwards, again rocky and cairned, then south west to Broad Crag.

I prefer this part of the walk to any other. It is predominantly a stonescape, with rough textures and hard, sharp angles dominating the scene. This is real mountain country; it incites your imagination and sharpens your awareness. It can bring a sunny smile or eke out a wind-lashed tear. A place for unashamed emotion.

A large gap separates Broad Crag from our objective. The Scafell side is steepest and great care must be exercised if there is any snow or ice hereabouts. An easing in the angle indicates that the summit is close and you'll soon arrive at a large pile of stones on top of an even larger pile of stones. Most visitors greet the summit in a typically English way. They don't climb onto the trig point, arms high, shouting something like 'Brilliant!' (Do they?) More likely they will shuffle around, find a place to sit, making comments like 'That last bit was a trifle steep.' Or "Ell, that were 'ard,' depending on county of origin.

However you approach your conquest, it's worth waiting a while. Sit down, relax. Look over at Gable. Those screes turn to fire in a winter's sunset. Perhaps the wind will be buffeting you, tearing at your jacket and forcing you to don your hat and gloves; or perhaps it will be still and silent and you can lean back on your sac, close your eyes and doze in the warm rays. I did just that on my last visit. I opened my eyes and gazed out at the mighty precipices of Scafell, and round to Pillar and Gable. Then, I refocused and examined the foreground and what I saw saddened me deeply. Virtually every boulder near the summit had litter crammed under it. I saw cairn after unnecessary cairn, bits of wood, part of an old cagoule. At that moment, the highest point in England was the lowest. We should be grateful that the efforts of National Park staff and of many volunteers at least prevent us having to walk knee deep in litter to get to our beloved rubbish heaps.

Turning to the west, the massif of Scafell itself presents the Lake District's finest mountain, a mecca for climbers and ramblers alike, but more serious than the Pike in that the descent back to this side is notoriously dangerous. Broad Stand is definitely only for climbers and once when I climbed the upper section of Lord's Rake it was made quite dangerous by a sudden cloudburst. The way to the south via Foxes Tarn is the only sure way of ascent and descent from the Mickledore side and this would add a good hour to your day.

Beyond Scafell stand the obscene towers of Windscale and let's hope it's blowing a stiff easterly.

I never like to retrace steps on a walk, but on this route I don't mind the kilometre or so of boulderfield before we can strike off to Great End, which is just 16ft (5m) short of the magic 3000 foot mark. It presents a gentle, rounded aspect from this side, unlike its northern flank — a steep, vegetated face sliced by steep, wet gullies which provide excellent winter climbs. A few years ago, we drove from Ambleside in the half light, down a silent, snowy Borrowdale to park at Seathwaite. As we walked through the farmyard, Stan Edmondson assured us that the snow was "'ard as concrete'. Great End looked superb, each gully a ribbon of white, tinged with delicate blues and greens. With the promise of a great day's climbing ahead of us, we geared up at the foot of the crag, only to find that a certain someone had forgotten his crampons. Recalling that I had already climbed Bowfell Buttress that winter in a pair of Dr Martin shoes, this was obviously going to be no problem and we had a great but rather slippery day, rather like trying to rock climb in roller skates and boxing gloves — which is also possible, but another story.

The descent from Great End to Esk Hause is straightforward and the stone-built, cross-shaped shelter is a fine place for the last bite or brew before the long descent to the valley. In misty conditions, take care to get on the right route here. A south-easterly bearing will lead off towards Angle Tarn, whereas the alternative possibilities will only lead to good business for the local taxi firms and a late tea.

Two descents, split by a short rise, lead to the tarn, a popular high-level campsite as can be witnessed by the rubbish and piles of stones. It is a fine situation, sternly overlooked by the sombre, broken crags of Hanging Knotts, which seem to seep water continually, discolouring the rock and creating a mosaic of black, red and grey against a dull green fellside.

Although Angle Tarn is a well used place, it retains a remote feeling, with open views down barren Langstrath and away north, and to the normal exit back to Langdale barred by a short but tough climb before the final descent.

There are a number of alternative (and more difficult) routes back from here, but I will describe the most popular one down Rosset Gill, and along the old pony track.

A bit of heavy breathing, some more peat on your boots and you're at the top of the gill. The old pony track goes off to the right, but the first long zig-zag is very wet and it appears that the authorities are going to encourage people to use the gill itself for the initial part of the descent.

Broken, blocky scree and boulderfield improve with loss of height, until an exit right can be made to join the pony tack. This has been rebuilt for much of the rest of its length to a high standard by the National Park Authority. Massive areas of eroded ground have been successfully re-vegetated and for the most part the new surface is comfortable to walk on.

Looking down Mickleden, there's still a long way to go, but brilliant views of Pike O'Stickle will hold your attention and motivate wilting muscles and rock-jarred knees. The end of the descent and the start of the flat valley bottom coincides with the junction with Stake Pass, which is an alternative way down. To reach the

top of the Pass from the tarn you must contour north east, then south east on a wet path. The descent consists of a long series of ancient zig-zags (which are much easier on the legs than the erosion-causing short cuts) which lead increasingly gently to the floor of Mickledon.

The valley is a psychologically difficult end to a long day, but the walking is easy. Watch out for the so-called rustler's sheep fold up on the left and very well hidden, and look closely at the cairns — some are evidence of ancient land clearance. Once you're past the fell wall, you've not far to go and before you get there, the long, worn out screes of 'The Sugar Loaf' and the enormous, smooth profile of Gimmer Crag will amply compensate for any end of the day blues. Eventually, a small rise is topped and the buildings of Middlefell Farm and the Old Dungeon Ghyll signal the day's end.

I suppose that there will inevitably be some readers who are among that breed of indefatigable characters with mechanical legs and hot-water-bottle inflating lungs. For you, the day can be extended by an ascent of Pike O' Stickle (which is easily reached from the top of Stake Pass), and by descending via Loft Crag to the New Dungeon Ghyll. I suspect that this option will be the least popular, but which ever route you choose, you should aim to end up at 'The Old' shortly after opening time. Perhaps you'll be able to lounge outside and enjoy the evening sun on Side Pike, or maybe you'll be inside, in front of a roaring fire looking at that fascinating painting of 'Black Jack'. It's a satisfying and relaxing end to a great day, a chance to go over the best and worst bits, to create everlasting memories. Aye, It's been a grand day.

Walkers take the road down to Mickleden, beneath Pike O' Stickle.

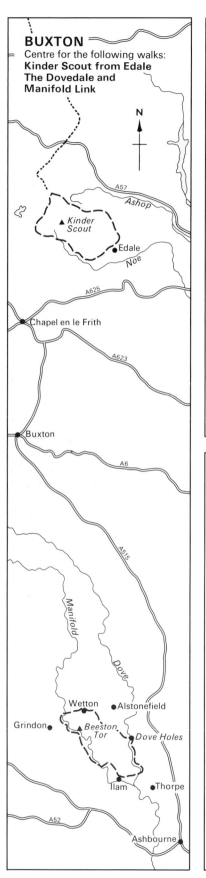

BUXTON
Centre for the following walks:
Kinder Scout from Edale
The Dovedale and
Manifold Link

N

A57
Ashop
▲ Kinder
Scout
Edale
Noe

A625

Chapel en le Frith

A623

Buxton

A6

A515

Manifold
Dove

Wetton
Alstonefield
Grindon
Beeston
Tor
Dove Holes
Ilam
Thorpe

A52

Ashbourne

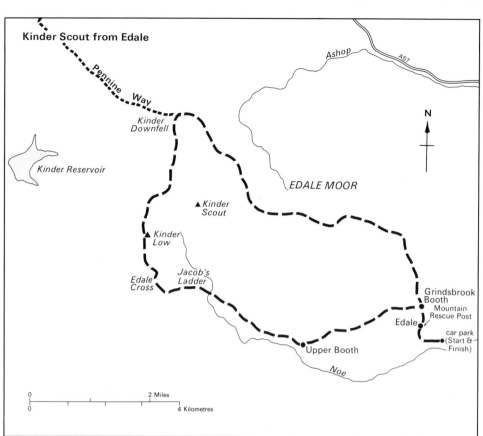

Kinder Scout from Edale

Ashop
A57
Pennine Way

Kinder
Downfell

Kinder Reservoir

EDALE MOOR

N

▲ Kinder
Scout

Kinder
Low

Jacob's
Ladder

Edale
Cross

Grindsbrook
Booth
Mountain
Rescue Post

Edale
car park
(Start &
Finish)

Upper Booth

Noe

0		2 Miles
0		4 Kilometres

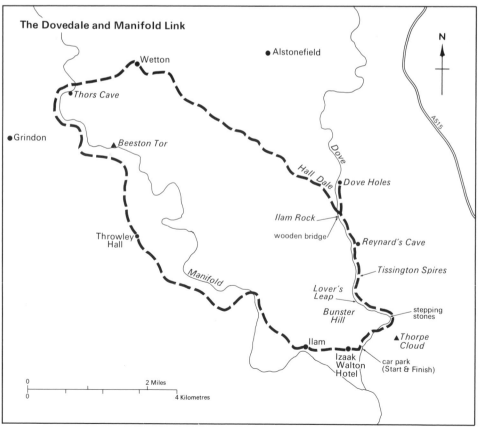

The Dovedale and Manifold Link

Alstonefield

Wetton

N

Thors Cave

Grindon

Beeston Tor

Dove

Hall Dale
Dove Holes

A515

Ilam Rock
wooden bridge

Reynard's Cave

Throwley
Hall

Tissington Spires

Manifold

Lover's
Leap

stepping
stones

Bunster
Hill

▲ Thorpe
Cloud

Ilam

Izaak
Walton
Hotel

car park
(Start & Finish)

0		2 Miles
0		4 Kilometres

BUXTON – Northern England

Buxton: Accommodation base for the following 2 walks: Kinder Scout from Edale; The Dovedale – Manifold Link.
Map Ref: SK 059735.
Location: Conveniently sited between the two walks described (Peak District, Derbyshire, Northern England).
Distance to Walks: 20mls (32km) south along A515 to The Dovedale Manifold Link. 11 mls (18km) north along A6 to Kinder Scout from Edale.
Accommodation: Every type including camping.

Population: 20,800.
The Town: An affluent spa town. Neat and attractive, it nestles delightfully beneath the High Peak District and has a clean and healthy aspect. The grand Opera House, fully restored to pristine glory, hosts both the British Walking and Mountaineering Conferences, (held bi-annually on alternate years). The interestingly domed building that is now the Devonshire Royal Hospital, reputedly the largest unsupported dome in Europe, was built to stable and exercise the Duke of Devonshire's horses.

Proof that the Peak District is popular with walkers is this Hiker's Bar at The Old Nag's Head, Edale.

The Walk: The Dovedale and Manifold limestone river valleys, The White Peak District (Stafford/Derbyshire, Northern England).

Accommodation Base: Buxton (see p101).

Maps: OS OD24 – The White Peak, L110-Sheffield and Huddersfield Area, T4-Peak District.

Start and Finish: At the foot of Dovedale from the large car park below the Izaak Walton Hotel (map ref: SK 146508).

Length: 12 mls (19 km).

Approx Time: 8^1/2 hours.

Ascent and Descent: 1940 ft (590m).

Difficulty: Straightforward walking on footpaths and tracks with some sections of untracked fields. A long walk but well interlaced with public roads making modification easy.

Access: Car to the foot of Dovedale below the Izaak Walton Hotel, (signposted from Ashbourne).

Seasons: All year.

Observations: A scenic and impressive walk taking in two classic limestone river valleys and the high ground between. A walk for all seasons: in summer the luxuriant trees and vegetation in the valleys gives a thousand shades of green and the heights are a mass of multicoloured flowers; in winter the distinguished physical features of Ilam Rock, Dove Holes, Thors Cave et al can be seen at their best.

NORTHERN ENGLAND: The Dovedale – Manifold Link by Bill Birkett

The Route

From the car park either cross the little wooden bridge, or continue along to the stepping stones then cross to the right of the River Dove (true left bank). Continue along, eventually to pass the Ilam Rock and wooden bridge to reach the Dove Holes, (2hrs). Return to the wooden bridge and continue along to a wall-stile leading to Hall Dale. Up this then cross fields to the road through Stanshope. Leave this just over the top of the hill, immediately past the farm, by a tiny stone squeeze stile on the left. Plot your way through unpathed fields (right of way marked on the map) through many more stone squeeze stiles, cross a little lane (useful marker), and on to Wetton (2hrs). Proceed through the village and leave passing the church on the left and take the low path, through fields, below Thors Cave (1hr). Many will want to view this feature and there are a number of paths to facilitate this. Drop down to cross a little bridge and gain the cycle track on the other side of the river. Continue along to the farm below Beeston Tor. Take the track to the right, immediately prior to the farm (there is no right of access along the Manifold valley), and continue up and over high ground to Throwley Hall. Follow roads to return to Ilam. Afterwards take the sign for Bunter Hill to cross the fields above the Izaak Walton Hotel to drop down to the car park and the starting point (3^1/2hrs, total 8^1/2hrs).

The Walk

The confluence of the White Peak District's two most scenic rivers (the Dove and the Manifold) occurs just downstream of this circular walk where, beneath the picturesque village of Ilam they join to become the Dove. This trek includes the best features of these two limestone river valleys; their flora and fauna, their pinnacles and caves, their mystery, grandeur and charm. First you go up the Dove passing all its most spectacular features then escape through the naturally foliated limestone rift of Hall Dale to cross higher ground, finally to gain and descend the Manifold valley.

The Dove begins along the southern corner of Axe Edge, and for much of its length (45mls, 72km) it forms the boundary between Staffordshire, to the west and Derbyshire to the east. Like the Manifold, Dove valley is the product of limestone, the rock of the White Peak, dissolving in rainwater. The result is the plethora of subterranean caverns. As the dissolving process continues so the roof caves in and resilient and softer sections of rock form, alternately, pillars and caves. These are the attractive physical features of Dovedale,

Ilam Rock and the Dove Holes, whereas the Manifold valley is more obviously still undergoing the process and it will be seen (in summer) that the section taken by this walk is often dry. The river disappears at Wetton Mill, for the water is running through a self-made passage below the apparent river bed to emerge, curiously, by Rushley Bridge. The famous British traveller Dr Johnson dropped in corks to ascertain the waters above and below were one and the same.

However fascinating these facts may be, the real attraction of these two wonderful valleys can be truly appreciated only by walking through them. Byron asked 'Was you ever in Dovedale? I assure you there are things in Derbyshire as noble as in Greece or Switzerland?' and Ruskin of the Manifold valley said: 'It is only in the clefts of it, and the dingles that the traveller finds his joy'. It's hard to meaningfully compare the exquisiteness and subtleties of these two unique valleys to anything else but I tend to agree with Ruskin — so let's get on and do the walk!

Our starting point was the large car park below the Izaak Walton Hotel on the banks of

Facing page: **Crossing the stepping stones from Staffordshire to Derbyshire.**

Below: **Farm buildings nestle below Beeston Tor, the largest limestone cliff you'll see on this walk. Spot the climbers.**

the Dove and it isn't far from here to cross over a little wooden bridge, following the path alongside the river. Immediately you are lulled by 'the charms of the valley as the river whispers by, a smooth but rapid flow trailing behind the long green weed. Brilliant white limestone scree tumbles from Cloud Thorpe across the path into the clear waters. The odd trout can still be spotted darting to the next stone and it's reassuring to know that the Dove is still famed for its fishing. This, from the days of Izaak Walton in the 1600s through the industrial revolution to the present day, is a fact to be appreciated.

Inevitably the next feature, the stepping stones crossing from Staffordshire to Derbyshire, are the focus of busy attention. But their appeal remains: dogs splash, kids run and grannies swoon at the high adventure. It was amusing to watch and photograph. After this many of the tourists disappeared, content at their distance achieved from the car, and the dale begins to show its thousand shades of green.

It's difficult, in the height of summer, to see all the rock features picked out in the many walk guides but a glimpse can still be had through the luxuriant canopy of leaves. They are worth mentioning by way of information. Before you start to climb the many polished limestone steps to Sharplow point, Castle Rocks and the 12 Apostles stand to the left. From here the tops of the Tissington Spires can just be seen further on to the right and, opposite, the pinnacles of 'Lover's Leap'.

On arrival beneath Tissington Spires it is found that they are sizeable lumps of limestone. Many rock climbs exist up their apparently blank and vertical faces but I do not recommend you to try; these rocks are strictly for the experts.

After a little way, again on your right, the first of the large caves can be seen: Reynard's cave is framed first by a large arch beyond which lies the cave proper and few can resist, as witnessed by the eroded track, taking a closer peek at this fascinating foxhole. The already narrow dale now becomes narrower and you walk above the water along a constructed wooden walkway to regain solid ground just prior to the bulging Lion's Head Rock. (Notice the little brass sign here tacked to the rock explaining the opening up of Dovedale for the public's enjoyment.) Greg (Cornforth) tried to climb the rock as I attempted to figure out why it was so named, but neither of us succeeded and the rock kept its secret. But not for long! To our delight we discovered the secret of how Lion's Head Rock got its name, when, just as we were rounding the big overhanging rock,

we happened to glance back.

Ilam Rock, a 90-ft (27m) high thin splinter of limestone really is impressive. Look carefully and you will see the rock climbers' nylon slings dangling outwards, gravity showing the true angle of the rock. A wooden bridge takes you across from Pickering Tor to the base of the pinnacle but first I recommend you continue along the river for a further few minutes to view the Dove Holes.

Quite suddenly the tranquillity of our little world was invaded by a most peculiar sound. It grew in strength as we walked and we could imagine it to be the high pitched hubbub of an angry swarm of bees or some flight of monster bats. But no, it was a high-spirited Brownie pack enjoying a field trip. No one could fail to smile at all that innocent, noisy excitement as they rushed from place to place discovering the wonders of their environment.

I'll leave you to discover the details of these super caves yourself before you either backtrack to the little wooden bridge by Ilam Rock, or alternatively wade the stream and then continue down the opposite bank of the river (true right). From the bridge continue along to the dry little valley of Hall Dale. Hall Dale is definitely worthy of separate mention, not least because it is a complete and sudden contrast to the section of Dovedale just completed. Here, tunnelled down the narrow valley we felt the wind on our faces to be chill, despite the sunshine and, to our right, saw the open hillside. Wild and uncropped meadow land (preserved by the National Trust) replaces the thousand shades of green down below and today the bank was a carpet of riotous colour. Rich British limestone country in the height of summer is hard to better for its varied plant growth and here you can see it at its glorious best. Immediately to your left a neat wall of white rock separates you from attractive mixed woodland but soon you gain the high lands between the two sunken river valleys and the character of the walk changes yet again.

The path takes you into the little hamlet of Stanshope and we followed the road for only a little way until the hill was topped, just past the farm. From here an obscure little stone squeeze-stile leads you into the fields. This stile is the first of many, most of them ridiculously tiny, but those of stouter build shouldn't worry unduly for it's possible to stride over the majority. The way across the fields is not well marked for there is no worn or distinguished track and the best advice is to keep the map to hand and attempt to follow the contours.

Midway from Stanshope to Wetton you cross a lane (squeeze stiles both sides) and this serves as a useful landmark. Immediately prior to this you encounter a small field which houses a curiosity. In the corner there is a typical feature of limestone terrain: a 12-foot (3.5m) diameter water bowl constructed to retain the rainwater from which the cattle or sheep may drink (limestone being porous there is little surface water). Traditionally they are all stone, tightly jointed by stonemasons to facilitate water retention, however this one must have leaked for it has been lined with concrete.

Wetton has a small cafe, pub and shop but we didn't delay, making straight for Thors Cave, the fearsome sentinel overlooking our section of the Manifold valley. It's worth having a look around. Inside it is almost cathedral like and is well illuminated by a further side entrance which, facing in a southerly direction, sucks in the sunshine. Then a drop down through what, in summer, is best described as a jungle, takes you over a little bridge to a surfaced track.

Beware of cyclists! This track is now an official cycle track and is very popular. It used to be the line of the Leek and Manifold Light Railway which operated briefly between 1902 and 1934 to transport the minerals won from various locations in the valley. Continue straight along, quitting the cycle track to follow the lane to the little farm below Beeston Tor — they run in parallel.

Beeston Tor is the largest limestone cliff you will see on this walk and look out for rock climbers, for this is one of the best climbing crags in the Peak District. We could see them, ant like, making their slow and deliberate progress up to the deep slash cave at two thirds height. It is known as the Ivy Gash and I had sat there myself only a few months before, looking down to this very path.

Just before the farm you take a right track which leads over high ground to Throwley Hall; there is no right of access along the river itself. Of course it was now completely dry but last time I had climbed on Beeston the river was in spate and it had been impossible even to cross over the stepping stones situated just above the farm.

After Throwley you follow the road through thorns and thistle. It seems quite a slog, probably because up to this point the route has been littered with quite spectacular features whereas now it is just pleasant. Ilam is another sudden contrast and with its quaint houses, school, Gothic cross and stone-arched bridge (the last bridge over the Manifold river) it adds another dash of class to this superb walk.

The sign says 'Bunter Hill' and fields are followed behind the Izaak Walton Hotel back to your starting point. 'Two and a half hours

huh!' said Greg. I had promised him a short walk before a few rock climbs but it had taken us slightly longer!

Fortunately he was grinning.

Reynard's cave, the first of the large caves, is framed by a large arch beyond which is the cave.

The Walk: Kinder Scout from Edale, High Peak District, Derbyshire, Northern England.
Accommodation Base: Buxton (see p101).
Maps: OS OD1 – The Dark Peak, L110-Sheffield and Huddersfield Area, T4-Peak District.
Start and Finish: Edale (Grindsbrook Booth), map ref: SK 124853.
Length: 10 mls (16 km).
Approx Time: 5hrs.
Ascent and Descent: 3100ft (945m).
Difficulty: A reasonably long high fell walk that can become extremely tricky in inclement conditions. The peat and deep water-worn runnels make the plateau section hard going and route finding difficult, although it can be circumnavigated avoiding these problems. From a scrambling point of view there are no technical difficulties.
Access: Car or train to Edale.
Seasons: April to November.
Observations: Although extremely popular the Kinder plateau is large and gives a feeling of solitude even on the busiest weekends. The plateau section has a good deal of soft peat and you will inevitably end up with it deposited somewhere on your person. Additionally the plateau is relatively featureless and a map and compass are essential. In wet conditions (the best time to view Kinder Downfall) the plateau can be avoided by traversing its edge, first westwards, along a clearly defined path.

NORTHERN ENGLAND: Kinder Scout from Edale by Bill Birkett

The Route

From Edale car park walk up the road to the village of Grindsbrook Booth. Take a tiny opening on the right signposted 'Pennine Way' and cross the stream by a wooden bridge to follow the track up Grinds Brook to reach the Kinder Scout Plateau (1903ft, 580m and 1¹/4hrs). Cross the plateau, following the Pennine Way on a compass bearing, to Kinder Downfall (1¹/4 hrs). This section is through softish peat and involves crossing water-formed runnels up to 20ft (6m) deep. In wet weather this can be sensibly avoided by traversing west along the edge of the plateau and then back along the edge to Kinder Downfall, so taking a circuitous and longer route. Follow the edge south to Kinder Low (2077ft, 633m and 1 hr) and from here drop to Edale Cross and on down the steps of Jacobs Ladder. Continue down to Upper Booth Farm and turn left through the farmyard to follow a track first up the hill then back down to Grindsbrook Booth. Stroll down the road to the car park (1¹/2hrs, total: 5hrs).

The Walk

Situated in the High Peak of Derbyshire this famous and extremely popular upland area can still provide a day of unspoiled countryside and variety. Greg Cornforth and myself set off to do this walk on the busiest of summer weekends and found to our joy that not only were our fellow walkers a pleasure to be with on the hill, but also that the whole popular trail was virtually litter free. In truth, once we reached the extensive and wild upland plateau it was if we were alone; birds cried uninterrupted and rabbits scurried for cover into the heather. If simple human pleasure is the yardstick by which to measure the ultimate consequence of the mass trespass of the 30s, freeing this superb upland area to all, then the event was an unqualified success.

'Twixt the stalwart blackness and grime of the north's great industrial centres (Sheffield to the east and Manchester to the west), the High Peak of Derbyshire stands aloof. The rocks may be dull brown and of roughly textured millstone grit, and the outlook wild and inhospitable (the acidic peat does not support lush vegetation), but the importance, the magnetism, of the Dark Peak far outweighs these petty observations. For a generation this upland area has spelt freedom to those economically fettered to the industrial realities of the flatter plains below. On these high places the wind blows without calling and the air is clean and sweet.

I'm a rambler, a rambler from Manchester way,
I get all my pleasure the hard, moorland way,
I may be a wage slave on Monday,
But I am a free man on Sunday. ('The Manchester Rambler', Ewan MacColl)

The walk described is situated on the highest of the High Peak, Kinder Scout, and takes in much that is best of this area that is so full of character. Once on the plateau itself this includes copious supplies of soft, wet, black peat and all parties should be aware of just what a direct crossing entails. Not to say that wallowing in peat isn't fun, of course, just that

Facing page: **Sculptures in the grit on Kinder Scout Plateau.**

Below left: **A family enjoys the walk up Grinds Brook.**

Below right: **Greg Cornforth leaps across a peat grough.**

Walking can be enjoyed by people of all ages. Above, on the left, a party of walkers rest at the trig point of Kinder Low, while to the right a brother and sister are obviously enjoying themselves in Upper Grinds Brook.

I think its best to be absolutely frank about the plateau before you actually get there. Many parties, especially those with children, opt for the circumnavigational route and there is a lot to be said for this.

We set off at the crack of noon on a day that seemed to be improving. Luckily it did and we had our fair share of sunshine, even if most of it was reserved for the trot back along upper Edale. Up through Edale itself passing the station, cafe, pub and church you soon reach the daintier Grindsbrook Booth and, a little way up the narrowing road, a signpost 'Pennine Way' pointing rightwards down a tiny alcove between wall and hedge. The inauspicious start, despite its slight beginnings, soon leads to more worthy pastures. The track immediately expands to reveal a wooden bridge crossing Grinds Brook and up the far bank a pleasant walk through fields and pleasantly mixed woodland leads you to green

bracken and purple heather, the colours of the hills.

Initially a track blazes up the hillside to your right. On this particular walk this is ignored as you carry on more horizontally through a gate to aim for the next batch of woodland. Today we passed a group of swallows settling on the power lines; we were in the last few days of July and it would be another month or so before they would wing their way back to hotter climes. It seemed as though they were having a tactical conference before they started their 8000-mile flight that takes them a little over 30 days. Beyond them, a tracked vehicle, belching fumes of diesel and bellowing sounds of radio communication climbed at a crazy angle to the remnants of a gritstone wall. Later, when we found the footpath to be in good order and the area litter free, I found forgiveness for the Park Rangers and their blatant intrusion into our quiet world.

The path winds its way beneath the stark grit edge of Upper Tor on the right skyline to eventually reach the narrows of upper Grinds Brook. Here you cross and recross the stream as the landscape quickly becomes harsher. A tumble of grit boulders makes the going more difficult and we found a lot more people here, slowed and struggling with the increased difficulties. In front of one party a young brother and sister were making light work of the problems and the young lad, sporting a plastered arm — evidence of a previous mishap — remonstrated with me on the advantages of his forked walking stick.

A final milieu of tumbled gritstone takes one directly up to the edge of the great expanse of the Kinder Plateau. Here the last steep section is taken directly as the main Grinds Brook bears off to the right. The edge is grit and one can look left to Ringing Roger, or right to Grindslow Knoll, along its curvature. But beyond, viewed between the two, Lose Hill and the other tors across on the far side of Edale offer a different profile, evidence of their different geology. Note the mushroom-shaped rock commonly named The Anvil. It is a typical grit feature to be found on these elevated and wind-blown grit escarpments. (The most dramatic collection of these rock pinnacles is at Brimham Rocks in Yorkshire.)

Next comes the crossing of the great peat desert (the Kinder Scout plateau), to the sometimes magnificent waterfall of Kinder Downfall. I say sometimes because in summer when conditions for the crossing of the plateau are at their most favourable, it is often dry. However when there is plenty of water about it becomes a spectacular water fall, perhaps at its best when a strong easterly wind, funnelled over Kinder Reservoir, sweeps up the gorge to Kinder Downfall blowing the falling water back up into the air and over its top.

From the southern edge of the plateau we left the solidity of the grit to follow a canyon through the peat; a delightful tunnel with a blue roof, a white sandy and gritty floor and walls of chocolate brown topped by a green wave of bilberry. Soon we were out again, temporarily on high ground and among the fascinating grit formations. We had a quick snack and rest and viewed the rocks, for all the world looking like Henry Moore sculptures, and also a tiny young rabbit which cowered in front of us. The youngster looked lost and misplaced, obviously disturbed by some passing rambler, but its camouflage was superb and we hoped this would protect it from the many predators that roam this barren plateau.

Back into the bog again and now we were alone, swallowed up by the immensity of the nothingness all around. The day was good, a fresh wind blew intermittently, the sun shone bathing us in its welcome warmth and we enthusiastically worked our way through the mire. Great canyons interrupted our steady progress and invariably these would be taken at speed with huge leaps into space followed by a soft landing in the peat on the far side.

The sharp calls of frequent dunlin brought the place to life and occasionally the large succulent cloudberry lay beneath our feet. Pools of white cotton grass waved in the breeze and if it wasn't for the total absence of man's form you could be forgiven for thinking you were traversing some forlorn First World War battlefield.

Over an hour passed before we came across anyone else — a group of ramblers adding a splash of colour to the sea of cotton grass that marked the end of the plateau. Soon we were again walking along a grit edge towards Kinder Downfall. Wind-curved rocks were piled together like a plate full of broad beans and just beyond lay the fall itself. It was dry but still powerful.

After a lunch spent sheltering from the sharp-edged wind behind a large grit boulder we made off for the highest point of our walk — Kinder Low! Swifts swooped past at a breathtaking speed seemingly, at times, only inches from the peat. Here the walking was easy and firm going and we were soon crossing the silvery sands to the trig point.

Here it is rather like a moon landscape and the trig point itself is perched high on grit boulders that stand above their sandy base. From here you tumble down to the rock bluffs and Edale Cross to follow the remains of a once substantial stone wall leading quickly to the head of Edale. Rapid descent down the stone steps of Jacob's Ladder leads to a quaint stone-arched packhorse bridge.

A good track leads on through a farm, though prior to this, note two derelict and ancient stone gate stoops on the left with square holes cut through their tops to take wooden rails. Carry on to reach the tiny hamlet of Upper Booth. At a telephone box turn sharp left through a farm yard. The going through fields is very pleasant but it seems a trifle unfair after all this way that you actually start walking up hill again. It's worth it and not far, and soon you sight the church spire and make the last tight squeeze through the final stile into a little wooden lane and down to Grindsbrook Booth and past The Old Nags Head . . . who am I trying to kid?

NORTHERN ENGLAND: The Cleveland Way by Bill Birkett

Above: **Looking across the plains to Sutton Bank and Whitestone Cliff.**

Facing page, top: **Captain Cook's house at Staithes.**

Facing page, bottom: **A walker stops to admire the beauty of Rievaulx Abbey.**

The Route

Day 1: Helmsley to Kilburn (10mls, 16km) via Rievaulx Abbey, Cold Kirkby.

Day 2: Kilburn to Osmotherley (14mls, 23km) via Sutton Bank, Sneck Yate Bank, Hambleton Hills.

Day 3: Osmotherley to Guisborough (22mls, 35km) via Huthwaite, Hasty Bank, Greenhow Moor, Battersby Moor, Kildale, Captain Cook's Monument, Roseberry Topping.

Day 4: Guisborough to Saltburn (8mls, 13km) via Charlton, Skelton.

Day 5: Saltburn to Whitby (20mls, 32km) via Skinningrove, Boulby Cliff, Staithes, Runswick, Kettleness, Sandsend.

Day 6: Whitby to Scarborough (18mls, 29km) via Robin Hood's Bay, Ravenscar, Hayburn Wyke, Cloughton Wykes.

Day 7: Scarborough to Filey (8mls, 13km) via Osgodby Point, Yons Nab, Filey Brigg.

The Walk

Statistically this walk is Britain's second oldest long distance footpath, officially opened in 1969. In practice it is one of the very finest long walks to be found anywhere in Britain. There is so much to see, so much history and so much natural beauty here that to those who know the area my seven-day recommendation for the walk may seem derisory. In its defence it must be said that it is a reasonable period to complete the route and appreciate the land through which you are passing. To those who will say that it is too short and that in fact, you could spend longer I entirely concur — a lifetime would not be too short a time during which to enjoy this superb area.

Physically the walk circumnavigates the high upland moors of North Yorkshire (from which some 370 million tons of iron ore were extracted in a little over a century), to find the north coast and to traverse along, passing the many fishing villages that once fed this land of plenty. The walking will suit most people for it is exceedingly pleasant and, taken in its entirety, demanding enough. Yet it is without the extreme difficulties and hardships to be found in the high mountains and wilderness areas.

The interest is diverse, ranging from the physical beauty of the hills, the flora and fauna to the fascinating historical background — the evidence of which is still to be found. It is not easy to point at one aspect of this walk and say it is that which makes it so enjoyable; there are so many different aspects that make the Cleveland Way what it is. But of its character, despite the proximity of the nearby industrial complex of Teesside, there is a pervading sense

of timelessness, and through the Cleveland Hills and passing the little fishing villages of the north east coast, little seems to have changed for two centuries.

Day 1: Helmsley to Kilburn

A short start but a very interesting day and thoroughly worthwhile despite the seeming lack of direction in descending to Kilburn, Rye Dale is a deep richly agricultural valley hemmed in on all sides by trees. The focal point of interest is undoubtedly the great ruined Rievaulx Abbey. This is not just another pile of stones, and is well worth the entrance fee to take a closer look.

It captivated Dorothy and William Wordsworth and it captivated me. As I stood by its massive sandstone pillars and beneath the pointed arches I honestly thought this was the most impressive building I had seen in Britain. The work is intricate, every curved stone being detailed minutely, yet the overall line flows elegantly. It is both exquisite and powerful; detailed yet magnificent. Perhaps it affected me so because it is a ruin, because the flying buttresses trace a naked line through the air unaccompanied, because the corbelling of the

The Walk: A long distance walk through the iron-bearing limestone and sandstone hills of Cleveland and along the large shale cliffs of the east coast, passing numerous quaint fishing villages (North Yorkshire, North-East England).
Maps: OS L93, L94, L99, L100, L101, T2 — North York Moors.
Start: Helmsley (map ref: SE 612839).
Finish: Filey (map ref: SE 126817).
Waymarks: Cleveland Way signposts and acorn plaques.
Length: 100 mls (161 km).
Approx Time: 7 days.
Difficulty: Fairly strenuous walking but without technical difficulty.
Access: Car.
Seasons: All year.
Observations: An excellent contrasting route of great character through the attractive hills of Cleveland and then along the cliffs of Yorkshire's east coast.
Accommodation: Hotels, bed and breakfast accommodation and camping.
Guidebooks: *The Cleveland Way* by Bill Cowley (A Dalesman Paperback), *A Guide to the Cleveland Way and Missing Link* by Malcolm Boyes (Constable), *The Cleveland Way* by Alan Falconer (HMSO).

masonry is laid bare to be appreciated, the eye not distracted by decoration. Perhaps to the practical minded this clarity of construction, set out like some detailed engineering drawing, makes it seem grander than it actually is.

They say the White Horse above Kilburn, 314ft (95m) long and 228ft (69m) high, was cut out by the village schoolmaster in 1857. You are asked not to tramp over the Horse. Kilburn village is the home of the Thompson oak carving workshop famed for its mouse signature on each individual piece of work.

Day 2 – 4: Osmotherley to Kilburn

Straight away on reaching the heights the spaciousness of the walk hits you. Past Sutton Bank along Whitestone Cliff, gliders fly silently overhead and limestone cliffs lay sheer beneath. Out in front lie the vast open flatlands that reach to distant Teesside and the iron town of Middlesbrough. Nestling in the trees further down from the cliffs is the mysterious Gormire Lake which nestles in what appears to be, but isn't, a volcanic crater. Dorothy

Wordsworth kept a journal of her Yorkshire visit and in it she described the following scene which could be the view from above this large cliff.

As we descended the hill there was no distinct view, but of a great space; only near us we saw the wild and (as people say) bottomless tarn in the hollow — seeming to be made visible to us only by its own light, for all the hill about us was dark.

This is walking at its best, not too strenuous but with splendid views and a feeling of position. The rocks below are oolitic limestone but it is the most peculiar limestone I know. It's more akin to a mixture of sandstone and egg-shaped blocks all loosely cemented together.

The walk along the edge of this upland area offers magnificent contrast: to your right there is the wild and desolate moorland of chattering grouse and purple heather whilst below and to your left lies the neat agriculture of the rich Cleveland plains and then beyond, the inevitable polluting smog of the Teesside industries. One thing about this mantle of pollution, is

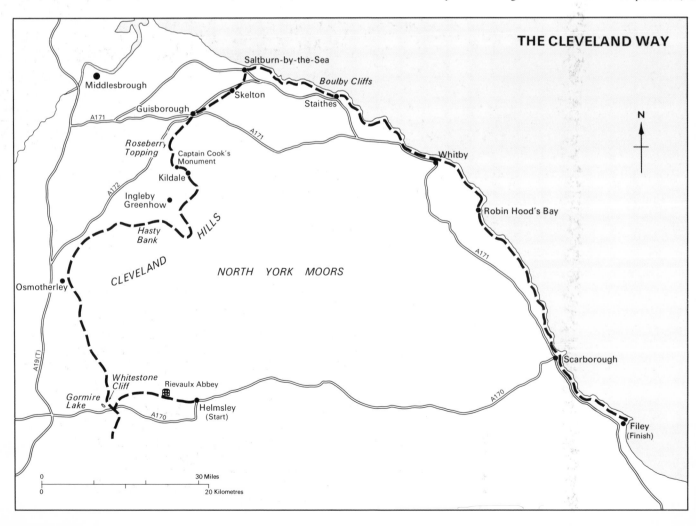

THE CLEVELAND WAY

that with the light diffusing and refracting on the foreign particles in the air, it does give the best sunsets to be had anywhere in Britain.

But the air on this walk is miraculously clean and brisk. Be well prepared for its force. John Ruskin wrote:

To get full expression of the very heart of the meaning of wind there is no place like a Yorkshire moor. Scottish breezes are thinner, very bleak and piercing. If you lean on them they will let you fall, but one may rest against a Yorkshire breeze as one would on a quickset hedge.

The rich agricultural land below is an additional factor which contributes to Yorkshire's prosperity and enhances the prospect beneath. It is a colourful patchwork of many different crops. The barley gives a silver sheen as it ripples with the wind. Wheat is the one with the fat head like the tail of a rattle snake; it gives us our daily bread. Oats, and

there are many hereabouts, are a darker colour than the rest and become golden after harvesting.

This path is also enhanced by the tremendous variety of trees and woodland to be found. Trees range from the dwarf larch to mature oaks and there is everything from the small coppice to large plantations. In autumn these hills are ablaze with colour. The naturalist will also have a field day and if you complete this walk without having seen a squirrel, red fox, roe deer, goldfinch, sparrow hawk or a buzzard then you were either not looking or you're just plain unlucky.

Osmotherley is a solid little Yorkshire town and many will put up here for the night. Afterwards you cross over the secluded valley of Scugdale — 'sunny Scugy' as it is known to the locals. Along Hasty Bank you may glimpse the sandstone pillars of the Wainstones where

Above left: **Walking along Sutton Bank, the rosebay willow herb in flower, The Cleveland Way clearly marked.**

Above right: **A climber above Whitestone Cliff surveys Gormire Lake below.**

113

many a rock climber from the industrial towns below, has cut his teeth. Notice how red the rocks are here and if you examine them closely you will see the iron nodules deposited in pockets. This section of the journey is shared with the exceedingly popular Lyke Wake Walk and unfortunately sections have been reduced to a veritable mud bath.

Above Ingleby Greenhow you cross the now deserted incline that was the old iron railway, an important artery that fed the iron of the Cleveland hills to the hungry and industrious Middlesbrough across the plain below. Middlesbrough grew in half a century from two farmhhouses and the remains of a monk's cell on the Tees mud-flats, to a leading iron town of 55,000 people and with exports of over a million pounds per annum. In 1877 there were 39 mines working in Cleveland.

The iron masters of Middlesbrough led the new technology and travelled the world selling their expertise; in Cleveland USA for example. Times change but Teesside still retains a strong position in the world of technology. I studied structural engineering here, a country lad alongside the whizz kids of 'Cleveland Bridge' and 'British Steel'.

Jet and alum mines also abound here and can be consistently found along the 900-ft (274m) contour. Jet is akin to a superior coal but is shiny (jet) black and can be cut — it was extremely popular in jewellery making in the past and it can still be found in Whitby.

Dropping down into Kildale (below the little climbers' crag of Park Nab), gives views across to Captain Cook's Monument. The inscription reads 'The celebrated circumnavigator Cap. James Cook, F.R.S. A man in nautical knowledge inferior to none, in zeal, prudence and energy superior to most.' Yorkshiremen describe Cook as the greatest Yorkshireman — so he must be something special!

He was a farm labourer's son from Malton and the lands he was born and bred upon you see below you now. From these humble beginnings in the 18th century, he rose to Captain in the Royal Navy and became a fellow of the Royal Society. He also sailed abroad on occasion!

The next summit is that of Roseberry Topping. Known as the 'Matterhorn of Cleveland', it presents a striking aspect when seen from the plains below. It is however 1057ft (322m) high and only an easy walk is needed to crest the summit. It once bore the Viking name of 'Odinsberg'. Not far below, Guisborough is a pleasant place to stop for the night.

From here to the coast at Saltburn is an area of some contrast as the industrial overflow competes with the agricultural lands. There are many fine horses to be seen in the fields around here, and there is an equestrian centre at Skelton. After the heights of the moors above, it is not particularly pleasant, but stick with it; this is a transition zone, for when you get to the coast the walk takes on a completely new dimension. This area is noted for its thick sea fogs, particularly in autumn, and if you should have the misfortune to encounter one of these then you can forget about walking for a good while.

Saltburn is a curious seaside town and despite the large and impressive 'Zetland Hotel' it never really made it as a tourist resort. Down by the sea the Ship Inn and its environs give a more traditional air. With the odd fishing boat pulled up onto the shingle you get some indication of what is to follow.

Days 5–7: Saltburn to Filey

The cliffs along from Saltburn are high, some 400ft (122m) and they are highest, although more broken, at Boulby. Keep away from the edges because they comprise loose shale which is constantly collapsing. In my student days I made a serious attempt to climb the most continuous of these cliffs but the rock gave way and I fell to the beach below. I was lucky in that my only injury was a twisted ankle. Despite the height of these cliffs there are many days when you can taste the salt on your lips.

Boulby is a maze of old alum workings and the cliffs below are frequently tunnelled. There is reputed to be a large vertical shaft leading down to a sea cave large enough to take a sailing ship. Supposedly the alum was shipped away from here. The name on the map 'Rockhole Hill' gives some credence to this tale. Look out for Celtic heads built into the ancient houses nearby. Tales of smuggling and smugglers also abound in these parts.

Staithes is an old world fishing village and is a place to be savoured. It's a tiny haven of shelter from the North Sea and appears to have been cut out of the surrounding shale cliffs. The available space for housing was used up many centuries ago so that nothing much has changed here. It is much the same as when James Cook served as an apprentice grocer here — his house down by the sea front bears a plaque. Tiny houses with red-tiled roofs perch on the steep hillside with narrow alleyways between, giving the impression that they are on the verge of sliding into the sea. But they have stood many a gale from the cruel North Sea and will stand many more.

In Cook's day there were 50 fishing cobles stationed here. (A Yorkshire fishing coble is a flat bottomed boat that can be pulled up onto the beach.) On 11 September 1886 a Great Coble Race was run from Staithes to Whitby. The race, over ten miles of open sea was won by the Staithes crew (beating the Northumbrian crew) in 1 hour 25½ minutes. The prize was a silver cup, £100 and the title 'Champions of the North Sea'. Today a few fishermen remain to retain the true character of this remarkable village. It is said that the men of Staithes drink beer with salt in it to remind them of the sea! Fish, or ling, pie is a traditional Staithes dish and the following ditty illustrates this (notice the similarity to the Cumbrian dialect — the Norse influence):

A dish for onny king
Is yan o them ling pies;
Steeas wimmin — an they're wise-
Knaws what ti deea wi ling;
Neea las sud git her ring
Till a ling pie she tries;
a dish for onny king
Is yan o them ling pies!

Whitby is quite amazing and still harbours a full fleet of fishing boats. Out of the town, at the top of a long series of stone steps, lies the ruined abbey. There are tourists to be found here in plenty, but somehow Whitby retains her character, one that has been shaped by the North Sea.

Robin Hood's Bay resembles the space when a bite has been taken from a lump of cheese. It is picturesque in the extreme. As you descend into the village you may notice a plaque commemorating a lifeboat rescue at sea. They brought the lifeboat overland through the snow and launched it here. Lives were saved through brave and hard working men pulling together; through community spirit. At the southern end of the bay, at Ravenscar, fossils abound in the shale rocks. It is famed for its ammonites which resemble coiled millepedes.

Scarborough is a nice town but it is not a place to linger on this walk. Better, with any time to spare, to pause for a while with the few remaining cobles of Filey Brigg in sight, to reflect upon your experiences on this rather fine walk, for you will now know perhaps, why Yorkshiremen are so proud of their heritage.

The shale cliffs at Staithes.

115

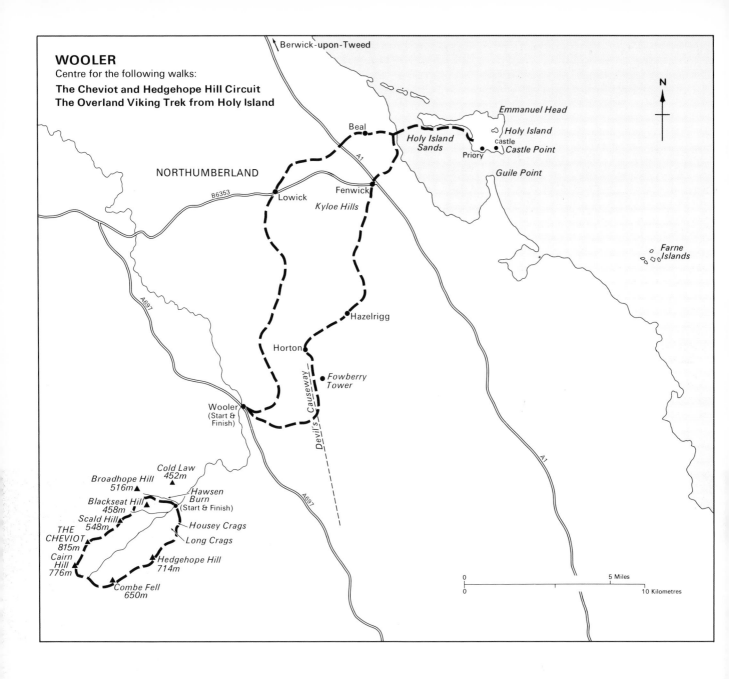

WOOLER
Centre for the following walks:
The Cheviot and Hedgehope Hill Circuit
The Overland Viking Trek from Holy Island

N

Berwick-upon-Tweed

NORTHUMBERLAND

Beal

Emmanuel Head

Holy Island Sands

Holy Island

castle

Castle Point

Priory

Guile Point

B6353

Lowick

Fenwick

Kyloe Hills

Farne Islands

A1

Hazelrigg

Horton

Fowberry Tower

Devil's Causeway

Wooler
(Start & Finish)

A697

A697

Cold Law
452m

Broadhope Hill
516m

Hawsen
Burn
(Start & Finish)

Blackseat Hill
458m

Scald Hill
548m

Housey Crags

THE CHEVIOT
815m

Long Crags

Cairn
Hill
776m

Hedgehope Hill
714m

Combe Fell
650m

0   5 Miles

0   10 Kilometres

WOOLER – Northern England

Wooler: Accommodation base for the following 2 walks: The Cheviot and Hedgehope Hill Circuit; The Overland Viking Trek from Holy Island.
Map Ref: NT 992280.
Location: On the A697 below the Cheviot Hills (Northumberland, North-East England).
Distance to Walks: 5mls (8km) The Cheviot and Hedgehope Hill Circuit, 16mls (28km) to The Overland Viking Trek from Holy Island,
Accommodation: Small hotels, bed and breakfast accommodation, camping.
Population: 2,000.
The Town: Wooler is a small market town, grey slated and solidly built with attractive sandstone masonry. Once it was extensively thatched but suffered a number of times from fire. The last severe fire, starting in the Three Half Moons Inn, was in 1862 after which the residents decided to re-roof with slates. This is a Border town with a strong Scottish influence and Scottish reivers raided many times. The townsfolk of Wooler raided in return and 'Hot Trod' was an English law of the day which allowed them six days to recuperate their losses and take revenge. After this period it became unlawful! To the north of the town a boulder known as 'The Battle Stone' commemorates the Battle of Hamilton Hill when over 10,000 Scots were beaten — the dramatic beginning to Shakespeare's *Henry IV*. Traditionally the buying and selling of the produce from the surrounding rich agricultural lands and the hiring of men and women was done on Fair Day. There were a number of these and they were accompanied by side shows and amusements. They were called 'Hoppens', Danish for Dance — hence the expression 'going to the village hop'. Today travelling fairs with their candy floss, hot-dogs and brightly lit mechanical devices still visit rural little Wooler.

The seasonal fair at Wooler offers instant entertainment for those who enjoy it.

NORTHERN ENGLAND: The Cheviot and Hedgehope Hill Circuit by Bill Birkett

The Walk: From the Harthope Valley up The Cheviot to follow high ground to Hedgehope Hill and down by Housey Crags (Northumberland, North East England).
Accommodation Base: Wooler (see p117).
Maps: OS L75, L80.
Start and Finish: At the end of the driveable section of road up the Harthope valley by the Hawsen Burn (map ref: NT 944225).
Length: 10mls (16km).
Approx Time: 6 hrs.
Ascent and Descent: 5300ft (1615m).
Difficulty: A straightforward mountain walk.
Access: Car.
Seasons: April to October.
Observations: The colours are at their best in autumn. The going underfoot is good except for the summit of Cheviot and the descent to Cairn Fell (part of the Pennine Way) which is a peat bog.
Summits: Scald Hill: 1798ft (548m), The Cheviot: 2674ft (815m), Cairn Hill: 2546ft (776m), Comb Fell: 2133ft (650m), Hedgehope Hill: 2342ft (714m).

The Route

Proceed up the Hawsen Burn out onto open heatherland just behind the slight summit rocks of Blackseat Hill. Traverse across to the shoulder that descends from Scald Hill, crossing the ravine of New Burn en route. (The regular route comes straight up this shoulder.) Up Scald Hill and along to the summit of The Cheviot. Continue along the fence line (peat bog) to drop down to the shoulder leading to Cairn Fell. Drop down left to the hollow of Scotsman's Knowe at the head of the Harthope Valley. Then up to gain another fenceline leading to the top of Comb Fell. Continue along the fenceline to gain the top of Hedgehope Hill. Steeply down its flanks and across to Long Crags, then on to a second

rocky knoll (Housey Crags) and round this to descend to and follow a path that leads to a little bridge directly below your starting point.

The Walk

A forgotten land, Northumberland rolls in great agricultural plains between the Tyne and the Scottish Border. To the east lies the North Sea and to the west rise a series of moors rolling over at their edges into waves of sandstone. At the northern end these gentle uplands steepen and rise to a height approaching 3000ft (1000m) — these are the Cheviot Hills.

What a day, the wind was fresh and the sun shone; twelve hours earlier things were not looking good and one could not have predicted that the day was going to be so fair. Deliberately I saved this walk for a day in autumn for that is the best time to be in Northumberland; when the high heather is coloured to its purple best and the lowland plains are a patchwork of green, brown, straw and yellow.

Virtually at the head of the Harthope Valley there is a sign saying that cars should not be taken any higher. At this point, where the Hawsen burn crosses underneath the road, there is ample parking on the grass area beside the road. The burn, despite indications to the contrary on the OS Landranger (1:50,000 series) does not constitute the usual path taken to reach the summit of the Cheviot; this lies a little further on through the plantation up ahead. However this handily situated burn cutting a small gorge through the hillside, provides an excellent start to the walk and is therefore the route I shall describe here.

Before we start I would like to make another comment on the OS Landranger maps covering this area: unfortunately the walk is split by the joint between the two maps and I recommend that before you start you put them together and make a study of the overall topography to be traversed. Then you will see quite clearly that we are doing a horseshoe walk around the head of the valley of Harthope.

As I set off up the brackened burn I found the picturesque little gorge was littered with rowan trees resplendent with masses of red berries. If you believe folk lore, we were in for a hard winter.

Despite giving the distinct impression that this way was hardly ever used, the path was a good one and criss-crossed the little burn many times. At one point the water has cut its way through a curious outcrop of rock which gives the impression of being crystalline and may well have been quartzite-sandstone metamorphosed, probably by some nearby heat source. Further up, a definite fault, bearing deposits of iron was plainly exposed.

Pulling out of the head of the burn you are able to fully appreciate the splendid autumnal colouring; of bracken just reddening in places, still green elsewhere and all the different shades of purple mountain heather. Suddenly now the great patchwork of colour that is agricultural Northumberland, unfurled itself to hit the steel, viking-eyed blueness of the North Sea. The grandeur of the scene, perhaps after the confines of the gorge, is most uplifting.

I must admit as I strode onto the flatness of the tops that there was a moment of mild panic! No path! And struggling to fit the maps together in the blustery wind (hence the advice to tape them together before setting out), for a

few moments I couldn't work out which was The Cheviot. There was no sign of anyone else to give a clue as to where the paths lay and I initially mistook the distant Hedgehope Hill to be The Cheviot itself. Broadhope Hill, behind, seemed somehow massive and much greater than the mere odd hundred metres indicated on the map. Preston Hill shimmered in the sunshine but the valley above Goldscleugh lay hidden from my position, adding to the confusion. Rocks below Scald Hill seemed substantial and were hardly hinted at on the map.

Eventually, using rucksack and camera to pin the sheets down, I took stock and worked out just what was what. Embarrassed at my ineptitude and lack of preparation I crossed over New Burn to find the motorway that was the regular route up Scald Hill and on up to The Cheviot.

Apart from the odd patch of peat the going underfoot is good, and as you pull out from steepness to see a cairn with a stick in it to your right over a wire fence, you have no indication of what is about to follow. Before going on it is perhaps worth crossing to the cairn because it gives the best view you will get from The Cheviot across to the distant Lindisfarne (Holy Island). The Cheviot is the final summit on the Pennine Way.

A great morass of soft peat follows and I defy anyone to reach the summit cairn without getting plastered in the stuff. The trig point floats like a desert island on a sea of soft mud and all you can do is work out which you think is the firmest and shallowest section of bog.

Three grinning people huddled on the eastern and leeward side of the concrete pillar cheered and laughed as I sank up to my ankles in the morass. The evidence of their crossing was plain to see and I huddled from the wind with them, quite pleased with my attempt. They were three Geordies from South Shields and we had a 'bit-o-crack' as we ate our lunch. Then it was the turn of another group of unfortunates. Spurred to great deeds by our cheering, one lad floundered to his knees and we thought we may have to rescue him. But he came out smiling and we congratulated him on his stout effort.

They, the original three, namely Neil Towler, Graeme Wallace and Geoff Crackett, were also on my round and I was glad to break my solitude and join them on the walk. The mud goes on for some way down the shoulder to Cairn Hill and there were times when the wire fence was utilised to pass over the worst bits. In a hollow a number of small ponds also required careful navigation but by the time the top of Cairn Hill is reached the worst is over.

Facing page: **Looking from Hedgehope Hill to Cairn Fell**.

119

It's a direct fall down to the col of Scotsmen's Knowe and as you drop you cross over a number of scree patches. The rocks here are red, giving the impression that they have been baked in an oven. The name Scotsmen's Knowe seems to suggest that this col and the entrance into the Harthope Valley served as a pass to the Scots at some stage in this region's turbulent past.

The ground in front resembles an ill-fitting toupee as a cap of peat seems to sprawl awkwardly over the top of Comb Fell, holed frequently and not quite managing to stretch over onto the higher Hedgehope Hill beyond. Geoff Crackett was not about to discover the delights ahead for he had pulled a ligament in his knee and hobbled off, cutting short his walk in the interests of self preservation. 'See you back at the car lads.'

'Well, he knows best. He's training to be a doctor', grinned Neil. So then we were three.

Once the fence line is gained, it is best to follow it all the way over Comb Fell and on up to the summit of Hedgehope Hill. The lads pointed to some great smoking chimneys in the distance where the Tyne snakes through 'Geordie Land' to the south east, and proudly informed me that was their town. They also explained that every weekend they left it to walk or to climb. Next weekend they were going potholing. In this age of polarised specialisation I admired their true spirit of adventure.

It seemed all too soon when we reached the top of Hedgehope Hill to shelter from the biting wind below the summit triangulation point. On the last steep slope I noticed that the tiny, wild, strawberry-like ground leaves were now golden brown and crunched beneath the boot, a sure sign of autumn as was the present wind temperature. Neil demonstrated the art of drinking from a Spanish goat's skin and Graeme pressed the shutter of my camera; hopefully to take my portrait as I perched in happy repose seated on the summit cairn.

You seem to descend back to the valley of Harthorpe in no time at all. It's steeply down at first but then becomes more horizontal as you pass the igneous outcrops of rock that form the knolls of first Long Crags and then across to the bastion-like Housey Crags. Below these latter rocks drops a well-marked path, a little bridge secreted over Harthorpe Burn and the end of a very pleasant and colourful mountain walk.

'Cheviot — why aye man, it's a canny walk.'

Above: **Neil Towler demonstrates the art of drinking from a Spanish goatskin by the trig point on Hedgehope Hill.**

Left: **Crossing the peat to the summit trig point of The Cheviot.**

Facing page:

Top left: **Easy walking downhill to Hawsen Burn, the start of the walk.**

Top right: **Looking up through the heather and ferns from Hawsen Burn.**

Bottom: **Graeme Wallace and Neil Trowler walk down to Scotsman's Knowe with Combe Fell and Hedgehope Hill beyond.**

The Walk: A long distance walk exploring Holy Island (Lindisfarne) then taking a circuitous route through varying countryside reaching and returning from Wooler, (Northumberland, North-East England).
Accommodation Base: Wooler (see p117).
Map: L75 Berwick-upon-Tweed and Surrounding Area.
Start and Finish: Holy Island (Lindisfarne), (map ref: NU 126420).
Length: 45mls (73km).
Approx Time: 2$^{1}/_{2}$ days.
Difficulty: A straightforward walk, a little undulating on the inland section.
Access: Car. Holy Island is connected to the mainland by a causeway and this is driveable when the tide is out which effectively means for the period up to 2 hours before high tide and 3$^{1}/_{2}$ hours after. Safe crossing times are clearly displayed on the road to the island and also on the island. (Note tides occur at approximately 12$^{1}/_{2}$ hour intervals.)
Seasons: All year.
Observations: A fascinating and attractive walk of quiet beauty. Historically Holy Island is of prime interest — the home of St. Cuthbert and the Lindisfarne Gospels — and still has a ruined priory and preserved castle. Even so inland, the cup and ring markings on the outcropping sandstone are plentiful and date at least back to the Bronze Age. There is plenty to see for the birdwatcher and botanist or anyone interested in natural history.
Accommodation: Inns and bed and breakfast accommodation.

NORTHERN ENGLAND: The Overland Viking Trek from Holy Island by Bill Birkett

The Route

Half Day: Holy Island (9mls, 14.5km). A walk round the periphery of the island to include those features which interest you most.

Day 2: Holy Island to Wooler (18mls, 29km) via the causeway, Beal, Plough Inn (West Mains), Kenstone, Hunting Hall, Lowick, Lowick South Moor, Hetton North Farm, Doddington Moor, Weetwood Hall, Clavering, Weetwood Moor.

Day 3: Wooler to Holy Island (18mls, 29km) via Weetwood Moor (south path), East Horton, Town Law, Old Hazelrigg, Cockenheugh (St. Cuthbert's Cave), Shiellow Wood, Fenwick Wood, Fenwick, Fenwick Granary, Beal Sands, the causeway.

The Walk

The rolling lands of Northumberland are now relatively quiet despite the combine harvesters that sweep through the golden corn. Its position above Newcastle, 'the northern capital of England', below the Scottish border and somewhere east of the famous Lake District goes some way to explain its current obscurity. It has not always been so.

The rivers of this quietly beautiful land have often run red with blood. When the Romans left behind their greatest military fortification, that of Hadrian's Wall in south Northumberland, they had already all but abandoned the region to 'the war-like peoples north of the wall'. The Anglo-Saxons took over and in 547

Ida became the first King of Northumbria.

Aidan arrived from Iona in 635 to set up an abbey on Lindisfarne (the name derives from his converts who were people from Lindsey in north Lincolnshire) and St Cuthbert became the most·famous bishop. This brief period of relative peace and tranquillity was shattered by the Viking fleet which proceeded to rape and pillage the people and their lands.

But the tale of Northumberland does not end there and it is worth just briefly bringing it up to date. The Scotland/England border repeatedly shifted north and south and it was Northumberland that always lay at the middle of these 'negotiations'. Marauding Scots known as the 'Border Reivers' took great delight in visiting Northumberland, and their intentions were not always honourable. In truth it worked both ways and the Northumbrians also travelled north for revenge on occasions.

Things started to calm down a little after the battle at Flodden. On a September day in 1513 Scotland suffered the greatest defeat of its entire, long and bloody history. For two days the English Army camped on the hills of Haugh Head on the eastern side of Wooler Water. They were led by the Earl of Surrey and were 26,000 strong. The opposition, however, under James 1st of Scotland, were just 4000 strong. Not surprisingly, the Scots were brutally defeated. The rivers and streams literally ran red with blood and not more than a half dozen prisoners survived this little episode. The Scottish song 'The Flowers of the Forest' was written in memory of the battle.

This walk starts then, from Holy Island — a more romantic little island you couldn't wish to find — and takes a circuitous trek that will enable you to discover the rural Northumberland countryside: refreshing, unspoilt, and in its own particular way a rather handsome land. To enjoy this trek and to discover just what they were all fighting about, you needn't spill one drop of blood. Merely tighten the laces and start the walk.

Facing page: **Harvesting in Northumberland.**

Top right: **Farmer and son straw burning on Holy Island.**

Middle right: **Susan Lund contemplates the mysterious Cup and Ring markings on Weetwood Moor.**

Bottom right: **Beware The Bull!**

Half Day: The Circuit of Lindisfarne (Holy Island)

First let me explain why I have given this a half-day status: it is because this circuit can be accomplished in half a day whilst allowing for any delays in crossing the causeway because of the tides.

My first sighting of Holy Island left a lasting impression of romanticism and fascination. A silver castle shimmered against a blue sky and above the cold grey North Sea; a castle in the air, on an island, and floating above the water was intriguing. It was many years before I actually had the opportunity to cross the causeway over to the island. The island was called Lindisfarne by Aidan's monks, but in 1802 a cell of Benedictine monks were granted the See of Lindisfarne and renamed the island 'Holy Island' to commemorate the holy blood that flowed during the invasion of the Vikings. Both names have survived.

Noting that the tide was well out I drove across, stopping midway to take some photographs. Today it was a mournful sight and both sea and sky were a sad grey colour, a cold wind blew and only the piping of the sands and the smell of seaweed broke the monotony. It felt very lonely and must have been even more so before the causeway was opened in 1954. Prior to this there was no permanent link with the mainland, and the route was across the sands. Marker posts were positioned on the line of this Pilgrim's Causeway only in 1886 and they remain as a ghost of the past.

In the distance we, Susan Lund and myself, had imagined that we had spotted a black plume of smoke arising from the distant hazy image of the village. Now crossing the sand dunes of The Snook, the smoke was confirmed and underneath, an orange wall of flame flickered, grasping and leaping as the wind drove it on. Full marks for dramatic impact but it wasn't the Vikings who had returned, merely the end of season straw burning.

As you enter the village you will find a field to your right which is open ended but surrounded on its other three sides by buildings. In it the straw burnt with a vengeance and all the smoke and sparks flew out of the open end. Chatting with the farmer he explained that he had waited three weeks for the correct wind conditions. He laughed at the recent law passed in Parliament which decrees that all straw burning should be done on certain days of the week. 'Sure I can burn up on the correct day but if the wind isn't right I'm not going to be too popular', he winked.

Most of this island is only 25ft (8m) above sea level but there is a hard whinstone dyke that has resisted the forces of erosion better than the rest and on this sits the abbey, and higher than the rest, Lindisfarne Castle. It seems natural, starting from the village, to circumnavigate the island in an anti-clockwise direction. This we will do, beginning amongst the ruins of the abbey.

The abbey is pleasant enough, well maintained and of neatly cut sandstone. I feel it necessary to delve again into the history as it is this that gives the island such a unique flavour. The sixth Bishop here was Cuthbert from 664-87 and for a century after his death Lindisfarne flourished. Then on 7 June 793 the Vikings came for the first time and Symeon of Durham recorded:

> They came like stinging hornets, like ravening wolves, they made raids on all sides, slaying not only cattle but priests and monks. They came to the church at Lindisfarne, and laid all waste, trampled the Holy places with polluted feet, dug down the altars and bore away the treasure of the church. Some brethren they slew, some they carried away captive, some they drove out naked after mocking and vexing them. Some they drowned in the sea.

In 875 the monks left the island with a number of holy relics. These included the body of St Cuthbert and the beautifully illustrated Lindisfarne Gospels. St. Cuthbert was carried about the countryside many times and is now thought to rest in the precincts of Durham Cathedral. His holy body was thought to be incorruptible and to retain all the physical features intact — as though he were but sleeping. His coffin has been opened twice

Lindisfarne Castle sits on a hard whinstone dyke that has so far managed to resist the forces of erosion better than the rest of the island.

since: once in 1104 and again in 1537 and the body was reported to be 'Sound, sweet, odoriferous and flexible' (850 years after his death).

But her history isn't the only attraction of the island: nature has much to offer too. Between the castle and the Abbey is situated a bay which is still home to a small fishing fleet. As you round it you will observe two cairned structures, like Egyptian Needles, on the sand spit that sticks out from the mainland. Ahead and out to sea the Farne Islands and Bamburgh Castle were highlighted black against a grey and scarlet sky. The distant islands gave the impression that a school of whales were heading full steam for the mainland.

Lindisfarne Castle is open to the public and despite the high charge, levied by the National Trust (who keep it in pristine condition), it is worth a look around. As you go you will find a vast area of sand that stretches across to Berwick and there are a number of cliffs with caves. Within this environment the bird life is outstanding and several species breed here including the ringed plover, oystercatcher and redshank all of which feed on the great numbers of shellfish, worms and crustaceans which inhabit the mud and sandflats. The wintering of geese is famous here and you can also see gannets, guillemots and the famous puffin with its red and orange striped beak.

With so much to see, you might find that on your return the tide has covered the causeway and you have to stay awhile longer — but don't panic, there are several inns where you can relax and enjoy a drink, a meal and talking to the locals.

Days 2 – 3: To Wooler and Back

The farm lands here are rich and support a number of different crops. The effect is a patchwork of different coloured, higgledy piggledy fields that stretch and roll to the distant haze that is the Cheviot Hills. The sheep have long Roman noses and the breed is known as Cheviot.

Rising from the plains are the high moors, upland areas of mature conifer, heather and outcropping sandstone. These little sandstone rocks are quite remarkable and some resemble actual waves, seemingly petrified in mid course. For the rock climber the best sandstone climbing in the whole of Britain is found here and you may see some climbers in action as you pass near Cockenheugh.

Before the high ground of Doddington Moor you will encounter the Devil's Causeway. Although difficult to see on the ground, the clue to its origin is in its remarkable straightness — it is of course a Roman road. There are many stylish buildings and the distinctive Scottish influence cannot be denied. Particularly elegant is the arched stone bridge over the River Till just after Weetwood Hall. Above this and of even earlier origin the cup and ring markings to be found on the moor itself are reputed to be of early Bronze Age, circa 1500 BC.

Certainly their purpose, they are frequent and widespread in these relatively soft sandstone rocks, is not known. Many theories are put forward but there is a distinct lack of hard evidence to support any one of them. The shapes vary in form and style but the basic pattern is of a hollow, the cup, surrounded by a number of concentric rings. It is likely that they had some purpose as they can be found on many important sites throughout Britain and Ireland.

It has been said that until recent times, in the distant Hebrides, the wives of crofters used to fill the cup with milk each morning. This has been linked with ancient fertility rites but of course the whole concept is pure speculation. The more thought you apply to the matter the more confusing it becomes.

Wooler was an important wool town and it is likely it was given that name because of this. Weetwood Moor again gives some excellent examples of the 'cup and ring' markings. These high grounds give excellent views but can often be stark and wind battered. When the trees (mixed conifer and deciduous) appear they are most welcome.

St Cuthbert's cave can be found towards the end of the Cockenheugh escarpment and one wonders if the terrified monks hid from the Viking hoards here. The drop down the far side of the Kyloe Hills is superbly wooded and contrasts strikingly with the rest of the walk. After crossing the main road and passing the Fenwick Granary soon you arrive back down to the sands and the sea.

You have passed through a remarkably peaceful and rural scene; a balance of nature and agriculture. But you cannot help but wonder, particularly when the old straw burns and the flames leap high, is Northumberland only resting before the next onslaught?

SCOTLAND: The West Highland Way by Tony Greenbank

The Walk: The West Highland Way was Scotland's first long-distance walking route. It runs for nearly 100 miles from Glasgow to Fort William on the west coast of Scotland — taking in the length of Loch Lomond, the ruggedness of Black Mount, the wilderness of Rannoch Moor, the great gorge of Glencoe and the old high-level Miltary Road from Kinlochleven to Fort William (North-West Scotland).

Maps: OS L41, L50, L56, L57, L64.

Start: Glasgow City Centre (most popular start); Milngavie (official start), (map ref: WS 555 744).

Finish: Fort William (map ref: NN 100 738).

Waymarks: Thistle motif on wooden markers.

Length: 93mls (150km) from Milngavie; 99mls (160km) from Glasgow.

Approx Time: 6–8 days.

Difficulty: The terrain gives varying surfaces underfoot from the hideously rough and uneven to remarkably good going. The route is usually straightforward to follow but map and compass should be taken in event of bad weather (or nightfall) and poor visibility. Roads are never far away should conditions indicate it would be more prudent to take to them.

Access: Rail, bus, car.

Seasons: April to November.

Observations: Midges can make the route a misery in the summer months. Spring or autumn would be a better time to undertake the journey. A water bottle should always be carried. Although a pair of shorts are ideal during warm days there are tracts of country with heather, dead or otherwise, which can prove uncomfortable on bare skin (track suit bottoms are ideal). A solution to wet boots — with a risk of suffering blisters as a result — is to walk the route with two pairs of training shoes. These seldom blister the feet, dry quickly and the reserve pair is light to carry. Loop-stitched ankle socks and thermal underclothing will also help to keep the body warm even though it may be wet. There are many variations to the West Highland Way. These are usually of a more serious nature, leading over high, exposed ground, and full mountain walking precautions should be kept in mind. The West Highland Walk itself is also serious, but being of lower level generally has more escape routes.

Accommodation: Hotels, inns, guest houses (B&B) and youth hostels are plentiful, but it does pay to book ahead if possible in those areas where there may be a limited choice during the holiday season.

Guidebooks: *The West Highland Way* by Tom Hunter (Constable).

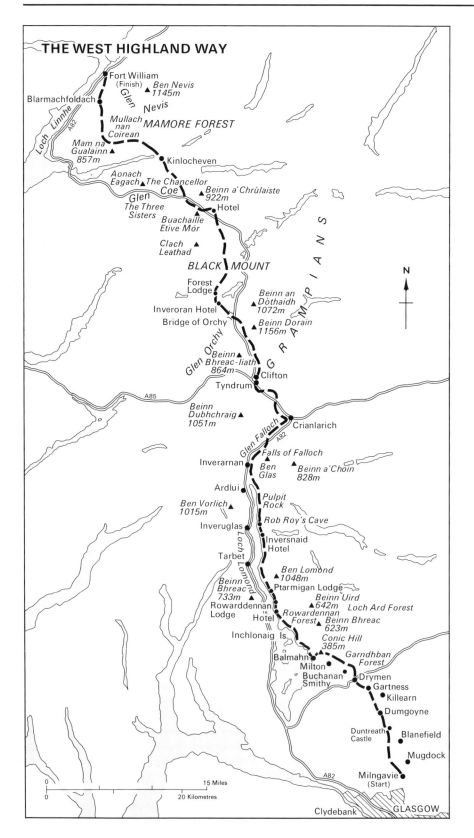

The Route

Day 1: Glasgow to Drymen (18 miles, 29km) via the Kelvin Walkway to the Antonine Wall and Milngavie. Then by The Allander Park, the west side of Craigallian Loch and the Blane Valley.

Days 2 and 3: Drymen to Crianlarich (33 miles, 53km) via the Garadhban Forest and Balmaha. Then by the east side of Loch Lomond to Rowardennan. Continuing via Inversnaid, Inverarnan, Beinglas Farm, the Falls of Falloch and Derrydaroch bridge to Crianlarich.

Days: 4 and 5: Crianlarich to Kingshouse Hotel (24 miles, 39km) via Tyndrum, the Inveroran Hotel, Bridge of Orchy, Victoria Bridge and Rannoch Moor.

Days 6 and 7: Kingshouse to Fort William (24 miles, 39km) via Devil's Staircase, Kinlochleven and the old Military Road to Fort William.

The Walk

North of the Border lies Scotland's largest city and seaport, a metropolis that is the home of a quarter of the country's population. This big city with its shipbuilding yards, docks, factories, tenements, and mean back streets had also one of the finest city centres in Europe — and one which justifiably is proving a major tourist attraction of the United Kingdom. Glasgow's marine and general engineering industries only started in the late 18th century. Before then the city had an ecclesiastical history dating back to the 4th century and was the main market and university town of West Scotland.

Glasgow is a city of fervent loyalties — religious, civic and national. Nowhere are these given greater expression than in the city's devotion to soccer. The greatest passions are aroused at an Old Firm match: Glasgow Rangers versus Celtic. I experienced this during a raw New Year's Day where the stadium was bisected in more ways than by the half-way line. On my right (and around me), Celtic's fans: to my left, Rangers. Rangers scored first and that half of the arena erupted, while to my right there was frozen stillness. When Celtic equalised the image was reversed.

The West Highland Way embodies both the frenzy and the freeze in its incomparable 100 miles (161km) from Glasgow to Fort William — and whatever the season. The reason is simple: the West Highland Way is a walk into freedom. It can be done by anyone who has the will to be free. At first when the idea grips, the mind cartwheels with the joy of anticipating some of the wildest and most scenic land in the world. Then comes its execution, possibly in elements so inclement it can seem all is lost, only for hope to be rekindled as each goal is struck along the way. That goal may be just reaching a bed for the night, but the reaction to achieving that may be no less than that to the equaliser so ably scored beneath the floodlights the day I visited Celtic Park.

The West Highland Way was Scotland's first long distance walking route. Officially opened in 1980 — and with all thanks to its creator Tom Hunter — it treads where Rob Roy strode around Loch Lomond, paces the very ground that R.L. Stevenson's heroes struggled across over Rannoch Moor (Europe's largest wilderness) and runs the gauntlet that the McDonalds ran through Glencoe's haunted Pass.

Buachaille Etive Mor can look benign or sinister depending on weather conditions.

The West Highland Way is dominated by the giant ridge of Drum Albyn which, carved from solid rock into a spectacular sawtooth chain by the agencies of fire, ice and water, soars up from the ocean — a true monarch of all its lovely lonely glens and glinting sea lochs along its way.

The last remnants of the great Caledonian Forest whose pines once covered the Highlands are here. There are sweeping new plantations of sitka spruce and lodgepole pine and airy loch waters with sandy beaches. Capercaillies and black grouse share the woodland with crossbills, woodpeckers and redstarts. On heatherclad hillsides golden plover, red grouse and curlew startle at the thud of approaching boots. And out there on the sub-arctic environment of the mountain tops, lives the golden eagle, ptarmigan and snow bunting.

John Hillaby wrote a foreword in Tom Hunter's *A Guide to the West Highland Way*. It embodies two good pieces of advice: 'If you are not a Scot you would be wise to look out for important Gaelic words on your maps, words such as CREAG meaning crag or cliff, and COIRE, a blind valley or corrie that almost always leads you nowhere except, often, to a CREAG on the other side. 'Ben' or its Gaelic equivalent BEINN is, of course, a hill which may be MOR (big), BEG (small), DUBH (black), RHUADH (red) and very often GLAS (grey) . . . Safety and comfort are matters of common sense. Remember always that it's almost as important to keep cool as it is to keep warm. Hyperthermia is nearly as dangerous as hypothermia. Wear clothes that can be zipped up or zipped down.

Accommodation is not always easy to find on the West Highland Way. Occasionally it may be necessary to quit the route to locate a sleeping place — and this, of course, adds to the distance you have to travel. A chain of youth hostels is one answer. There are hotels and guest houses (B&B) along the way too. Certainly the route lends itself to backpacking with frequent idyllic pitches in oases of wonderland.

A truly magical journey on foot now awaits you. Here is what you will remember most, never to forget.

Day 1: Glasgow to Drymen

Glasgow, the third most populous city in Britain, is — for an industrial city — fortunate in having over 70 imaginatively laid out public parks. This fact gives the West Highland Way a unique approach. Although the route proper does not begin until the town of Milngavie, 6 miles (10km) away, the linked walkways through Glasgow's parks gives the walker a flying start from the city centre.

It is via Kelvingrove Park and the Kelvin Walkway, then, that the West Highland Way truly begins. Kelvingrove Park is only minutes from the city centre, and the Botanic Gardens are the place to make for . . . a 42-acre spread of changing floral displays and exotically-filled glasshouses which form a fitting prelude to the wooded banks and grassy slopes flanking the River Kelvin.

The path from the Botanic Gardens takes the east bank, passing beneath the lovely Kirklee Bridge (amongst others) and presently perhaps the Glaswegian's greatest fortune is glimpsed — the grandeur of its surrounding countryside. The Campsie Fells lie almost within the city and how their skyline draws the walker on! On through Dawsholm Park (following the yellow markers of a nature trail and passing a bird sanctuary), the parkland green gives way to the oily right-hand verge of a busy road that is the necessary route to Milngavie.

Just north of the large roundabout at Canniesburn Toll the road meets the Antonine Wall. Built around AD 142 by Emperor Antoninus Pius to extend from the Forth to the Clyde, this wall served for half a century as the north-west boundary of the Roman Empire. It was intended to supersede Hadrian's Wall but was finally abandoned. Even so it is Scotland's most important Roman work to survive — a turf and clay rampart on a stone base with a ditch and a military road running parallel to it. More forts were positioned along this wall than on Hadrian's Wall as fiercer resistance from the marauding Picts was expected — and met with. A small section of the wall is preserved within a fenced enclosure.

The dormitory town of Milngavie feeds the walker ingeniously on to the West Highland Way via its War Memorial (Douglas Street), a lane of shops, a river bridge (over the Allander Water) and an old railway line to leafy Allander Park. Continuing through the edge of Mugdock Wood, a muddy path is presently reached overlooking the river Allander Water.

Craigallian Loch is skirted on its west side, the path then switching over past the eastern fringe of Carbeth Loch — and here are ghosts of highwaymen and stagecoaches, for this was the route they once took. The Way continues with views that make the heart beat faster: the Blane Valley unfolds away below, the Strath-blane Hills reach up to extinct volcano Dumgoyne and Ben Lomond beckons in the distance.

The West Highland Way follows the Blane Valley by a disused railway line and pipeline taking water from Loch Lomond. Although there are padlocked Water Board gates at road crossings, adjacent stiles give access. Watch out for wild birds along the route, and — in autumn — for the salmon which come up the river Endrick to spawn at the hamlet of Gartness. Watch too for the first view along the Way of Loch Lomond, glimpsed from the minor road leading on to Drymen village.

Days 2–3: Drymen to Crianlarich

The romantic mix of loch, birchwood, mountain and glen offers an invitation on this next section of the West Highland Way that is irresistible. Ahead is Loch Lomond 23 miles (37km) long, spangled with 30 islets. And with Ben Lomond adding its magic presence . . .

From Drymen the West Highland Way begins along the A811 road before sheering off along pleasant footpaths through the Garadhban Forest, an ocean of larch and spruce offering more tantalising glimpses of Loch Lomond.

It is from the summit of Conic Hill, the next objective, that the view does all credit to its position — a unique vantage point on the Highland Boundary Fault where plains and mountains are seen across the waters of the loch as clearly separated as if by a ruled line. Descending from the ridge of Conic Hill to the public car park at Balmaha, there is now beautiful walking through a variety of terrain from the greenery of oakwoods to shadowy coniferous forest and with a profusion of wildlife and flowers to be seen along the way. A feature of the landscape is also the many fine bays around the loch, scented by bluebells and rowan blossom and favoured by trout and pike.

Loch Lomond, the largest lake in Great Britain dominates this scenery. It is also the loveliest loch in Scotland. Soft green hills gently cushion its banks in the south, but further north they soar to the sky on both the Stirlingshire side to the east and the Dumbartonshire side to the west.

The scenic appeal of Loch Lomond owes much to its islands. Irish missionaries from the 5th century built monasteries and nunneries here — safe in the knowledge their position would deter marauders. It is believed St Mirren founded a monastery in the 6th century on the largest island, Inchmurrin. By the time the hamlet of Rowardennan is reached (seasonally opened hotel and youth hostel) the route is about to become even better.

Rowardennan is a popular base for the ascent of Ben Lomond (3192ft, 973m) as well as the starting point for a splendid walk along the eastern shore of Loch Lomond — this route a long-popular gem is now incorporated into the West Highland Way.

From Rowardennan pier, strike north to Ptarmigan Lodge, then by forestry road and footpath along Loch Lomond to Rowchoish (William Ferris Memorial Shelter) and the Inversnaid Hotel. The views of the triple-peaked Cobbler carved from wild, twisted rock are seen superbly across Loch Lomond.

Rob Roy, the Robin Hood of Scotland (immortalised by Sir Walter Scott), once owned a small estate near here called Craig Roystan. It spreads from the shores of Loch Lomond to the base of Ben Lomond, and here the walker may see giant-horned goats, golden eagles and peregrine falcons. Even the elusive wildcat has been sighted hereabouts.

From the Inversnaid Hotel a path continues north to Rob Roy's Cave — a natural cavern at the foot of a precipice near the loch. It is also known as Bruce's Cave as legend has it Robert the Bruce licked his wounds here after defeat in battle.

The going now becomes more difficult. Tom Hunter advisedly suggests extra time be allowed in his guide to the West Highland Way. The terrain is a higher-level and rugged wilderness of rocks and fallen trees. However, beyond Douane the going improves along a better track by the loch side, continuing north by Ardleish and Dubh Lochan to the bridge of the River Falloch at Beinglas Farm.

Past the justly famous Falls of Falloch the route climbs over exposed moors where ancient remains of the old Caledonian Forest can be seen. Eventually both the Falloch and the A82 road are crossed and the path follows the old — and in poor repair — Military Road built by William Caulfield (successor to General Wade) which is followed to the little village of Crianlarich.

Days 4–5: Crianlarich to Kingshouse Hotel

Continuing at first along the Military Road, the West Highland Way continues north, climbing through trees, then descending to the Oban railway line. After crossing under a railway bridge, then crossing the main road, the land around Kirkton Farm is reached. Care is requested here as the West of Scotland College of Agriculture has various experimental schemes in operation here.

The route now skirts the ruins of St Fillian's Chapel or Priory. The shell has considerable historical and religious significance and invaluable relics found here can be seen in the National Museum of Antiquities, Edinburgh.

Tyndrum is the next step along the way. It is

approached via a pine wood below the popular tourist village which has two railway stations: one on the Glasgow to Fort William line; the other, the Glasgow to Oban Line. Tyndrum is then left by the natural route of the old Glencoe road which skirts the bases of Beinn Odhar and Beinn Dorain and follows the West Highland Railway. Of all the peaks in Scotland Beinn Dorain must be one of the most photographed — a spectacular cone alive with red deer and of such wild scenic appeal it lifts the spirits the rest of the way to Bridge of Orchy.

The small village here is set amongst marvellous countryside. As the West Highland Way proceeds towards the Inveroran Hotel — a traditional staging post where William and Dorothy Wordsworth stayed in 1803 — the views of peaks like Stob Coir an Albannaich (the Highlandman's Peak) are breathtaking. So too is the setting of the hotel in native pine trees by the lovely Loch Tulla.

Inveroran is left by road for a mile to Victoria Bridge which it crosses to end at Forest Lodge. A sign says: 'Drove road to Glencoe. No vehicles', and this is the continuation of the West Highland Way. Rough at first, the walking becomes more comfortable as the route approaches Ba Bridge. But what remoteness! Corrie Ba above is said to be the largest corrie in Scotland and looks the very essence of wild territory.

Rannoch Moor is the next objective. The barren moorland scene has changed little since R.L. Stevenson used its 20 square miles as a setting for his novel *Kidnapped*. He described it as being 'as waste as the sea.' Certainly it is a serious proposition.

Although the West Highland Way traverses one edge by a fair track, the flat expanse of the moor where lochans glitter and flash is an extremely intimidating sight. It also stirs the soul. It is unique and magnificent. As a massive nature reserve it is one of the finest anywhere — 60 square miles once covered by the pines of the Caledonian forest, now bereft of these splendid giants apart from a few surviving specimens on the islets of lochs Ba and Laidon. Contrasting starkly against the dark peat lie the bleached skeletons of that former woodland.

Rare grasses, sedges and mosses flourish on Rannoch Moor. And purple heather too. The curlew, snipe and greenshank are denizens of this wilderness realm — along with myriads of rainbows that on a misty day glow and quiver in the rain.

On the run-in to the Kingshouse hotel the track descends from 1450ft (442m) and brings the traveller face to face with the great crags of Buchaille Etive Mor. This pyramid of perfection stands guard over Glencoe and Glen Etive. It completely dominates the Kingshouse.

Days 6–7: Kingshouse to Fort William

Glencoe is one of Scotland's wildest and most famous glens. Running from Rannoch Moor to Loch Leven in Inverness-shire, it channels between magnificent mountains — like Bidean nam Bian and Am Bodach.

It was here in 1692 that a Campbell commander and company of soldiers accepted the hospitality of the MacDonalds for nearly a fortnight, and consequently turned this beautiful place into the Glen of Weeping. Rising at 5am, the Campbells started a massacre in the middle of a blizzard. MacIan, the aged chief of the MacDonalds, was killed. His two sons, however, escaped to the hills with other survivors of the massacre.

The West Highland Way rather than following the ravine of Glencoe rejoins the old Military Road until it meets the main road. This is followed to Altnafeadh — a cattle stance where drovers rested their cattle on the route-march south. Once again the Military Road is gained and followed, a highway that since the 1750s linked Stirling with Fort William.

The Scottish Six Days' Trial is an international event in the motor cycle trialist's calendar. It is an exciting and gripping event, the only pity of it being the wheel tracks on the route ahead are becoming so obvious, they are threatening erosion. The Devil's Staircase is a case in point, the zig-zags of this steep gradient are badly tyre-mauled.

From the top of this famous hill pass, the views of Glencoe and Black Mount can be panoramic, while in a northerly direction good visibility will bring Ben Nevis and the Mamores into focus.

The path gives excellent walking from the summit and on past the steely spread of the Blackwater reservoir. Eight miles (13km) long, its water is held back by half a mile of dam, constructed in the early 1900s by thousands of labourers using pick and shovel. These men would make the journey to the Kingshouse hotel for drinking sessions, some perishing each winter on the return climb. In springtime it was not unusual for deer stalkers to stumble on anonymous corpses as the snow melted.

The descent brings great views of the Aonach Eagach ridge, a mountaineering three-star classic. When the track joins the access road to Blackwater Reservoir near the power station, both the town of Kinlochleven and

Loch Leven — a sea loch — can be seen.

Kinlochleven has had in its time the ambience of an Alaskan gold rush boom town. Soon after the turn of the century thousands of labourers were employed to build the then largest aluminium plant in the United Kingdom. Gambling, brawling, drinking and the rest were the order of the day, and all amid a squalor that quite belied the beauty and solitude of the mountains encircling the head of this wild and remote loch.

The remaining 15 miles (24km) to Fort William from Kinlochleven begins along the A82, but soon a signpost saying 'Public Footpath to Fort William' leads the traveller up Caulfield's Military Road again.

Gradually climbing westwards above the northern flanks of Allt Nathrach, the scenario becomes enormously impressive as Loch Leven, guarded by big hills, is viewed from this aerial vantage point. Climbing still higher, the track looks on to Stob Ban (3274ft, 998m), snowy with quartzite scree in certain lights.

After three miles along the old Military Road the former stalker's house (Tigh-na-sleubhaich) recalls memories when the Mamore Forest was celebrated for its deer, and Henry VII hunted this countryside. At 1000ft (3050m) the track tops out with vast mountain panoramas in every direction.

Mam na Gualainn (2603ft, 793m) bulks hugely to the south and is seen at its best from Lairigmor. There are also powerful views across Loch Leven to Glencoe if a diversionary path is taken from Lairigmor to Callert.

A pair of binoculars is useful for picking out the small islands near Loch Leven's south shore. Here seals can be viewed lying on the rocks, swans nest on the island and there are also herons. The islands were the home of the early missionaries. The largest one, for example, is called Eilean Munde after St Fintan Mundus who built a church here.

Eilean Munde has three landing places. As the isle was used by the MacDonalds, the Camerons and the Stewarts for burial purposes, these are called the Ports of the Dead. A reason for island cemeteries was that the wolf survived in Scotland until the 17th century and island graves were removed from its ravages. It is said that those MacDonalds killed in the 1692 Massacre of Glencoe are buried here.

The West Highland Way heads on west from Lairigmor, shortly to aim north, before descending gently and keeping the Allt na Lairige Moire on its left. Three miles on from Lairigmor, Caulfield's Old Military Road is forsaken for a path through forestry plantations at Blar a' Chaoruinn.

As the path strikes across the flanks of Sgorr Chalum and swings left towards the col to the left of Dun Deardail, the south-west ramparts of Ben Nevis, Britain's highest mountain at 4408ft (1344m) looms magnificently into view.

The West Highland Way heads north over the col and descends through thick woodland. Follow the markers with care until a good forest road is reached which then guides the traveller safely back down to earth into Glen Nevis. A final stretch by forest and public road to Bridge of Nevis marks the end of the official West Highland Way.

Looking across Loch Linnhe from near Fort William.

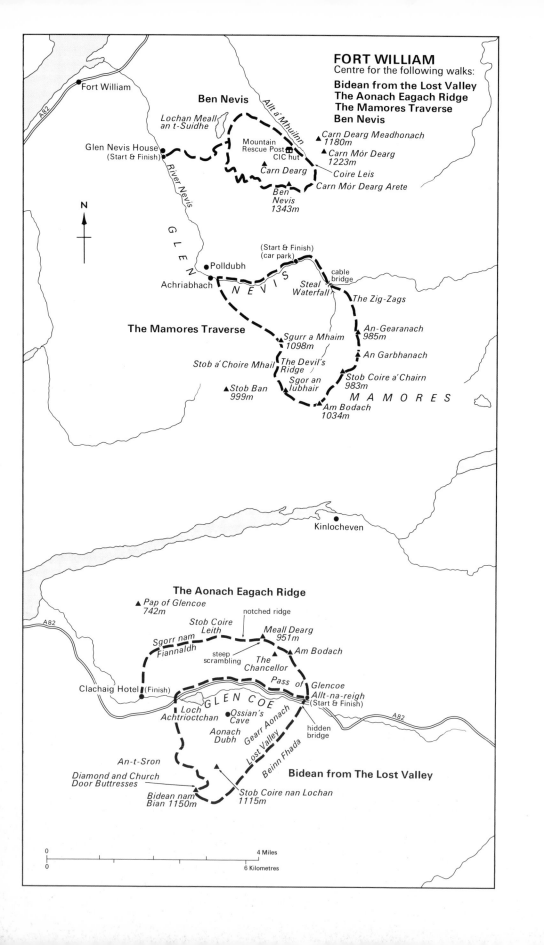

FORT WILLIAM
Centre for the following walks:
Bidean from the Lost Valley
The Aonach Eagach Ridge
The Mamores Traverse
Ben Nevis

Fort William

A82

Ben Nevis

Lochan Meall an t-Suidhe

Allt a' Mhuilinn

▲ *Carn Dearg Meadhonach 1180m*

Glen Nevis House
(Start & Finish)

Mountain Rescue Post
CIC hut

▲ *Carn Mór Dearg 1223m*

Carn Dearg

Coire Leis

Carn Mór Dearg Arete

River Nevis

Ben Nevis 1343m

G L E N

N

● Polldubh

(Start & Finish)
(car park)

cable bridge

Achriabhach

Steal Waterfall

The Zig-Zags

N E V I S

The Mamores Traverse

▲ *An-Gearanach 985m*

▲ *Sgurr a Mhaim 1098m*

▲ *An Garbhanach*

Stob a' Choire Mhail

The Devil's Ridge

Sgor an Iubhair

Stob Coire a' Chairn 983m

▲ *Stob Ban 999m*

M A M O R E S

▲ *Am Bodach 1034m*

● Kinlocheven

The Aonach Eagach Ridge

▲ *Pap of Glencoe 742m*

notched ridge

Stob Coire Leith

Meall Dearg 951m

Sgorr nam Fiannaidh

steep scrambling

The Chancellor

▲ *Am Bodach*

Pass of Glencoe

Clachaig Hotel ▌(Finish)

Allt-na-reigh
(Start & Finish)

A82

G L E N C O E

Loch Achtrioctchan

● *Ossian's Cave*

Aonach Dubh

Gearr Aonach

hidden bridge

Lost Valley

Beinn Fhada

An-t-Sron

Bidean from The Lost Valley

Diamond and Church Door Buttresses

Bidean nam Bian 1150m

Stob Coire nan Lochan 1115m

0			4 Miles

0			6 Kilometres

FORT WILLIAM – Scotland

Fort William: Accommodation base for the following 4 walks: Bidean from The Lost Valley; The Aonach Eagach Ridge; The Mamores Traverse; Ben Nevis.

Map Ref: NY 739102.

Location: Situated along the south shore of Loch Linnhe on the A82 below Ben Nevis.

Distance To Walks: 21mls (34km) south along A82 to Glencoe and the start of Bidean and The Aonach Eagach Ridge; 3mls (5km) north along A82 then up the Glen Nevis road to the youth hostel and the start of Ben Nevis; 7mls (12km) north along A82 then up to the head of Glen Nevis to start The Mamores Traverse.

Accommodation: Every type with camping in Glen Nevis.

The Town: Fort William is a thriving town that retains its Highland charm. Situated along the shore of Loch Linnhe and at the very foot of the great Ben Nevis it is amidst the best of the wild Scottish Highlands. Every veteran rainsoaked mountaineer has sought comfort in 'Fort Bill'. There are numerous restaurants and cafes and I have found that above the 'Nevis Sport' shop to be as good as any other in town for a light meal or drink. High quality haggis and Aberdeen Angus steak can be bought in the main street butchers. There are a number of small supermarkets, a modern cinema, a museum, frequent discos and many other distractions to idle one's way through a period of inclement weather. Note: The Clachaig Inn in wild Glencoe is best sited for the Aonach Eagach and Bidean walks and is a traditional mountain inn of great character. There is also free camping beside the road here and it retains a precious air of camaraderie often lost in the more formal and organised campsites.

Walkers on the Aonach Eagach Ridge. (Photo: Ronnie Faux.)

The Walk: A mountain walk up through the Lost Valley to the summit of Bidean nam Bian (Glencoe, North-West Scotland).
Accommodation Base: Fort William (see p133).
Maps: OS L41 – Ben Nevis, T7 – Ben Nevis and Glencoe.
Start and Finish: The upper large pull-in, on the south side of the A82 Glencoe road just below the Allt-na-reigh cottages (map ref; NN 174566).
Length: 7mls (11km).
Approx Time: 7hrs.
Ascent and Descent: 7000ft (2130m).
Difficulty: A high mountain walk requiring navigational competence and including some moderately difficult scrambling in descent.
Access: Car to Glencoe.
Seasons: May to October.
Observations: Superlative and contrasting mountain scenery with a huge vista from the summit. This mountain walk threads the easiest line through a wild mountainous region and is surrounded by large cliffs and precipitous slopes. Magnetite is present (particularly near the rocks of Stob Coire nan Lochan) and compass readings should be treated with caution. Good and settled weather essential.
Summit: Bidean nam Bian: 3773ft (1150 m).

SCOTLAND: Bidean from The Lost Valley by Bill Birkett

The Route

Drop down to the old road and along until the path takes you, over railway sleepers and wooden walk ways, over boggy bits, to a hidden bridge over the gorge. Up, over a stile, and left into the woods and tumbled rocks surrounding the burn of Allt coire Gabhail. Take the best looking track into the Lost Valley (valley between Beinn Fhada and Gearr Aonach). Up this, and at the top take path above right bank of gorge. (Care; very exposed.) Up and slightly left to a steep pull out onto the ridge. Traverse easily to the summit of Bidean nam Bian (4hrs, 3773ft/1150m).

Take the steep ridge down towards Stob Coire nan Lochan but at its base, by a small cairn, drop down left with a little moderate scrambling to follow scree to a little lochan (this looks much worse than it actually is!). Follow down the stream only to the large cliff of Stob Coire nam Beith then bear left underneath it until another small stream can be seen issuing from An t-Sron. Drop down to this and follow it. After some little scrambling next to the stream move left onto the shoulder of An t-Sron. Down to the road bridge then up the road back to starting point.

The Walk

Glencoe is possibly the most dramatic of all the Highland Glens and it cuts its way through the heart of some quite spectacular mountain scenery. These mountains, by British stand-

ards, are big. The highest, remotest and most rewarding summit in this prized collection is that of Bidean nam Bian.

Simply driving down the pass reveals the scale and savagery of this one time volcanic region. After the Meeting of the Waters, The Three Sisters, Beinn Fhada, Gearr Aonach and Aonach Dubh come into view to the south (left). Each present great faces of sweeping cliff beyond which can be seen a ridge of equally impressive stature. They can be considered to be fingers emanating from a great hidden hand behind. That fist is, of course, the complex Bidean nam Bian.

I will, with this walk, describe a circuit that takes you through some of the most breathtaking scenery, eventually to find the very summit of Bidean. There are harder and possibly more spectacular approaches but this path surpasses them all for variety and, additionally, it takes a

route that is without undue technical difficulty. It ascends the Lost Valley to explore the secrets therein, and continues up past cascading waterfalls to eventually gain the heights before traversing to the summit. Afterwards we will descend down Coire nam Beith to sample further the forceful rock architecture of the volcanic cauldron that formed Glencoe long ago, and on to regain the road by the bridge just below Loch Achtriochtan. Following up the road, a little way to the starting point, displays yet more of Glencoe's attractions and is a worthwhile end to a very fine walk.

Make doubly sure you are in the correct car park and heading for the right valley before you start. It's surprising just how many people make a mistake here. If you are aware of the possibility of making an error you will be alright, because Gearr Aonach, the middle sister, is definitely the most blazon. Her

Above left: **Looking down the stony track to The Lost Valley.**

Above right: **A walker looks over the edge of the waterfall at the head of The Lost Valley.**

Facing page: **Bidean nam Bian, its descent ridge in the centre, is seen from Stob Coire nan Lochan.**

135

precipitous form, a sheer and naked bastion of rock, stands proudly above and to the right (west) of Coire Gabhail — the Lost Valley.

It's only a short way to the steep wooden steps leading down to the bridged river gorge while above, over a broad stile, the well-defined path leads into the trees and tumble of boulders that hide the entrance to the Lost Valley. Always here, there is a sense of exploration as the path weaves in, over and around the rocky debris washed from above. You may find it best to cross over the burn but paths and false trails lay in all directions and it really is not possible to be specific as to which course is the preferable. In fact, of the many times I've taken this track I have always followed a different route through this maze of stone and birch.

Entrance to the Lost Valley is marked by a sudden clearing and a huge boulder just to the right. The contrast could not be more effective for in front of you now lies a long, flat-bottomed valley, clear of trees and obstruction, with immense and sheer walls rising on either side. Looking to find the tops of these precipitous rock walls you have to strain your neck. First you walk on stream-washed pebbles, and then sheep-cropped grass but you will note that even the stream has disappeared in this secret valley.

It is said that the MacDonalds hid their cattle up here during troubled times and it is easy to understand why. But quite apart from its anonymity this is a very special place. Today, in the sunshine, it was light and attractive with none of the threatening blackness that often pervades the now hidden Glencoe. Would that the MacDonalds had been here on the fateful 13 February 1692, when 38 men, women and children were slaughtered in cold blood and the rest scattered to die in the snow swept hills, instead of down in the valley beneath.

At the head of the valley the path takes the right side of the burn which now reappears, to occupy a deep, smooth-walled rock gorge. The roar of the water becomes deafening and a number of side streams falling clear into the abyss seem to intensify its depth. Possibly due to the roar of the water drowning the sound of our footsteps, two red deer appeared nonchalantly on the hillside just above us. (I had now been joined by a fellow lone walker.) Maybe it was a trick of the light but they both appeared huge.

The path meets the rim of the gorge at a superb waterfall which comes in from the right. Here, because the route circumnavigates over the top of the fall, the path becomes incredibly exposed and it is vital to keep a cool head. But the path is adequate and should pose no problems if care is taken.

It is now a steep pull up and out onto the ridge and today I was forced to climb a great snowfield. (This is not recommended to those without both an ice axe and the ability to use it.) Really it shouldn't have been there for it was midsummer! But there it was and as I pulled out onto the ridge I was alone again. Reluctantly my companion, with inadequate footwear, had had to turn back.

The view is big and of mountains in all directions, with long curving ridges monopolising the aesthetics. Walking along the ridge is a gentle affair and grass lies either side of the stony track. Warm air rushed past from the corries below and quite suddenly a raven swooped over with the airstream. It passed only a few feet in front of me, its arrogance heightening the intense feeling of loneliness.

Now there is the intense feeling that you are a long way from civilisation; a mere pinhead of humanity amidst a vast wilderness of mountains. But there is a magnificence in this harsh desolation and a feeling that, above all the others, Bidean is the leader of the savage pack. There is the awareness that this is a very special mountain and a feeling of pride knowing that you are going to set upon its remote summit.

A cairn stands on the top and the view in front, behind and on all sides is of mountains — large open mountains each with unique form and colour. Across to the Mamores and Ben Nevis, behind to those of Glen Etive and between the Buachaille Etive Mor and Sgorr Dhearg; fantastic. Lunch was cut short by a distinctly sharp change in wind temperature and direction and I headed down the ridge towards Stob Coire nan Lochan.

The ridge is made up of large red blocks and in the little col at its foot, from a small cairn, one begins a steep descent into the upper reaches of Coire nam Beithach. From above, this looks pretty horrifying but in execution it is quite reasonable and involves only a short section of moderately difficult scrambling.

Looking back to Bidean, when safely at the bottom of the scree, you will see the magnificent rock climbing buttresses of the Diamond on the left, and Church Door on the right. In the basin below, a tiny lochan feeds a stream which is followed for a while until further down, as the corrie widens out, you move over to the left under another massive rock face — this is Stob Coire nam Beith. Here you continue left until it is possible to move down to a further stream. Carefully note that the original stream must be quitted as it falls over rock steps and cliffs.

A little scrambling, then you leave the burn

to move down the shoulder of An t-Sron. Almost simultaneously as you escape from the confines and into the open, the roar ceases. Funny, you didn't hear it when you were next to it, but now the silence is golden. High above, the rock faces of the West Face of Aonach Dubh smile in the evening sunshine and, below, the little white farmhouse (and Mountain Rescue Post) of Achnambeithac moves into view. After the wild remoteness of my mountain walk it felt like I was arriving home.

A shower caught me by the road and I sheltered below the bridge. The centre span over the Glencoe river effectively dated the new road: 1929. Up the road, past the Loch, I just had a chance to get a sighting of the great gash of Ossians cave, high above on the face of Aonach Dubh, before the rain returned in earnest. A moped pulled alongside. It was the lone walker who had been forced to turn back at the head of the Lost Valley; a friendly Irishman, he had strapped a bottle of ginger beer onto his back mudguard. With a smile he de-topped it and handed it over saying 'Congratulations'.

Ginger beer in the rain never tasted so good.

Walkers climbing over an unusual stile; Gearr Aonach above.

The Walk
The famous knife-edge Aonach Eagach ridge running east to west above the Glencoe valley.

Accommodation Base: Fort William (see p133).

Maps: OS L41 – Ben Nevis, T7 – Ben Nevis and Glencoe.

Start: Car park below the Allt-na-Reigh (Map ref: NN 174567).

Finish: Clachaig Inn, (map ref; NN 128568).

Length: 4¹/₂mls (7km).

Approx Time: 5hrs.

Ascent and Descent: 6330ft (1930m).

Difficulty: A serious and exposed mountain walk with a steep scrambling section dropping down from the end of Am Bodach to the ridge proper (this first drop is the most difficult bit) with more passing the 3rd pinnacle on the notched ridge.

Access: Car.

Seasons: May to September.

Observations: Carefully note there is no easy or safe descent along the entire ridge between Am Bodach and Sgorr nam Fiannaidh. The scrambling sections involve both feet and hands, are very exposed, but can be tackled by walkers of reasonable fitness (a cool head, however, is essential). Regarded by many as the finest ridge walk in mainland Britain — a tremendous expedition.

Summits: Am Bodach: 3085ft (940m), Meall Dearg: 3119ft (951m), Stob Coire Leith: 3080ft (939m), Sgorr nam Fiannaidh: 3173ft (967m).

SCOTLAND: The Aonach Eagach Ridge by Ronald Faux

The Route
From the car park follow up the shoulder of Am Bodach. As the shoulder steepens take the left path to follow up the front of the buttress to gain the summit. Along to the end of the spur (note the pinnacle of the Chancellor to the left) and make the steep exposed scramble down to the ridge proper. Continue along to the central peak of Meall Dearg. Fence posts lead along the ridge to the Crazy Pinnacles. Pass two on their south side (fine views of Glencoe!) after the third dip into a notch and move north round the rock to climb a short chimney onto the next pinnacle, the knife edge and further pinnacles until the ridge eases and widens. Fence posts appear on the stretch along to the cairn on the peak of Stob Coire

Leith. A level walk follows to the top of Sgorr nam Fiannaidh. Take the easy scree westwards to the head of the Clachaig Gully (danger — keep out of this gully). Go to the right (west) of this to drop directly down to the Clachaig Inn.

The Walk
Few mainland mountain ridges rival the Aonach Eagach, the huge mountain wall that gives Glencoe a good deal of its gloom. The rise is steep from the valley along a four-mile front of scree shoots, cliffs and deep gullies to a ridge which millenia of rain, gales and ice have honed to a sharp knife edge along which the pathway runs.

In summer time it is a pleasant scramble, never desperate and always exhilarating. In

winter, when ice plasters the Crazy Pinnacles of the great notched ridge — which is the English translation of the Gaelic — then the Aonach Eagach can set a formidable challenge. Short days of sunlight in these latitudes and fickle weather have caught out many parties on the ridge and there are no easy escape routes from either side between Am Bodach and Sgor nam Fiannaidh.

The first decision is whether to make a west-east or an east-west traverse. The attractions of starting in the east are that Alt-na-Reigh, the group of whitewashed buildings just west of the Meeting of Three Waters, is several hundred feet higher than the Clachaig end of the ridge. The rock scrambling is evenly distributed in both directions with no sections particularly better in one direction than the other. The views unfold more dramatically heading westwards but the clincher, after a

long day on a waterless ridge, is that the final eastbound pathway leads to the very door of the Clachaig Inn.

There is a car park about a quarter of a mile down the glen from Alt-na-Reigh and a clear track cuts back across the shoulder of the glen to join the main path rising from the road. It winds up the side of a deep ravine and in ninety minutes reaches the summit of Am Bodach 3,085ft, (940m) and a level stretch of the ridge.

On a fine day the path usually attracts a large number of parties and even when clouds choke the Glen so that the ridge and the summits of Bidean nam Bian and its lofty neighbours stand out like dark islands in a white sea, the route may attract its crowds. An Teallach and Liathach have similar sharp-edged qualities but they are far more remote from urban Scotland than Aonach Eagach and in winter time when snow conditions in the

Above left: **Starting out on the Aonach Eagach Ridge with a view down to Glencoe.**

Above right: **The difficult descent that begins the ridge proper.**

Facing page: **The dramatic main section of the ridge with Ben Nevis peeping through the notch.**

Walkers on the Aonach Eagach Ridge. (Photo: Ronnie Faux.)

Lost Valley and other north-facing corries are prone to avalanche, then the ridge gives an excellent and much safer alternative.

My last traverse, east to west, was on a July afternoon with plenty of mist around to give the atmosphere of a much higher mountain. There were several parties around and an interesting variety of scrambling styles. One group from the Hash House Harriers was making slow but hilarious progress and in contrast there was a solitary, high-speed individual training for the Himalayas who moved along the ridge as if his feet were on castors. He skilfully slipped past the Harriers as a girl called Joyce was resting a boot on the party leader's head. 'You worry about your hands dear, I'll direct your feet,' he said. The party progressed with a great flailing of feet and much hesitation but did actually complete the ridge in less than eight hours. Joyce admitted that she had never set foot on a real mountain before and that she hated heights. Their experience may give a guide to others although the inexperienced would be well advised not to attempt the traverse in poor weather. The ridge quickly loses its atmosphere of a carefree scramble and becomes a serious proposition when the clouds fall and the wind starts blowing.

It is a high ridge and links a string of Munros (peaks of more than 3000ft). Beyond Am Bodach, west-bound, I would repeat that no attempt to escape southwards into the glen should be made until the summit of Sgor nam Fiannaidh has been reached. There is a feasible escape route down a steep gully slightly to the east of Meall Dearg but it is not advised in any but the most extreme circumstances. In bad visibility it could be mistaken for one of its lethal neighbours and the scree in the gully is poor quality. The best course and most probably the quickest for an average party is to keep right on to the end of the ridge.

From Am Bodach (3085ft, 940m) the path gives only an occasional hint of the ridge to come, twisting down between outcrops of rock before swinging upwards to the rounded summit of Meall Dearg (3118ft, 950m). The path is always clear from cairns, scratch marks and smoothly polished rock and the fact that there is frequently only one way possible. The 'Crazy Pinnacles' start shortly after the descent from Meall Dearg and are the notches in the Notched Ridge where the edge has been ground and compressed into a narrow section of rocky teeth. Some can be out-flanked by scrambling below the lip of the ridge, others are more difficult to avoid and give enormous exposure but always on large, sound holds.

This section requires concentration and the Hash House Harriers roped themselves into an intrepid chain to tackle it. A rope is a reasonable precaution here, particularly in bad weather. At the dip before Stob Coire Leith (3080ft, 940m) the difficulties ease and soon the ridge widens and levels out giving an easy walk to the final summit.

The choice is a descent into the Glen from Sgor nam Fiannaidh or a continuation to where the ridge wings northwards towards the Pap of Glencoe. It is proper to include the Pap although this adds a couple of miles on to the route and the latter stages seem to have little association with the main ridge itself. We cut down to meet the steep path that climbs beside the Clachaig Gully, and that proved a mistake. There can be few worse examples of erosion than this switch-back track, bounded by a sheer cliff dropping into the gully and marked by a notice at its foot, warning that it is not advised for walkers attempting the Aonach Eagach ridge. By the time we read it we were on the road and striding unstoppably towards a pint.

We took five hours from car park to pub with half an hour's rest on the ridge, which is quite average. Winter conditions may add at least two hours or more to that time and we were quietly congratulating ourselves at keeping up a healthy pace when one local hero confessed to completing the ridge within two hours. That was in the days before the present generous licensing laws were introduced in Scotland. 'I was running fast as I could,' he admitted, 'the pubs were going to shut.'

SCOTLAND: The Mamores Traverse by Bill Birkett

The Route

From the car park continue up the path into upper Glen Nevis. Cross the river, to the Steall hut, by way of the wire rope bridge and along past the great waterfall to gain the zig-zags leading up to the shoulder of An Gearanach and along the ridge to scramble up and then off the second peak (An Garbhanach). Descend to the hollow and then steeply up to the summit of Stob Coire a' Chairn (not named on the OS maps). Along to plunge down its shoulder to the col below Am Bodach, then the steep long pull to the summit (5hrs, 3391ft/ 1034m). Gently down and along to crest Sgor an Iubhair. Zig-zag down to the start of the ridge and along to top the little peak of Stob Coire á Mhail then drop slightly to the narrows of the Devil's Ridge itself. (A little pinnacle can be scrambled over directly but it is easier to circumnavigate.) Continue up to the structured summit cairn of Sgurr a' Mhaim (6½hrs. 3601ft/1098m). Take the long, but

The Walk: A horseshoe mountain walk rising from and returning to Glen Nevis taking in a logical round of Mamore peaks including the Devil's Ridge (North West Scotland).

Accommodation Base: Fort William (see p133).

Maps: OS L41 – Ben Nevis, T7 – Ben Nevis and Glencoe.

Start and Finish: Car park at the head of Glen Nevis (map ref: NN 168692).

Length: 9½mls (15km).

Approx Time: 9hrs.

Descent and Ascent: 10770ft (3283m).

Difficulty: A sustained mountain walk with some easy scrambling along An Garbhanach and the Devil's Ridge. The going underfoot is good and the path well defined.

Access: May to September.

Observations: An aesthetic walk of great beauty, peace and solitude.

Summits: An-Gearanach (1st peak): 3230ft (984m), An-Garbhanach (2nd peak): 3199ft (975m), Stob Coire a' Chairn: 3226ft (983m), Am Bodach: 3391ft (1034m), Sgor an Iubhair: 3284ft (1001m), Stob Coire á Mhail 3281ft (1000m). Sgurr a Mhaim 3601ft (1098m)

hidden and can only really be seen from the heights that encircle it or from within the group itself. For this reason the Mamores carry an air of mysterious fascination. The odd glimpse that can be had, along the Kinlochleven road or from Glen Nevis, only serves to heighten this intrigue. Even looking on them from the tops, Ben Nevis, the Aonach Eagach, Bidean, have an irresistible charisma that draws you towards them. Their opaquely white quartzite tops always give the impression that they hold a light snow covering and often, because of the pastel shades of schist and vegetation below, they seem suspended above the summer haze; a gossamer of floating peaks.

I have entitled this walk a traverse, because it does take in a fair number of the Mamores tops, but in practice it forms a logical horseshoe; climbing from and returning to the beautiful Glen Nevis. From the backbone of peaks running parallel to and between the valleys of Glen Nevis and Kinlochleven a number of spurs drop conveniently into Glen Nevis. We link two of these spurs, going up the saddle-shaped An Garbhanach, and along to reach the backbone peak of Am Bodach at the head of the horseshoe, and then return down the Devil's Ridge and Sgurr a' Mhaim. It is a walk that will fill every expectation you hold for these secretive hills.

Glen Nevis is delightful and somehow, although it is dominated on both sides by mountains, it is impressive without being oppressive. Immediately you leave the car park to begin your venture into the upper parts of the Glen it is easy to see why mountaineer W.H. Murray described it as having Himalayan character. Even before the rock walls narrow in and you near the roar of the gorge there is much to excite and admire. The mixed woods of oak, birch and Scot's pine are light and airy, harbouring the sweet smell of honeysuckle and fern. Below, through deep rock walls, the torrent crashes into pools and boulders wetting the air with its spray.

As you pull into the flatness of the upper reaches of the Glen it is the mighty Steall waterfall, up ahead, that is the finest spectacle in a grand scene. It has a clear fall of some 360ft (100m) and is reputed to hold a greater flow of water than any other tall fall in Scotland. To reach it dry you must cross the stream by way of the steel cable strand bridge; this is an adventure in itself!

Our route goes right up underneath the great fall and from here it appears to tumble forever before it meets the light of the sky high above. Underneath it appears to be spectacularly beautiful with the black protuberances of rock, causing division into many different streamlets

Above: **The author on the wire bridge crossing to Steall Hut and Steall Falls.**
Previous page, left: **Walker on Devil's Ridge.**
Previous page, right: **Along the Devil's Ridge with Stob Coire a' Mhail behind.**

uncomplicated fall down the shoulder directly to the road bridge at Polldubh. Back up the road to the car park.

The Walk

This group of mountains lies pretty well

and cascades, milking the water. Despite its great height and volume of water it gives the impression of gentility rather than savagery and, even standing right at its foot, craning your neck to see the heights, it does not threaten.

In late spring there is a profusion of blue hyacinth along left before you start to take the zig-zags that follow the stairway to the heights. At the bottom you cross a little burn to join the steeper flanks; be careful here for the rock is now quartzite and very slippery when wet. You do not need a broken leg at this stage — you would miss the entire collection of Mamores about to be bagged!

I took the zigs and the zags at a reasonable pace with occasional rests to look across at the huge lump of the Ben. As is very often the case clouds hung over her top and she seemed to be sulking — allowing only occasional glimpses of the North-East Buttress. Totally lost in my own thoughts, with only the distant rumblings of the frequent waterfalls, I was just pulling out of the steepness and onto the shoulder when my reverie was broken. Silently, suddenly, a golden eagle powered into my vision. Right there in front of me and not 25ft above,

the great king of the mountains and glens glided unruffled. The effect, from my almost semi-conscious trance to total awareness, could not have been more forceful. It was one of the most exciting sights I have ever seen in the mountains.

It circled above in menacing fashion, looking every inch of its six-foot wing span, laconically gaining height until it headed off towards the direction of Aonach Beag on the far side of Glen Nevis. Within seconds it became a pinprick and then it was gone — showing the true speed of its flight and its mastery of these high places.

I was still a little shaky as I pulled onto the shoulder to admire the view across the horseshoe to Sgurr a' Mhaim and up to Am Bodach. This is an excellent vantage point and gives an early view of the circuit along to the Devil's Ridge. Across the corrie beneath the summit quartzite of Sgurr a' Mhaim the folding of the underlying mica schist looked peculiarly like the slick combing of a spiv's hair. A single shaft of sunlight lit the hanging basin that fed the stream which falls behind the car park starting point. It already looked far away.

Above: **Steall Falls.**

Below: **Looking from Sgor an Iubhair to Devil's Ridge and Sgurr á Mhaim.**

Walking up broken rocks, some appeared as though they had been quarried and built into random walls. But I think not; it was just the natural layering of the schist that gave this impression. A large triangular patch of snow snuggled comfortably into the hollow before the first distinctive summit cairn of An-Gearanach was reached. It looked, for all the world, like some giant size nappy and I resisted the temptation to take a whooping slide down it; there was still a long way to go and I could feel a cold east wind blowing up.

From the first peak I could see a small figure outlined against the ghost grey sky on the second conical peak — that of An Garbhanach. Between these peaks stretches a sharp saddle-shaped ridge. As I crossed this a lamb cried in one of the corries below, and looking down, to the silver snaking burns to my left and right, brought home the very real nature of the exposure. To gain the top of the second peak involves some scrambling on steep ground and brings your eye to focus on the translucent pinkness of the rock.

The descent and rise to reach Stob Coire a' Chairn was rewarded when the sun decided to break through in earnest. It highlighted a party of pins on the Devil's Ridge and all the many patches of snow lying still on these shapely hills. This summit is the first we reach that lies along the backbone of the Mamores. The ridge on the left comes from Na Gruagaichean but we continue down to the right to the dip below Am Bodach.

This peak for some reason is not marked on the OS Map which, luckily, does not detract at all from its strategic position. One can see right down the corrie of Allt Coire na Ba to the pocket-size Kinlochleven far below, then on to the Aonach Eagach, Bidean and over in the distance the Buachaille Etive Mor; 'The Great Shepherd of Etive', presents a proud outline. But down below I thought I saw a figure move and thought fit to investigate.

Sure enough down in the recess below Am Bodach I finally encountered the lone figure first spied on Am Garbhanach. It turned out to be a fellow Cumbrian by the name of John Quine. Virtually a next door neighbour it seemed strange that we should meet here, in these mountains, for the first time. After a spot of lunch we panted up the steep ground leading to the summit of Am Bodach together. The sun picked out the moody sea blue of Loch Leven to perfection.

After the previous ups and downs, gaining the top of Sgor an Iubhair is no problem. It has a curious rocky crown which is a mixture of vivid white on indifferent brown and resembles the white plaster on red brick effect found on a demolition site. Through it run thick white veins of pegmatite.

Dropping down into the col I felt a sense of anticipation for the name Devil's Ridge had awoken my mountaineering instincts. The view of Stob Ban from here is most impressive, and resembles, in some respects, the Swiss Matterhorn. Beneath it, like some precious jewel, a small lochan shimmered in the sunshine. The first section of ridge to the little rise of Stob Coire a' Mhail seems fairly hospitable but thereafter the ridge is sensationally exposed.

Looking to the screes tumbling from Sgurr a' Mhaim (the highest and last peak of our walk) had me blinking twice for the white quartzite scree really does look like fresh snow. But now you must concentrate on the path ahead. It isn't actually very difficult in practice, the name Devil's Ridge conjuring up far more potency than the physical reality, but one must be steady. A blocky pinnacle in the middle of the dip is the trickiest section but most will drop slightly below this and avoid any problems.

On the top there is a large structured cairn and magnificent views, particularly of Ben Nevis. In the distance a hooter blasted and we assumed it was knocking off time at the aluminium works in distant Kinlochleven. Hot and thirsty I ate some snow from the long and perfect wave that crested the distinctive horseshoe rim of Sgurr a' Mhaim; that feature which is so prominent when viewed from Ben Nevis. The thought of radioactive contamination from the Chernobyl disaster was, admittedly, on my mind but if it was there its invisibility lulled me into a sense of security.

First we walked along the snow wave then headed down the shoulder directly for the road bridge at Polldubh. From snow to rock was an interesting transition. Even when comparing the rock to the colour of the snow the quartzite appeared to be incredibly white and it crunched like cinders beneath our feet.

The long sweeping shoulder falls smoothly and elegantly for almost 3500ft (1067m). From the summit to the bridge the descent is straightforward, giving a real feeling of elation as you swoop down this considerable expanse of mountain, unrestrained and unhindered into the welcoming Glen Nevis.

The trip uphill back along the road beneath high rocks and ancient pine can be missed by arranging suitable transport, but provides a contemplative end to a day that has explored some of the secrets of a fine mountain region. A walk that has investigated, but in no way dispersed, the aura of intrigue surrounding these distant, white, remembered peaks.

SCOTLAND: Ben Nevis by Bill Birkett

The Route

Cross the new bridge from the youth hostel to gain the Observatory (tourist track). At the top zig-zag above Lochan Meall an t-Suidhe break left to the valley of Allt a' Mhuilinn (stream marked on map). Continue up the burn past the CIC climbing hut (3hrs) into Coire Leis. Entering into the upper Coire it is best to take the smooth glaciated slabby rocks centrally. Depending on the prevailing conditions/snow cover either keep right under the cliff to gain the shoulder or follow a line out leading diagonally leftwards onto the Carn Mor Dearg Arete. At the end of the arete move up over the field of large boulders, aiming for the marker rods, to eventually gain the summit and the ruins of the Observatory (6hrs, 4406ft/1343m). Follow the well defined tourist way down — taking great care in the initial stages to keep clear of the large gullies cutting towards the track (3hrs, total: 9hrs).

The Walk

Seen from the usual vantage points below, the Ben seems quite gentle, softly rounded, a benign and sleeping giant. The plain fact is that Ben Nevis is Britain's highest mountain, standing at 4406ft (1344m) above the level sea, and the sea loch, Loch Linnhe, virtually laps her toes. Despite the rapid rise from the sea the summit is all but shielded from view behind the shoulder of Meall an t-Suidhe and consequently the drama of the transition is lost.

However her bulk cannot be hidden and for anyone other than the casual tourist, passing it by with little more than a second glance, there

The Walk: A high mountain walk circum-navigating the great north face of Ben Nevis to gain its summit (Glen Nevis, Fort William, North West Scotland).
Accommodation Base: Fort William (see p133).
Maps: L41 – Ben Nevis, T7 – Ben Nevis and Glencoe.
Start and Finish: Glen Nevis Youth Hostel (map ref: NN 128718).
Length: 9mls (14km).
Ascent and Descent: 8950ft (2728m).
Approx Time: 9hrs.
Difficulty: A high mountain walk, strenuous and including a little easy scrambling. Only to be tackled in good conditions and at the right time of year. Navigational competence essential.
Access: Car.
Seasons: June to September.
Observations: A great mountain walk offering unequalled cliff scenery and gaining the highest summit in Britain. On a clear day the mountain vista is incredible. Keep off any snow that lays near the edge of the cliffs — it may be corniced.
Summit: Ben Nevis (highest mountain in Britain): 4406ft (1343m).

is always that inexplicable air of malevolence. The back 2000-ft (610m) north face is all but hidden from view yet something, perhaps a sixth sense, tells you there is danger here — and adventure too. In truth she can be both savage and merciless, or beguiling and intoxicating. The mountaineer knows her as 'The Big Bad Ben' because of her immensity, and unforgivingness. Winter conditions here can be fiercer and more demanding than those in the arctic and any mistakes are paid for; dearly. But to those that take her on a good day and, from the summit, experience the vastness of the wonderful, endless mountain world all beneath; to them will be made known the ultimate feeling of mountaineering elation.

Only a hill; yes, looked at from below
Facing the usual sea, the frequent west;
Tighten the muscle, feel the strong blood flow,
And set your foot upon the utmost crest.
There, where the realms of thought and effort cease
Wakes on your heart a world of dreams and peace.
('A Hill' by Geoffrey Winthrop Young).

I think the route of this walk takes in all of the very best of Ben Nevis and shows you the sights, without difficulty, generally only viewed by the climber. The tourist trog is quitted at Lochan Meall an t-Suidhe and a traverse made round into Coire Leis to follow underneath some of the greatest cliffs and mountain climbs in Britain. After gaining the ridge that runs along to Carn Mor Dearg the summit is gained from the 'back' of the Ben. The tourist route now taken in reverse is by far the quickest and best way down. Almost a pilgrimage, the trip to the summit taken this way becomes a spectacular and interesting walk.

Outside the youth hostel a new and stronger bridge replaces the old iron affair but otherwise little has changed since I first climbed the Ben — aged nine! It was busy then and its popularity has not waned in the slightest. After only a little way steep ground takes you quickly to the old Observatory track and the strenuousness eases — but the slog goes on. Ignore the crowds, you will be leaving them soon, and appreciate the unfolding beauty of the wooded Glen Nevis down right and the blue waters of sea lochs Eil and Linnhe behind. Your immediate environment and focus of attention, the path in front, is dominated by the attractive granite.

An aluminium bridge shone metallically in the sunshine and seemed, although not unattractive in itself, akin to an alien extra-terrestrial invasion on the rocky burn, over which it spanned. I guess the original construction, built to facilitate the Observatory in 1883, must have been washed away. Logically I

couldn't really fault the choice of material, light to carry up, quick to assemble, and produced just round the corner, using the very waters of the Ben; although my personal preference would have been for the natural granite.

Very soon I was above Lochan Meall an t-Suidhe and pleased to leave the tourist track behind and traverse left into the valley of the Allt a' Mhuillin; to solitude and the great black cliffs of the north face I know so well. Here lies the true character of the Ben.

Apart from an occasional patch of peat the path is a good one and the first feature to make itself felt is a huge dark realm of rock that climbers know as the Nordwand face. In winter it is plastered white with snow and ice, but much of the rock is too steep to hold snow, and consequently shows through black. It is a grim and formidable sight and was first climbed by the late Ian Clough, a great pioneer of Scottish climbing, who also made the first British ascent of the North Face of the Eiger. (His young companion on that ascent was Chris Bonington.)

As you move round, an even steeper lump of rock comes into view — the Great Buttress face of Carn Dearg — and this is the playground of the extreme rock climber. The striking corner, up the middle, is known as the Centurian and was climbed by the late Don Whillans. By the time you arrive at the tumbling burn of the Allt a' Mhuillin its music and clarity provides welcome relief to the austere magnificence of the surroundings.

As you follow on up its bank you arrive at the CIC, Scottish Mountaineering club hut. (Note this is private and access is only open to a few select climbing clubs.) This is situated in the most incredible mountain environment and it is from here that you can see all the most prominent features of this world famous climbing arena. Let me mention three of the great ridges of the Ben which provide a tremendous challenge to climbers whether in summer or winter, to see if you can pick them out for yourself.

On the far right, beyond the buttress of Carn Dearg, starting high on the cliff, swoops Castle Ridge. It strikes up the heart of the obvious castle-like feature placed between two gullies. Just to your left from the initial rock pinnacle of the 'Douglas Boulder' is the longest and most striking of them all: The Tower Ridge. Over to the left silhouetted against the sky the mighty profile of the North-East Buttress goes on up and up. Every winter there is a multitude of climbing fatalities on these cliffs and, usually without exception, someone is avalanched from the Castle Gullies.

Previous page: **Ben Nevis, Britain's highest mountain (4406ft, 1344m), seen from Caol.**

Below: **The aluminium bridge low on the tourist track.**

I sat awhile to eat and have a break and as I looked up at the huge snowfield still remaining (snow lays permanently in the corries and gullies on the high Ben Nevis) in Coire na Ciste vivid memories of past adventures came back. Of the day I soloed the Nordwand and how on my descent down South Castle Gully (a climb in its own right), the powder snow avalanched and I slipped down the hard ice knowing that I had literally only seconds to stop myself before my specialist short ice picks would become useless to arrest the fall. I stopped, but on my return to the CIC hut noted that both front points of my crampon had been broken clean off with the force required to stop. How I went out again, the next day, with borrowed equipment onto the North-East Buttress in gale force blizzard conditions. Hard days! Then at the end of our stay how good it was to return to the Fort with feelings of accomplishment and satisfaction and most of all that it was so good to be alive.

The entrance, up the red granite glaciated slabs, into the high amphitheatre of Coire Leis does not present any problems; it is best taken centrally. In the deserted bowl of rocks you may spot a corrugated zinc survival hut sheltering down low. Whatever, you now cross the boulder field to climb steeply, with a little scrambling, onto the biting sharpness and exposure of the knife-edge ridge that is the Carn Mor Dearg Arete. This final approach, especially if the snow still persists at the head of the corrie, can be taken working out diagonally leftwards. There is no path here so you must use your own judgement taking stock of the prevailing conditions. But if there is no snow it is better to traverse up under the cliffs to the right.

Today it was perfect with clear blue skies and a sun that beat relentlessly down, but even so on my arrival onto the arete the slight wind bit coldly. I was glad to nestle in the rocks, semi sheltered, below its crest. This is the very heart of big mountain country and just to be there is an absolute privilege. You can almost hear the glaciers crunching and grinding as you survey the surrounding features. Massive hanging valleys, crashing waterfalls and the cliffs of truncated spurs abound but it is their scale, and not their frequency, that is impressive.

A tumble of sizeable boulders and a steep tiring pull now separate you from the summit and you aim up for the alloy marker rods fixed into the rocks at regular intervals. But before you leave the arete observe the iron signpost 'Abseil posts 50ft intervals for roping down only' which provides an escape route for winter mountaineering parties.

As I set off up past the large cornice forming the rim around the head of the Coire Leis it let off a noticeable crack. It remained intact, but I knew it to be only hovering, awaiting the moment when the sun would sap its strength to the point whereby it would let go completely, and plunge into the abyss below. Take careful note and stay off the frequent cornices you will see flanking the cliffs beneath the summit.

You suddenly seem to arrive at the cluster of walls and cairns that mark the summit and the site of the old Observatory. There are a number of things that immediately vie for your attention. First you wonder about the strange derelict-looking structures and buildings, second you are overwhelmed by the marvellous feast of mountains all around your feet and thirdly there is the compulsive urge that pulls you to the edge of the North Face to admire the breathtaking cliff scenery.

Of the first, mainly, the structures are those of the Observatory that was in operation for 20 years and opened in October 1883, though the highest, apart from the summit cairn itself, supports the corrugated tin emergency hut. It now appears stilt like and ridiculous but in winter, when it is often used by mountaineers trapped or benighted on the summit, the snow lays deep and the hut becomes level with the shifting surface of the Ben. This gives some little idea of the severity of the winter conditions up here.

There are some interesting recordings that were made in the Observatory and I will repeat a few here for your interest:

1884 Feb 16th — Owing to storm, every observation taken by two observers roped together at 20h. As soon as Mr. Omond went outside door of snow porch, he was lifted off his feet and blown back against Mr. Rankin, who was knocked over.

1886 Apr 21st — Meteor as bright as first mag. star seen at 23h. 5m. It went from Pole Star towards W.N.W. horizon and left a train about 10° long at a height of about 50°, which remained visible for a second.

1887 Oct 29th — At 1h. 5m. St. Elmo's Fire was seen in jets 3 to 4 inches long on every point on the top of the tower, and on the top of the kitchen chimney. Owing to the number of jets on each cup of the anemometer, this instrument was quite ablaze . . .

While standing on the office roof watching the display, the observer felt an electric sensation at his temples, and the second assistant observed that his companions' hair was glowing. At 1hr. 15m, the accompanying hissing noise ceased, and the fire vanished from every point the same instant.

1891 Apr 13th — Beautiful snow crystals falling in the afternoon . . .

1892 Sep 21st — A magnificent aurora seen from 20h. till midnight. There were three distinct arches from W. and S. to N.E., with shifting streamers shooting to the zenith.

Looking across the North Face of Ben Nevis.

Ensconced in the ruins, on my arrival, I found a green tent and two Royal Marines in attendance. Equipped with a radio they had been acting as safety cover for the Three Peaks Yacht Race that had just taken place. We had 'a crack' and I borrowed their finely pointed tin opener to fix my sophisticated camera — you can always rely on the Marines in a jam!

The view is best admired on your way down the tourist path when, on a clear day, picking out the Cuillins of Skye, the Paps of Jura and even the Ochils to the south east is quite easy. My everlasting memory, as a nine year old, was to observe the horseshoe-like top of Sgurr a' Mhaim, over in the nearby Mamores and to think that if I was actually higher than that (which I knew I was), then I had really arrived as a mountaineer!

Many will want to look over the edge along the cliffs and it is an amazing sight to see the immense tower ridge now down below you to your left. But if you do look, take extreme care and never walk out on snow, it could well be a cornice and liable to collapse; always ensure there is solid rock beneath your feet.

A speedy descent down the zig-zags of the tourist track can be made but be extra cautious as you leave the summit because a number of deep gullies in the cliffs plunge very close to the path. Don't go too fast, admire the splendid view, and obey the erosion direction signs taking you across towards the Lochan Meall an t-Suidhe. On this day the sky was a graduated blue; high above it was black-blue and as the eye dropped to the horizon it lightened to powder blue and then grey. A perfect way to end the perfect mountain day.

Ben Nevis is a brilliant mountain walk, and taking the route I've described, you are rewarded with the prize of Britain's highest summit. But it is only to be tackled in good conditions and at the right time of the year. It can snow at any time on the Ben, and the weather changes fast, so don't take any chances. It's just not worth it. As my friend, one of Britain's greatest mountaineers, the late Don Whillans, so rightly said:

The mountains give and the mountains take.

Facing page, top: **The great cirque of cliffs above the CIC hut.**

Facing page, bottom: **Above the snowy North Face looking west.**

Above right: **Looking along the Carn Mor Dearg Arete to the Ben.**

Below right: **Descending the zig zags on the tourist track, Loch Eil below.**

SCOTLAND: The High Tops of the Cairngorms by Cameron McNeish

On the heights of Cairngorm.
(Photo: John white.)

The Route

Day 1: Tomintoul to Lochbuilg Lodge (10^1/2mls, 17km).

This could be either done on a summer evening or treated as a half day.

Day 2: Lochbuilg Lodge to Loch Avon (14mls, 23km) via Carn Dearg, Carn Drochaid, Clach Choutsaich, Leabaidh an Daimh Bhuidhe (Ben Avon), Beinn A'Bhuird — North Top, Mòine Bhealaidh, Lairig an Laoigh, Fords of Avon.

Day 3: Loch Avon to Garbh Choire (8mls, 13km) via Cairngorm, Ben Macdui, Allt a' Choire Mhóir, Lairig Ghru.

Day 4: Garbh Choire to Achlean (12^1/2mls, 20km) via Cairn Toul, Sgor an Lochain Uaine, Braeriach, Mòine Mhór, Carn Bàn Mór.

The Walk

Loch Builg lay like quicksilver in its high Grampian cradle. At its far end the skeleton of Lochbuilg Lodge was etched against the hillside, a sad remnant of its former glory. No ghillie rows his laird onto the waters of the loch these days. No more does the lodge echo to the crash of shotguns. A world past, replaced by this ghostly silence, broken only by the throaty whispers of grouse and the plaintive call of the golden plover.

Aye, it's a lonely place is Loch Builg, but for all that there is a great freedom here. A freedom born of the wide open skies and the wide rolling hills; big Grampian hills that don't compare with anything else. No soaring peaks here; no mighty pinnacles. Few Sgurrs here but plenty of Carns. Rounded hills but big hills, leviathon hills whose scale is hard to grasp at first acquaintance.

I had walked in from Tomintoul, six miles or so of easy walking on an old right of way. A comfortable start. Tomintoul is the highest village in the Highlands where the locals speak in the broad dialect of Aberdeenshire, a farming county, but not the farming of the south. The farming heritage of high Aberdeenshire is a craggy granite one, a heritage of grappling with savage elements, a heritage of bothies and bothy ballads.

But beyond Builg this world is left behind and replaced by the high hills of the Cairngorms, an Arctic world, a place well worth exploring for the simple reason that there is nothing else like it in this country.

Day 1: Ben Avon and Beinn á Bhuird

Over breakfast I checked my route for the

The Walk: A long distance high mountain walk taking in the six highest summits of the Cairngorms: Ben Avon, Bienn a Bhuird, Cairngorm, Ben Macdui, Carn Toul and Braeriach (The Cairngorm Mountains, North-East Scotland).

Maps: OS L36 Grantown and Cairngorm.

Start: Tomintoul on the A939 (map ref: NJ 170187).

Finish: Achlean, Glen Feshie (map ref: NN 852976).

Length: 45mls (73km).

Approx Time: 3½ days.

Ascent and Descent: Day 1: 500ft (155m), Day 2: 4,300ft (1310m), Day 3: 5,250ft (1600m), Day 4: 8,550ft (2,600m), Total = 18,600ft (5,665m).

Difficulty: A long remote high mountain walk that is extremely strenuous and serious. There are no technical difficulties.

Access: Car (a pick-up must be arranged unless the Aviemore finish is taken).

Seasons: May to August.

Restrictions: The stalking season begins in August and extends to mid October. Details must be sought locally to determine if stalking will affect the area through which you plan to walk. For Glen Avon (Inchrory) Estate telephone Tomintoul (08074) 256.

Observations: Essentially this is a backpacking route and a tent should be carried (although refuge can be sought in the bothies). In all but perfect summer weather this is a mountaineering expedition of the highest calibre. One must be extremely well prepared, physically and mentally, and have the correct equipment and the ability to use it. Beware in this remote high mountain region of rapidly changing weather conditions. Possibly the finest expedition of its type in Britain.

Accommodation: Hotels and Bed and Breakfast accommodation in and around Aviemore. Camping in the mountains.

Summits: Carn Dearg: 2533ft (772m), Carn Drochaid: 2438ft (743m), Stuc Gharbh Mhor: 3648ft (1112m), Mullach Lochan nan Gabhar: 3681ft (1122m), Leabaidh an Daimf Bhuidhe (Ben Avon): 3842ft (1171m), Cnap a' Chéirich: 3845ft (1172m), Beinn a' Bhuird — North Top: 3924ft (1196m), Cairngorm: 4084ft (1245m), Cairn Lochan: 3983ft (1215m), Ben Macdui: 4295ft (1309m), Cairn Toul: 4241ft (1293m), Sgor an Lochain Uaine: 4116ft (1255m), Braeriach: 4248ft (1295m), Carn Bàn Mór: 3451ft (1052m).

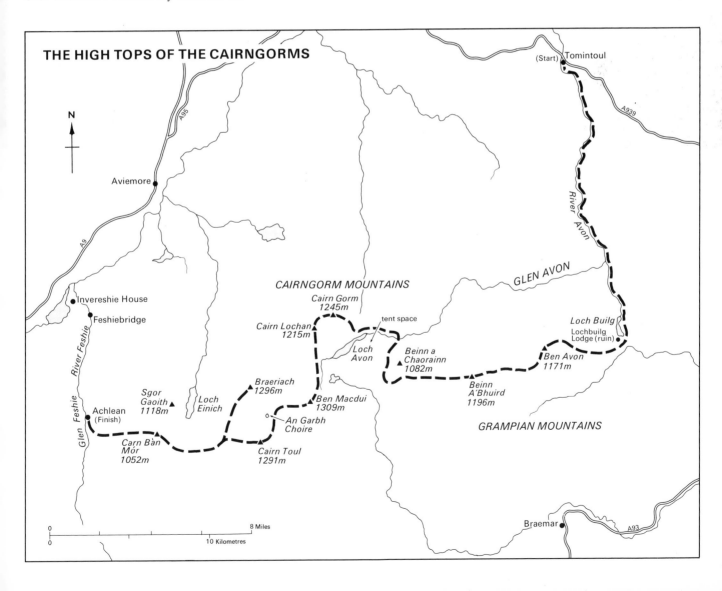

THE HIGH TOPS OF THE CAIRNGORMS

next three days. Three days which would take me over the six highest Cairngorm hills, over three very different high plateaux, over the biggest tracts of land over 2000, 3000, and 4000ft (610-1220m) in the country, and three days which would undoubtedly confirm to me that these are the finest walkers' hills in Britain.

The lie of the land is kind to the expedition planner for this particular ploy. The six tops break up evenly into three days of two tops apiece; Ben Avon and Beinn a Bhuird on the first day, the classic traverse from Cairngorm to Ben Macdui on the second, and the superb high level traverse of Cairn Toul and Braeriach on the last day, before dropping down through the Rothiemurchus Forest to finish in Aviemore, or over the Great Moss to finish at Glen Feshie. Many walkers take longer to enjoy this route, filling in time with visits to other Cairngorm tops, and some walkers do it in a shorter time; indeed it's been bashed inside twenty-four hours. Three full days, with an evening walk in from Tomintoul and a half day walk out through Rothiemurchus or Glen Feshie nicely fills a long holiday weekend.

Loch Buildg lies at the eastern extremity of Ben Avon, a hill that is almost a mountain range in itself. It's a big, complex mass of muscly shoulders which bulge out in every direction, throwing up a series of tor-studded tops. The name of the hill, Avon, is obviously taken from the river which scours its northern flanks. Celtic scholars believe the name to be taken from Ath-fhinn, the bright or fair haired one. A local legend tells how the wife of the great Fionn MacCumhail, or Fingal, slipped when crossing the river, and was swept away to her death. Fingal named the river in her memory. The name, incidentally is pronounced 'A'an.'

A rough path runs westwards from the ruin of Lochbuilg Lodge and climbs the heathery slopes of Carn Dearg, Ben Avon's easterly outlier. Beyond Carn Dearg, I abandoned the path and crossed an area of high moorland, led on by the sad crooning of a golden plover. How I love this bird of the high lonely places. Soon the path, sketchy in places, begins to climb more steeply, until the great granite wart of Clach a'Chutsaich, or Coutt's stone, comes into view. Like most of these Cairngorm hills, Ben Avon keeps her real secrets for those who take the trouble to climb her heather-covered flanks. She's not a hill to gaze up to for scenic splendour, but rather a hill to gaze down from, north and west towards the other Cairngorms of the Central massif, the great rounded tops which have been scoured and shattered by glaciation, cleft by great ravines and corries,

cliff girt trenches and high lochans.

From the Coutt's stone, an easy high-level crescent takes you round the gravelly plateau to the summit of the mountain, Leabaidh an Daimh Bhuide (the Couch of the Yellow Deer) at 3843ft (1171m). Immediately west of the summit, the plateau abruptly ends. Huge cornices often hang out over the edge here, with a steep drop into the great Garbh Choire (the Rough Corrie). Away below the acres of scree and rubble the waters of the Slochd Mor roar northwards into Glen Avon. Our route to Beinn a' Bhuird lies across the top of this big corrie, and along a narrow and rocky ridge known locally as the Sneck, from the Gaelic 'snaig', or notch. Great corries fall away on either side and it's a superb position with rock buttresses soaring up to the green slopes of Cnap a Chleirich to the south west.

The summit of Beinn á Bhuird, (pronounced Ben a Voord) is distinctly uninteresting. It lies some 3924ft (1196m) above sea level, but more often than not clouds drench these high parts and visibility is limited to a few rock strewn feet. In conditions like this good sharp navigation is vital. These plateaux are broad and featureless, with few footpaths and easy landmarks. However, when the weather is good the next stretch of the walk offers some superlative views of the rest of these Cairngorm mountains. As you descend from the summit to the broad, high-level moorland below you, you gaze into the bowels of Coire Etchachan, with Beinn Macdui, Britain's second highest mountain, ahead, which you will be climbing tomorrow.

The deep trench of the Lairag an Loaigh separates the Avon/a'Bhuird massif from the Central massif, just as the Lairig Ghru will separate your next day's hills from the last day's walk on the western massif. These two great glens cut their way across the granite of the Cairngorms, both long and distinct mountain passes of some grandeur. The story goes that cattle drovers once took their cattle through the rough defile of the Lairig Ghru, but that the younger kye were taken through the Lairig an Loaigh because it wasn't so rough. Hence its name of 'Pass of the Calves'.

Our route takes us northwards through the Lairig an Loaigh to the River Avon, where Fion MacCumhail lost his wife to the roaring waters. On the far side of the river there is a howff, a rough bothy made of stones and turf and a certain amount of twentieth-century concrete. It's a miserable place and I'd recommend a tent. If you're going to camp, don't stop here but follow the river to where it flows out of Loch Avon, the loch that is one of the most precious jewels in this Cairngorm crown.

Facing page, top: **The high tops of the Cairngorms. To the left Cairngorm, right of centre the Lairig Ghru and to the extreme right, its head in the clouds, Braeriach.**

Facing page, bottom: **On the Moine Mhor.** (Photo: Cameron McNeish.)

I've often lain outside a tent beside this loch, the clear waters of which are said to be haunted by a kelpie, a kind of water horse. The situation is remote, with the great square cut bulk of the Shelter Stone crag at the far end of the loch. Hemmed in between Beinn Mheadhoin and Cairngorm itself, Loch Avon, with the great slabs of the Garbh Uisge providing water courses for thousands of tons of water is a place of great atmosphere. An old local rhyme goes:

The waters of A'an they rin sae clear,
Wad beguile a man o' a thousand year.

An alternative start to the next day could be a walk right round the loch, but on this trip that time wasn't available. First thing in the morning I had to wet my feet in the infant River Avon, and start out on a big climb towards Cairngorm, the third of the Cairngorm Big Six.

Day 2: Cairngorm to Ben Macdui

On the south side of Loch Avon, the Saddle, a low col between the slopes of A'Choinneach and Cairngorm, offers the best start to the climb. A rough path runs up the slope from the lochside to the col, which separates the Loch Avon basin from the long glen at Strath Nethy. I'm a great believer in getting the worst of the hard work finished early in the day, and that was certainly the case today. I arrived at the summit of Cairngorm hot and sweaty, as the mists rolled back to reveal the relative gentleness of the rest of the day's activity. I say relative, for the scenery is far from gentle, however easy the walk may be in terms of effort. This high-level walk from Cairngorm to Ben Macdui is one of the classic trade routes of the highlands, a high-level walk which rarely drops below 3000ft (1000m). The route is well marked by a worn footpath, and cairns over the rougher parts, but if you have time, deviate from the path to enjoy the wild views down towards Loch Avon, or down into the great scalloped corries of Coire an t' Sneachda and Coire an Lochan.

A weather station, operated by Heriot Watt University, adorns the broad summit of Cairngorm. At 4,064ft (1245m) Cairgorm is the fifth highest hill in the country, and is a very good viewpoint. Sadly, Macdui disappoints from this angle, appearing merely as a rise in the far terrain. But Macdui's splendours have yet to come, for he keeps his glory for those who penetrate these Cairngorm hills and not for those who take the soft option of the chairlift to the top of Cairngorm.

The ski development on Cairngorm is cause for much debate. There is little doubt that it is ugly and environmentally damaging, but that is the price we pay for a ski development in an area in which regeneration is very, very slow. A threat which is much more insidious is the erosion caused by the numbers of people on areas like the Cairngorm/Ben Macdui plateau, and ever more recently, the Cairngorm to Loch Avon routes down to the Saddle, down Coire Raibert and down Coire Dhomhain. This pressure has simply been brought about by easy access to the summit of Cairngorm by the chairlift which operates all the year round.

The Cairngorm plateau itself is a good place to linger. In high summer you are likely to see dotterel (that semi-tame bird of the High Arctic), snow buntings, ptarmigan, peregrine and very possibly, a golden eagle. Reindeer, escapees from the herd which is kept on the lower slopes of Cairngorm, can sometimes be found wandering these high parts in summer, looking for lichens or sandwiches from the tourists.

The track from Cairngorm to Macdui is an obvious one, but I wandered off it, just beyond Coire Domhain, to where the slopes of Beinn Macdui hurl themselves downwards to Loch Avon. This view of the loch is one of the finest in the Cairngorms. Here the waters of the Allt Bhuidhe run through great cornices and snow tunnels before tumbling down great red granite slabs to the loch below. Very close by lie the great cliffs of Stag Rocks and the Hell's Lum crags, and to your right lie the precipices of the Shelter Stone crag, looking incredibly steep and sustained from this angle.

I didn't linger too long here this morning, for there is still a fair bit of walking to be done on this second day of the walk. It is a gentle stroll to follow the waters of the Allt Bhuidhe and in the warm summer sunshine it's a beautiful walk. But the weather isn't always so benevolent. It was here in 1971 that fourteen schoolchildren died in driving snow and bitterly cold temperatures, a salutory reminder of how conditions up here can indeed kill.

And yet, when the sun shines and the cock snow bunting is full of song, it's hard to imagine the terrible times of a Cairngorm blizzard. Hard too to imagine that you're sitting at almost 4000ft (1220m) above sea level. When conditions are kind I can't think of any place I'd rather be, along with the wide open skies and the spaciousness of these big Grampian hills.

The wander up to Ben Macdui is straightforward: across a boulder field, with the ubiquitous cairns marking the way, up a short gravelly pull, across vivid red screes and onto the last little rise which leads to the south summit of Macdui, at 4,300ft (1310m) the second highest mountain in Britain, and the reputed lair of one Ferlas Mor, the 'Great Grey Man'. It was Professor Norman Collie who began the stories of Ferlas Mor sightings back at the beginning of the century. This illustrious mountaineer, who was also a well-known practical joker, told of a ten-foot tall ghostly figure who takes one footstep in the scrunchy snow to every two of yours, a figure which follows you until fear overcomes you and you flee for fear of your life. It's all good stuff, and the stories are just right for those candlelit nights in the bothy.

From the summit of Macdui I took stock of the next stage of the walk. From this great Cairngorm/Macdui massif, the great trench of the Lairig Ghru separates the western massif, the Braeriach/Cairn Toul plateau, and beyond it, the vastness of the Mòine Mór and the Glen Feshie hills.

I wasn't too sure whether to stay the night at Corrour Bothy, which lies in the Lairig Ghru below the black ramparts of the Devils Point, or camp somewhere in the Lairig. In view of the fact that it was summer, I opted for the camp. This made planning a bit simpler. Such is the popularity of the Lairig Ghru route nowadays that the bothies are usually busy, and I tend to prefer the solitude of a tent and a westerly breeze coming in the open door, rather than the scent of someone else's breakfast being cooked over the tumult of bodies trying to get away for the day.

The direct descent from Ben Macdui into the Lairig is a long purgatorial route over very large scree blocks. South of the summit, the Allt Clach nan Taillear has formed a shallow corrie, and a very rough path leads down towards Corrour, but I didn't particularly want to travel that far south. Ideally, I wanted to be able to set up my tent at the mouth of the An Carbh Coire, the Big Rough Corrie that is made up by Cairn Toul, Sgurr and Lochain Uaine, and Braeriach. I therefore decided to go north again from Macdui, and follow the stream known as Allt a Choire Mhoir. Again it's quite a long way off the mountain into the depths of the Lairig Ghru, but another advantage of coming off at this point is that you can generally cross the infant River Dee without too much of a problem. Further down, the river widens and generally you can only cross near the Corrour Bothy where there is a bridge.

Day 3: Cairn Toul and Braeriach

Having spent the night near the tiny howff of An Garbh Coire, I awoke to the prospect of a steep pull up onto Cairn Toul. It was quite tough but I knew that once up there I would be high all day long. In actual fact, although the ascent of Cairn Toul is steep and rocky by its north-east ridge, it does offer spectacular views which improve by the minute. And half way up the ridge, the lochan (which Cairn Toul shares with Sgor an Lochain Uaine) makes a

Loch Avon viewed from the Cairngorm Plateau. (Photo: Cameron McNeish.)

welcome, and scenic rest place.

Cairn Toul, at 4241ft (1293m) is one of the most attractive Cairngorm summits. When viewed from the west, the hill appears broad and stunted, hence its name 'Hill of the Barn'. But seen from the south and east she is the most pointed of all the Cairngorm tops. From the summit, a superb high-level ridge runs around the rim of An Garbh Coire to Braeriach, one of the really high-level walks in Scotland.

Coming off Cairn Toul you climb again to Sgor an Lochain Uains (the Hill of the Green Lochan), which is generally known as Angel's Peak. I suppose this is to balance up Devils Point which lies further south in the Lairig Ghru. I think we have to be careful about anglicising our Gaelic names, for once the original names drop from everyday use they are soon lost and with them goes a little more of our Gaelic heritage.

Enjoy this high-level ramble around the red screes, and you realise why these hills were once known as the Monadh Ruadh (the Red Hills). The great cliffs of Braeriach are seamed and riven by great gullies and cracks, offering superb sport in winter for snow and ice climbers. There is a lot of potential in these vast crags for new routes in winter, but unfortunately you need the combined luck of good weather, good snow conditions, and time to tramp into this isolated corrie and explore.

Stop by the infant River Dee as it cascades over the edge into the corrie, and consider that in a few miles this rushing stream becomes one of the most important rivers in Scotland as it flows serenely through the Royal country of Braemar and Ballater and then into Aberdeen where it joins the anonymity of the North Sea. Braeriach is only a short hop from here, the summit lying on the edge of a precipice. Braeriach, at 4248ft (1294m) means 'Bridled Upland', and is the third highest hill in the country. Braeriach is a wonderful mountain, with no less than seven great corries gouged out of her flanks. The exploration of these corries, in one long walk, makes a very interesting and rewarding couple of days out, and I would urge you to return and get to know this mountain better.

Our route now leads across another high plateau, westwards towards the Mòine Mór and the Glen Feshie hills, but those who want to finish near to Aviemore are best to continue northwards, down into the Lairig Ghru via the ridge of Sron na Lairig and then down through the forests of Rothiemurchus to Coylumbridge, and then by road to Aviemore.

I preferred to finish in Glen Feshie, and was rewarded by the wide open spaciousness that the Mòine Mór, the Great Moss offers. This is the land of dotterel and ptarmigan, of red deer and eagle. Below lies the great trench of Gleann Einich and I've often sat on the edge of this vast plateau and watched the flight of the eagle, spiralling high above the loch. In autumn this area comes alive with the primaeval sound of the red deer rut, that great lustful belly roar of the stags mixed with the cacophony of migrating geese as their great skeins fly in formation over the top of these hills for the south. In winter, when the moss is white under snow, then it becomes a paradise for ski touring, with long easy slopes and big distances to be covered at a high level. But now in summer it's a place to linger, to listen to the melancholy crooning of the golden plover, to wish you had another night to spend in this high place. But you haven't, so its over Carn Bàn Mór, and down the Foxhunter's Path to Achlean to, hopefully, a waiting car, or a long walk down Glen Feshie to Kincraig or Kingussie. A very fine private hostel lies at Ballochcroick in Glen Feshie, an opportunity to get a good meal, a hot shower, a soft bed and build yourself up to face civilisation again.

SCOTLAND: The North-West Wilderness by Bill Birkett

The Route

Day 1: Dundonnell to Shenavall (map ref: 066810) 8mls (13km). Take the little track leading off from behind a cottage to follow it into a high corrie. Follow the stream until forced out left then continue to the head of the corrie above the stream. Proceed up the shoulder to Glas Mheall Mor then drop into the gap to follow the final steep slope leading to the summit of Bidein a' Ghlas Thuill. The ridge of An Teallach can be seen to the south and is reached by first descending to the shoulder below the next summit. Very steeply ascend to the summit of Sgurr Fiona. The ridge can be followed, with a little scrambling and great exposure, to Lord Berkeley's Seat and then carry along to Corrag Bhuidhe.

Alternatively a lower level path traverses (to the south) under the summits — both descend to the col of Cadha Gobhlach. Steeply up to the top of Stob Cadha Gobhlach (unnamed on the map) and then along a little ridge to the summit of Sail Liath. Drop down the long easy shoulder to the path leading around to Shenavall. (Alternatively this path could have been followed in from Corrie Hallie.)

Day 2: Shenavall to Carnmore (map ref: 978769) 7mls (11km). The Abhainn Srath na Sealga burn must be forded (you will get wet and take care in spate conditions — it may not be possible to cross) then cross the bog to the private shooting lodge of Larachantivoire by fording the Abhainn Gleann na Muice Beag. Follow the path on the west bank and on up to

Carnmore Crag with a building just visible to the bottom right, giving scale to the crag.

Near the start with Dundonnell and Little Loch Broom below.

Gleann na Muice Beag. Continue passing Lochan Féith Mhic'-illean to descend to Carnmore.

Day 3: Carnmore to Inverewe 9mls (15km). Cross the causeway between Dubh Loch and Fionn Loch to follow the path along to Kernsary. (Note to *not* take the steep path left that goes over to Letterewe but cross the burn low down, afterwards do *not* take a false path that leads rightwards to Fionn Loch or its environs. Keep left to pass Loch an Doire Crionaich. Dropping down to Kernsary is now very peaty.) From Kernsary take the path leading above the north shore of Loch Kernsary to follow down to Sròndubh and so to Inverewe.

The Walk

High in the remote north west of Britain there is a secluded world of high mountains and wild glens. The mountains are of the ancient Torridonian Sandstone, their shape and position the stuff from which dreams are made. The great U-shaped glens were sculpted by glaciers long since departed. On their flanks will be found mammoth cliffs reaching to the heights and on the valley floor, mountain burns tumble while black lochs ponder. In the air floats the golden eagle, king of the sky; and down below the red deer, monarch of the glen, freely roams. A wild and lovely wilderness of breathtaking height and depth, of rock, of peat and water.

Beinn Alligin, Liathach, Beinn Eighe, Slioch, An Teallach, Stac Polly and Suiliven, the great mountains of the north west are all names which tug at the heart of the discerning mountaineer. They are all magnificent yet there is none finer than that of An Teallach, The Forge. Surrounding it amongst the area that is known as the Fisherfield Forest (although there is hardly a tree to be seen), there lies what has been described as the last great wilderness in Britain.

This walk which I have called 'The North-West Wilderness', climbs An Teallach taking in seven summits over 3000 ft (915m), and explores the very depths of this superlative, wild Scotland. The first day is a hard and strenuous mountain day, of that there is no doubt, but the next two days are straightforward in their execution and the allowance of two days, as described, is a relatively mild target. You must be self sufficient however, and able to deal with all emergencies — out here you are definitely on your own.

Day 1: An Teallach, Dundonnell to Shenavall

Before you set off I would remind those who don't feel up to An Teallach or are unable to get to climb high because of poor weather conditions, that there is an alternative way to reach Shenavall. Starting from Corrie Hallie, this way is much more in keeping with the standard of the rest of the walk though few would want to miss the magnificent An Teallach. Conversely those intent on ticking off the Munro's will take in all ten summits in this group rather than just the seven I have included.

Roy Garner and myself started from the Dundonnell Hotel on a day that could have gone either way. Over the sea it was black and most threatening, yet An Teallach remained persistently clear, the sunlit centre of a bowl of rotating cloud. 'Well there's only one way to find out', said Roy, setting off.

First you pass the skeleton of a bleached and rotting rowing boat and then climb over a wire fence to gain the track behind the cottage. As we gained height the rain blew in from little Loch Broom spitting at us gently and the sight behind with rainbows that seemed to be collecting at the head of the loch already looked very wild. But the threat came to nought and the sun again broke to tempt us on our way.

The rocks are the attractive pink of the Torridonian Sandstone and from the smooth and sculpted slabs protrude pebbles of both red and clear quartz. As we entered the upper corrie you cross a level plateau of broken rocks and this was obviously the terminal moraine of the final glacier to hang here. Above this it appeared pretty hostile and the wind was now strong and cold.

As we followed up the flat bottom of the river the day began to rapidly deteriorate. At least the walking was quite straightforward at the moment. Stopped by a waterfall we moved out left and then along towards the nearing head of the corrie. Roy's tubular framed rucksack began to whistle a monotonous and

Roy Garner studying the map at the west end of Loch an Doire Crionaich.

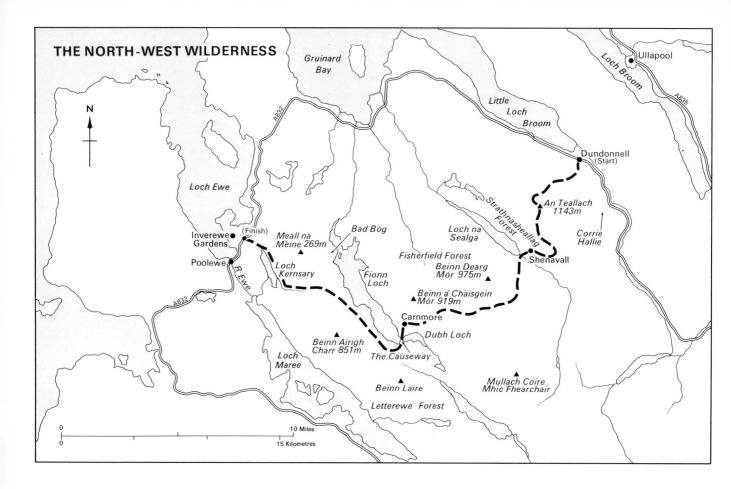

THE NORTH-WEST WILDERNESS

The Walk: A long distance walk that must be backpacked, and which takes in the spectacular heights of An Teallach and then goes on through the great highland wilderness along Glean na Muice Beag and Fionn Loch between Shenavall Carnmore and Inverewe, North West Scotland.

Map: L19-Gairloch and Ullapool Area.

Start: Dundonnell Hotel (map ref: NH 090880).

Finish: Inverewe Gardens (map ref: NG 863818).

Length: 24mls (39km).

Approx Time: 3 days.

Ascent and Descent: Day 1: 9300ft (2840m), Day 2: 2500ft (760m), Day 3: 1150ft (350m).

Difficulty: The first day is a spectacular and high mountain walk but without undue technical difficulty. The second two days are, for the most part, on reasonable paths but the going is rough in places and the area is extremely remote.

Access: Car to Dundonnell Hotel and return from Inverewe by bus (note times and frequency vary so the bus service must be checked locally).

Seasons: May to September.

Restrictions: The area is to be left alone during the stalking season which starts the first week in September and continues to late October.

Seasons: May to September.

Observations: Primarily this is a backpacking route although Shenavall has a mountain bothie open to walkers/mountaineers in need of shelter (if used you should support the Mountain Bothies Asso-

ciation whose address can be found in *Climber* magazine). Ample camping space outside. Carnmore has a barn at the end and this is reserved, by agreement with the BMC and the estate, for walkers/mountaineers in need. It is no more than a shell with a roof on and is suitable for emergency only. Camping here must be discrete and outside of the fenced area around Carnmore. For walkers who consider the severity of An Teallach to be too demanding, Shenavall can be reached by a track from Corrie Hall (map ref NH 114850).

Accommodation: Inns and B&B at either end, camping within the wilderness (or emergency shelter in Shenavall or Carnmore).

Summits: Glas Mheall Mor: 3217ft (980m), Bidein a' Ghlas Thuill: 3484ft (1062m), Sgurr Fiona: 3473ft (1059m), Lord Berkeley's Seat: 3436ft (1047m), Corrag Bhuidhe Buttress: 3075ft (937m), Stob Cadha Gobhlach: 3145ft (959m), Sail Liath: 3129ft (954m).

unrelenting tune. He was very proud of this; it appealed to his ingenius inventiveness.

Finally we pulled onto the shoulder where the wind was ferocious. It was an effort to stand up and the racing clouds offered only tentative glimpses of what might have been. An Teallach on a clear day is a group of

summits. Today it was virtually a fight for survival and although no lightweight, I was blown off my feet on two occasions. No joke on these exposed rocks — it's an awfully long way down to Loch Toll an Lochain.

So I will have to say a few words on An Teallach as it might have been and as it should be seen. From the highest summit, Bidein a' Ghlas Thuill, the view to the ridge in front is one of the most impressive sights in the British mountains. Although the sandstone is bedded horizontally, its top has been eroded in such a manner as to leave a sharp knife edge, above which point is a number of dramatic pinnacles. The summits that make up the ridge are, in order, Sgurr Fiona, Lord Berkeley's Seat, Corrag Bhuidhe, and some way below these will be found Corrag Bhuidhe Buttress. The rocks and scree plunge for 1700ft (518m) to Loch Toll an Lochain cupped below.

It's very exposed and from the pencil pinnacled top of Sgurr Fiona extreme caution must be exercised. The descent from the last and most southerly top involves what is known as the 'bad step' and here there is scrambling of some difficulty. If in doubt it is best to traverse, descending from the summit of Sgurr Fiona, along the path that flanks the south-west slopes of the ridge.

The view across to Beinn Dearg Mor is superb and this is a most impressive-looking mountain. It resembles a volcanic cone from which the side facing you has been blown. Further to the left, at the foot of this mountain, your destination up the great wilderness valley of Glean na Muice beckons. It is a desolate yet irresistible sight.

So down we go to the col of Cadha Gobhlach and then up to the summit above, Stob Cadha Gobhlach, and along the little connecting ridge to Sail Liath. The way down the broad ridge ahead gives no problems and at the bottom you pick up the cairned moor path to Shenavall.

The little farm house of Shenavall is a little haven of humanity in a hostile environment. The very name has a romantic ring to it and I guarantee you will not be disappointed. As we arrived we found we were not alone. In our soddened rain and wind-lashed state we were more than a little happy when the two occupants lit a roaring fire and offered us mugs of steaming tea.

Shenavall, with a roaring fire and hot tea, when the wind howls outside and the rain beats on the window: that is the place to be.

Day 2: Shenavall to Carnmore

We woke to rain and the sight, through the bespattered window, of the little rowan tree outside being bent virtually double. But once I got my half pint Optimus stove singing throatily beneath a pan of water it didn't seem so bad. Roy, whom I had been at school with many years ago, entered into a highly technical discussion on the lighting of derelict mines to the best advantage in order to take record photographs. This was currently his passion which over the years has ranged widely. A few years ago he had been the northern Rally Champion in a car he had built largely himself — he certainly backs up his theories practically. As I passed him the tea and a bacon buttie fresh from the billie I reminded him of a poster that had hung in the old Kelswick Grammar School. It pictured an ape stuffing a screwdriver into a live electrical socket with some appropriate warning beneath. Some wag had written across it, in large letters, the words: 'Garner's Brains, Birkett's Features.' We both laughed. The sun broke through and it was time to be going.

The first objective was to ford the swollen waters of the Abhain Srath na Sealga burn, the second to negotiate a bog and the third to cross the Abhainn Gleann na Muice to the private shooting lodge of Larachantivore. At least we didn't have to pronounce their names!

After this the track is good all the way to distant Carnmore and the setting could not be wilder. As you wind up the side valley of Gleann na Muice Beag it is very noticeable that the high ground to the right and behind you is sandstone but to your left the great smooth-faced cliffs are those of granite. As you start to zig-zag and gain the level whereby you can look across the forlorn Loch Bienn Dearg there are large boulders of obvious volcanic origin. These lava rocks exhibit contraction cracks which formed as they cooled, and large pockets where gas bubbled through the once molten rock.

The traverse past the lochans of Lochan Féith Mhic-illean is horizontal and easily accomplished. There are good views up to the red screes of Ruadh Stac Mór. But the sight about to greet you is in many ways the most impressive of all. As you proceed down the hanging valley above the burn of Allt Bruthac an Easian it is as though you are entering into the mountains of the moon; so white, sheer and smooth are the granite rocks here. They rise on either side and straight up ahead, across the as yet invisible space of the Fionn Loch glen; the huge slabs of below Beinn Làir glisten. Climbers call these mighty rocks the 'Ghost Slabs' because of their unreal white appearance.

As you reach the rim of the hanging valley and proceed to wind your way down towards Carnmore the grandeur of the scene becomes even more apparent. The Dubh and Fionn Lochs flood most of the valley floor and the mountains rise higher and higher above your head as though you are about to be swallowed. The portrayed image is the very epitome of wilderness.

Carnmore is a rather grand looking shooting lodge but our destination was the tiny hovel at the end of the now deserted barn to the west. Outside the lodge stood an aquatic wheeled vehicle (an Argo Cat - All Terrain Vehicle) which explained how these hunters reached their killing fields.

Above the buildings lies a tremendous cliff face well known to the rock climber. It is called Carnmore and it and the pinnacle-like buttress of Sgurr na Laocainn dwarf the lodge reducing it to a mere pinprick of white amidst this huge wilderness. If you look up to the cliff you will see that at about half height there is a large sculpted recess out of which lies the best rock. The best rock and therefore the best rock climbs! A climb called 'Dragon' goes up a grooved corner from the left-hand side of the recess and 'Gob' traverses beneath the obvious overhangs that cross above the right-hand side. They are both fine climbs and looking up at

them now brought back vivid memories of the day I climbed them.

Of course we were 'dossing' here in this barn on that occasion also and I remember we walked in on a day that started wet but came out sunny as we arrived. Being keen and fit we stole straight up to the cliff to do our climbing. In the barn were a group of Glaswegian lads who had been ensconced there for six days. Six days of unremitting rain during which time they couldn't rock climb. On this, the first fine day, they were in such a damp, bedraggled state it was all they could do to sort out their equipment and get 'psyched up' for the next day. The next day it was raining!

Roy and I were privileged to see a beautiful sunset, a breathtaking sight of scarlet turning to moody purple and finally just a lighter afterglow in the enveloping blackness; superb lighting, the effects of which were heightened by the vast loneliness of this god given land. As we sat, making the final brew of the day, the candle flickering, I thought I saw a slight movement outside. Snuffing out the candle we looked through the open doorway; a herd of red deer stealthily and soundlessly passed by. It is at times like these that you realise just why you 'rough it', why you walk, why you climb and why you seek the freedom of the hills.

Day 3: Carnmore to Inverewe

The causeway divides Fionn Loch from Dubh Loch and crossing it serves as an abrupt reminder that man can indeed control the environment however savage. On this third day in the north-west wilderness the emotions generated by this humble structure were by no means unpleasant — later when you return to the concrete jungles you may feel differently. In front and above, the ghostly slabs look stark and formidable.

There is a little lochan on your left that contrasts mightily with the scale of its surroundings. Lilies grow in its waters and a tiny island, virtually only a single rock, supports a solitary rowan. It wouldn't be out of place in a miniature Japanese garden and I'll warrant that if the day is hot and the sun shines you will seek to examine more closely the clear cooling waters.

On your way down you will pass under a number of impressive cliffs. At the base of one by a little lochan lies a jumble of blocks whilst above yawns a huge concave black-stained face. One can't help but think that if the same event were to recur with you underneath there would be absolutely nothing that could be done to escape the inevitable. Walking beneath these cliffs is a rather humbling experience.

Now as we were into our third and final day

the sun began to shine in earnest. Bees suckled the sweet heather and wheatears bobbed in abundance. Only a faint wind stirred the long orange-tipped grass. As we descended from the wilderness the path begins to break up a little and there is much soft peat. It is much better to descend, rather than ascend this type of going. On the dry bits long hairy caterpillars wiggled their way across our track.

Soon you take the stile over the large deer fence and enter a small wood of immature conifers. A number of things seemed to herald the end of our wilderness walk. Firstly there was the different colours, the green of conifer and yellow brown of bracken but more striking than this was the regained sensation of smell; pine, resin sweet, and bracken, aromatically pungent.

We turned right at Kernsary to walk along above the north shore of the loch. From here there are tantalising views back into the wilderness from which we had just emerged and also to the big world of mountains beckoning in the distance. Up a little hill and then the white walls and multicoloured roofs marked the end of the wilderness and the return to civilisation.

It was with mixed emotions that we viewed the rusty abandoned tractor and the old hay stacks in the random little fields. A feeling of disappointment because our wilderness trek was over. Yet also a feeling of satisfaction because we had achieved our goal. But the sun shone and as we passed through an 8ft (2m) high tunnel of gorse the pods popped like gunfire and the seeds scattered on the ground all around us. Next a rowan hung red with berries, then a field bright yellow with flowers lead through a farmyard to the open road. In front the blue sea and that good smell of salt.

The end of a trek over the high mountains, through flooded burns, past charming lochans and great cliffs. An experience of coldness and heat, of easy and hard terrain. An observation of the red deer in their wilderness home and of the sun setting magnificently over Fionn Loch. The end of something that is more than a walk: it is really a journey of discovery. A search into the wild north-west wilderness that reveals not only the natural world in all its glory, but also something about fraternity; of hot tea and a place by the hearth shared. When you discover these things you have found yourself and you have found freedom.

The end of the walk, but who could be sad on such a day and in such a land as this?

Top: **Descending through the plantation before Kernsary.**

Bottom: **Looking from the barn at Carnmore towards the shooting lodge with A' Mhaighdean in the distance.**

PORTREE – Island of Skye

Portree: Accommodation base for the following 4 walks: The Red Cuillin Horseshoe: The Black Cuillin Pass via the Harta and Lota Corries; The far Northern Round of Skye; The North Ridge of Skye.

Map Ref: NG 483435.

Location: At the end of the A850, 34 mls (54 km) from the Kyleakin (To Kyle of Lochalsh) car ferry.

Distance To Walks: 9 mls (15km) south along A850 to the Sligachan Hotel and The Red Cuillin Horseshoe and The Black Cuillins from the Harta and Lota Corries; 20mls (33km) north along the A855 (east) to the start of the North Ridge of Skye; 18mls (27km) north along the A855 (west) to the start of the Far North Round of Skye.

Accommodation: Every type from camping, bed and breakfast, to hotel.

The Town: A little sea port nestling in a sheltered inlet between the cliffs and heights of Ben Chracaig to the north and Ben Tianavaig to the south. A romantic and unspoilt centre of civilisation in a remote wilderness area. The town is raised above the harbour and steps lead to the quay and the boats bobbing, in the clear sea. The attractions are many and include freshly baked bread, and freshly caught fish (at its simplest and very best in the Pier Hotel Restaurant). Gaelic is frequently spoken here and the local character is courteous and friendly; life moves at a slower pace and people have old-fashioned values. Celidhs occur most weeks in summer and at the Tongadale Hotel Bar taped music features local and traditional artists.

Note: On the way to Portree you pass the Sligachan Hotel, the starting point for two of the walks described here. For this reason and because it is traditionally the base for mountaineering on Skye it should also be considered as an alternative centre. The hotel itself offers excellent accommodation and today there is a campsite fully equipped with facilities such as showers, shop etc.

A double rainbow over Portree Harbour.

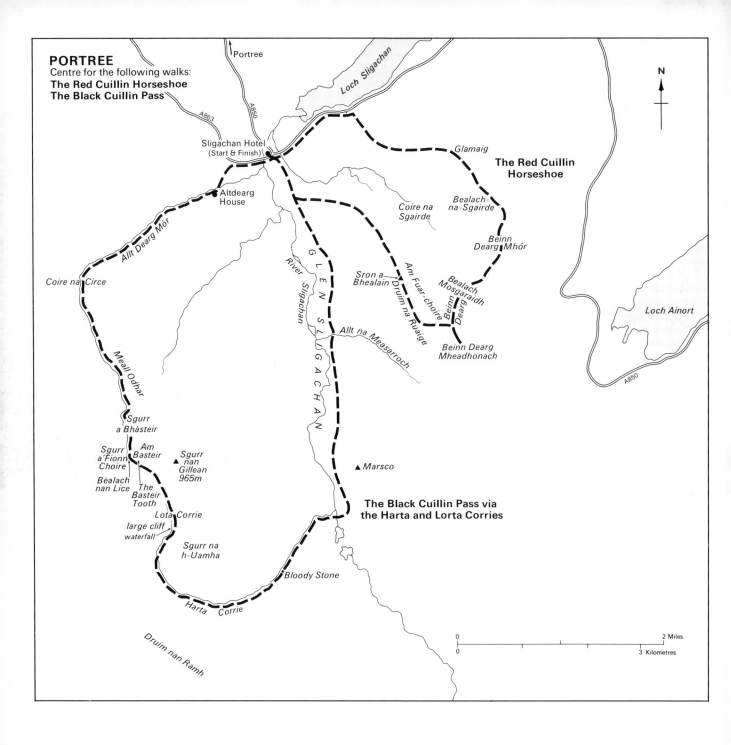

PORTREE
Centre for the following walks:
The Red Cuillin Horseshoe
The Black Cuillin Pass

Portree

A863

A850

Loch Sligachan

Sligachan Hotel
(Start & Finish)

Glamaig

**The Red Cuillin
Horseshoe**

Altdearg
House

Coire na
Sgairde

Bealach-
na-Sgairde

Beinn
Dearg Mhór

Coire na Circe

Allt Dearg Mór

River Sligachan

G L E N   S L I G A C H A N

Sron a
Bhealain

Am Fuar-choire

Druim na Ruaige

Beinn Dearg

Bealach
Mosgaraidh

Allt na Measarroch

Beinn Dearg
Mheadhonach

Loch Ainort

A850

Meall Odhar

Sgurr
a Bhàsteir

Sgurr
a'Fionn
Choire

Am
Basteir

Sgurr
nan
Gillean
965m

Marsco

Bèalach
nan Lice

The
Basteir
Tooth

Lota Corrie

large cliff
waterfall

Sgurr na
h-Uamha

**The Black Cuillin Pass via
the Harta and Lorta Corries**

Bloody Stone

Harta   Corrie

Druim nan Ramh

0   2 Miles

0   3 Kilometres

Facing page: **Looking from the
shoulder of Beinn Dearg Mhor
across the end of Glamaig to the
volcanic cone of Dun Caan on
distant Raasay Island.**

SCOTLAND: The Red Cuillin Horseshoe by Bill Birkett

The Route

From the Sligachan Hotel cross the old bridge to proceed up the Glen Sligachan path until a small stream comes down from below the end of Druim na Ruaige. Follow this to circumnavigate a small area of peat bog and continue to the end of the shoulder. Straight up this to the first summit, Sron a Bhealain — 1407ft (429m) — then along the flat open ridge of Druim na Ruaige to rise up and then follow a zig-zagging path up red scree to the summit ridge of Beinn Dearg. First proceed rightwards to the summit of Beinn Dearg Mheadhonach (2139ft/652m, 2¹/₂hrs) then back along the ridge passing a cairn to stop into Bealach Mosgaraidh 1676ft (511m). Pull up to the summit of Beinn Dearg Mhor (2402ft/732m,

1hr). Walk along then drop. Scree running ability will greatly speed the descent, to Bealach na Sgairde (1351ft/412m, ³/₄hr.) Straight up again to gain the Sgurr Mhairi summit of Glamaig (2543ft/775m, 1hr). From the summit cairn keep to the west (Sligachan) side of the shoulder and either aim for the road (so avoiding bog) or the Sligachan Hotel (again scree running ability will greatly speed the descent). (2hrs, total 7¹/₄ hrs.)

The Walk

Physically separated from the Black Cuillins only by Glen Sligachan, the gentler Red Cuillin mountains display a much more reasonable weather temperament. The sunshine can often be seen illuminating their beautiful red-orange

The Walk: The Red Cuillin Horseshoe, Isle of Skye, Scotland.
Accommodation Base: Portree (see p163).
Maps: OS L32-South Skye, OL8-The Cuillin and Torridon Hills.
Start and Finish: Sligachan Hotel, the junction of the A850 and A863 (map ref: NG 486298).
Length: 7¹/₂mls (12km).
Approx Time: 7¹/₄hrs (without scree running).
Ascent and Descent: 7964ft (2427m).
Difficulty: A straightforward mountain walk of no technical difficulty. The going is good underfoot. Escape is easy. Steep rises make it strenuous.
Access: Car or bus to the Sligachan Hotel.
Seasons: April to October.
Observations: Because the weather is often better here than in the Black Cuillins, the going is good underfoot and the escape simple, this mountain walk is frequently in condition.
Summary of Peaks: Sron a Bhealain: 1407ft (429m), Beinn Dearg Mheadhonach: 2139ft (652m), Beinn Bearg Mhor: 2402ft (732m), Sgurr Mhairi (Glamaig): 2543ft (775m).

rocks, when their bigger brothers are lost in the rain and gales. Why this should be doesn't really matter, it simply means that you can walk here when, as often as not, the Black Cuillin are ruled out because of weather conditions.

As you proceed along the ridge, where the horizontal begins to tilt, the grass loses its grip and the reddest of Cuillin rocks bare themselves for your ascent to Beinn Dearg (The Red Peak). The scree is zig-zagged by a good path and the walking is decidedly pleasant. The rock is hard, fine grained, and has broken in such a fashion that it is small enough not to break up your rhythm; it is also angular enough to be relatively stable underfoot.

When you hit the top it is quite breathtaking for you find yourself on a well-defined ridge with steep ground and uninterrupted scree falling to Loch Ainort 2000ft (610m) below. Here we walked rightwards for a few hundred feet to the summit of Beinn Dearg Mheadhonach a convenient and, because of the heather and bilberry carpet, cosy location to have a break.

The view across to the huge dark cliffs of Bla Bheinn (pronounced Blaven) is absolutely superb. From this angle too, the redness of the scree tumbling down from The Big Red Peak to the green of the heather, poised above the aquamarine blue of the Inner Sound, is something you must see. The day we were there the multiple array of Scalpay, Raasay, Paybay, Longay and the Crowlin islands, shone like emeralds forming a complex patchwork of land and sea before the Inner Sound finally lapped onto the Scottish mainland. This scene to the east could not have contrasted more starkly with that of Sgurr nan Gillean under its mantle of angry cloud. It was as white is to black or as summer to winter.

Proceed back along the ridge, passing the cairn, and drop smoothly into the Bealach Mosgaraidh then climb steeply to the highest of these red peaks. The rocks here are simply a joy to be amongst; their colour, their form, their texture all radiate a quality that feels clean and pure. We joined another two parties who were sheltering on the east side of the mountain, to eat a belated snack before we set off again to descend the aesthetically stooping shoulder.

It ends abruptly with a little cone and then you plunge rapidly down to the Bealach na Sgairde. We, John Hargreaves and myself, scree-ran this section. Obviously this is considerably quicker than walking and it took us, from the summit of Beinn Dearg Mhor to the bealach, only twenty minutes.

Although Glamaig appears intrinsically red

Top: **Sunlight and storm looking from Drum na Ruaige to the Black Cuillin.**

Bottom: **Dropping into Bealach na Sgairde with Glamaig above.**

when viewed from afar, here you notice a colour change in the rocks. They become, at close quarters, distinctly bluey grey. It's a long, long way from the col up to the summit of Glamaig towering over 1000ft (305m) above, but really you know that, although escape contouring down left is tempting, you have got to do it, for ascending Glamaig is the ultimate objective of this walk.

Remember, as you slog up its steep flanks that Glamaig has been ascended, from the Sligachan Hotel, in 37 minutes; a record apparently set some time ago. It's worth it when you get to the top and you're greeted by luxuriously spongy turf, to take the final stroll along to reach the summit cairn. The clouds were now just beginning to close and we had but little time to admire the commanding view: north to the Storr and its Old Man, west across the Inner Sound to the Applecross hills and down to the eye-catching volcano-like cone of Dun Caan on the Island of Raasay.

Because of the rapidly worsening weather we scree-ran like fury straight down the Sligachan side of Sgurr Mhairi to gain the main road alongside the shore of Loch Sligachan. The gulls and the lambs cried and the rain fell in buckets.

This walk is a revelation for a Skye mountain walk because the going is firm and easy. Only at the start is there a boggy section and this, with a little prudence, can be successfully negotiated without wetting the feet. For the rest of the way it is either sound turf or amiable scree. It is, in addition to all these little advantages a very fine mountain walk taking in the Red Horseshoe of Sron a Bhealain, Druim na Ruaige, Beinn Dearg Mheadhonach, Beinn Dearg Mhor and culminating in the magnificent cone of Glamaig.

Technically it is an easy walk but it is strenuous and needs a little perseverance to make the steep haul from the hollow of Bealach na Sgairde to the summit of Glamaig. Fortunately escape from any point on the walk is easy and this makes it worth an attempt when the weather could go either way. The rule in Skye being, of course, when you can see the mountains it's going to rain, when you can't it's already raining!

All the morning it had lashed rain but now with a few shafts of sunshine and the occasional sight of blue flitting above at high speed, we thought it time to try. We were lucky for the whole of the Red Cuillin cleared so we could enjoy their distinct colour resplendent against the blue sky. Across the glen, Ossian and the gods battled on, the clouds never fully lifting from the rocky Sgurr nan Gillean. Occasionally they would rise to reveal a huge basin

of snow below where the scree and rocks of Coire Bhasteir should have been at this late end of May. But then down the clouds came, sending out ugly black showers that raked Glen Sligachan, amazingly to stop somewhere short of our walk.

There are a number of small variations to start this walk but really there is nothing between them. The one we chose was to proceed down the Glen Sligachan path until a little burn cuts down, and then to walk up alongside this to gain the end of the shoulder of Sron a Bhealain. Just before we gained the shoulder we had to cross a small area of bog but this was easily circumnavigated to the right. In retrospect an approach initially alongside the Allt Daraich, taking you less directly to the shoulder, may well have avoided some of the bog we encountered.

Once on the shoulder the going is fine. You quickly gain height and rapidly begin to command excellent views. The summit of Sron a Bhealain falls easily and before you now, the remarkably open ridge of Druim na Ruaige puts you in a tremendous position both to admire the perfect symmetry of Glamaig to the north, and also to pierce the very heart of the jagged Black Cuillin over to the south west.

The different perspective here allows you to see that Glamaig, which appears to be a perfect cone from below, does in fact extend out in a long lower ridge from its highest summit, Sgurr Mhairi, to its second summit, that of An Coileach. Now seen through the gap of Bealach na Sgairde with the sun alternately lighting the sweeping red screes of the conal Sgurr Mhairi, and then the long steep face joining the two summits, it looked most attractive. (It was tempting to extend our walk to take in this second summit, and I'm sure that extremely fit parties will make a point of doing so.)

Before you too, the magnificent form of Marsco adds a further dimension to the grandeur. The day we were there, with most of the Black Cuillin obscured by cloud, Marsco almost stole the show from Glamaig; almost but not quite. Really they are so different in form that it is difficult to compare one with the other. Indeed when the sun is high in the sky, and before it dips westwards to plunge into the sea, there can be few more wonderful sights to the lover of wild places, than the sun shining directly down Glen Sligachan illuminating the graceful Glamaig and the powerfully poised Marsco.

The Red Cuillin viewed from the south across Loch Ainort. Beinn Dearg can be seen on the left, Beinn Dearg Mhor in the centre and Glamaig to the right.

The Walk: A route along Glen Sligachan and up through the Black Cuillins via the Harta and Lota Corries, Island of Skye, North West Scotland.

Accommodation Base: Portree (see p163).

Maps: OS L32-South Skye, OD8-The Cuillin and Torridon.

Start and Finish: Sligachan Hotel, the junction of the A850 and A863 (map ref: NG 486298).

Length: 11mls (18km).

Approx Time: 10hrs.

Ascent and Descent: 6000ft (1830m).

Difficulty: A walk involving no technical difficulty but due to its altitude, length and remoteness it should be considered to be extremely tough. (Possibly the most difficult walk described in this book.)

Access: Car or bus to the Sligachan Hotel.

Seasons: May to October.

Observations: A compass *cannot* be relied upon due to the presence of magnetite. This is a high and remote mountain walk taking the walker into the heart of the mountaineers's world of the Black Cuillin. Execution is straightforward but escape is not easy and the consequences of misnavigation serious. Under no circumstances should it be tackled in poor visibility or inclement weather. Because of the large cliffs separating the Harta and Lota Corries this route is not recommended in reverse.

High Points: Bealach nan Lice: 2940ft (896m), Sgurr a'Bhasteir: 2951ft (899m).

THE ISLAND OF SKYE: The Black Cuillin Pass via the Harta and Lota Corries by Bill Birkett

The Route

Cross the old bridge from the Sligachan Hotel then follow up the path along the west side of Glen Sligachan and on under the flanks of Marsco. When the Lochan Dubh are in sight take a right-angled right to enter the Harta Corrie. Note that when you are in line with the south of the Sligachan River as it flows down Harta then you are on the correct path (2hrs, 4mls/6km). Attempt to keep along the bank of the river as soon as possible (bog elsewhere) and stay with it up into the Harta Corrie passing the Bloody Stone. Continue to the bend and cross the burn to continue up various waterfalls to enter the upper Harta

Corrie. Ascend into the Lota Corrie to the right of the large waterfall. Aim for the obvious notch of Bealach nan Lice — the Basteir Tooth stands overlooking the right side of the gap. First follow a small stream but quickly leave this for the easy buttress to the left. (2000ft, 610 m of ascent from the upper Harta Corrie, 4¹/2 hrs, 2940ft/896m.)

Follow the ridge to the summit of Sgurr a Bhasteir (2951ft/899m) and continue down the ridge slightly to the right with a little easy scrambling to arrive on the plateau top of Meall Odhar. Continue along to drop down its snout detouring left at the bottom (care needed) to avoid some small rock buttresses.

Gain the north bank of the Allt Dearg burn and down past the Alltdearg House (boggy) to gain the road and then the Sligachan Hotel (3½hrs, total 10hrs).

The Walk

The Black Cuillin have long been the spiritual home for British mountaineers. Their spectacular form, the stark nakedness of the rough gabbro rock, their solitude and height combined with the sheer romanticism of the Island of Skye make it so. The great Cuillin Ridge, a long and difficult mountaineering expedition, is the brightest jewel in the crown but it includes sections that are reserved for the technical rock climber and indeed, for the average walker, the Black Cuillin are inhospitable and inaccessible.

This trip takes the walker into wild solitude, along Glen Sligachan and up through the Harta and Lota Corries, over Bealach nan Lice to kiss the heights and experience some of Skye's most magnificent mountain scenery. It passes under the mighty tooth of Am Basteir (The Executioner) and provides unequalled views of the most romantic peak of them all — Sgurr nan Gillean. It then takes you gently down the ridge of Sgurr a Bhasteir to the rock pools of the Alt Dearg burn and eventually back to the Sligachan Hotel — the historical base for many a mountaineering adventure. This walk offers the non-climber the opportunity to sample, in safety, the world of the mountaineer.

The Black Cuillin stretch some six miles from Gars-bheinn — the most southerly of them — to end with the towering peak of Sgurr nan Gillean, situated above and beyond the lonely Sligachan Hotel. It is this peak (Peak of the Young Men), with its position and distinctive form, that enchants every traveller to Skye. This mountain encompasses all the mystique and savage beauty of the magical Cuillin, and from the Sligachan Hotel, our starting point, it is worth studying its intricacies because this will acquaint you with the topography of the area through which you are going to descend and will impress upon you the logic of the route.

Saddle shaped, the high peak of Gillean lies to the left, and to our right Am Basteir ends with the gap that is our point of access from the Lota Corrie — Bealach nan Lice. Even from this distance the great Basteir Tooth can be seen to overhang the gap, looking like the notched steel of an executioner's blade. Look carefully, and the triangular peaked ridge (Sgurr a Bhasteir) emanating from this notch (and forming the right wall of Coire a' Bhasteir), can be seen as the line of descent you will take to the Allt Dearg burn.

The day before, I had coincidentally met John Cleare who had been blown down from his latest photographic assignment in the Hebrides, and had invited him to accompany me on this walk. The weather was unsettled and I wasn't sure that my planned trip was going to be a practical proposition — but that night Gillean, a blonde-haired and blue-eyed native of Skye (named after the mountain) had pointed to stars beginning to twinkle in the clearing west and predicted that the morrow would be fair. It dawned with one single lenticular cloud high in the sky over Sgurr nan Gillean and the rest was blue, blue, blue.

Down in the depths of the U-shaped valley the linnets sang and patches of lush lime green grass added a dash of luxuriance to the unfolding heather and rock wilderness. The silver snake of the Sligachan river looped its way north as we walked virtually due south. High, above, the pyramidal bulk of Marsco and the Red Cuillin lay to our left, and to our right the tower-like pillars of Gillean stood out starkly against the white snow which lay, still thick, in the corries of the Black Cuillin. In that moment summer arrived on Skye.

You're more than half way along beneath Marsco, with the Lochan Dubha in sight, when you take a right-angled right to head off up into the remote and wonderful Harta Corrie. You are on the right track if your line of travel heads for and along the left side of the Sligachan burn issuing from the corrie. From the flanks of Marsco, the cliffs and rocks of Sgurr Beag and Sgurr na h-Uamha, over the way, are impressive enough but, as you progress into the corrie the unbroken steepness continuing for 2000ft (610m) above you is dramatic almost beyond words.

Few can remain unintimidated as, in front, you spy two resolute marker stones. In the distance, over to the right, a large but anonymous sentinel stands where the corrie bends right, but nearer, to the left, stands the larger and infamous Bloody Stone. The path takes you to this boulder and few will pass it without at least a circumnavigatory inspection. Of its history there are different explanations. Charles Weld wrote in his *Two Months In The Highlands* in 1865: 'Half-way to Camasunary you come to the entrance of Hart O'Corrie, a dark purple glen. The jaws of this gloomy gorge are set around with huge rocks; one which is much larger than the rest, is called the Bloody Stone, from a shepherd having lost his life up there.' But more recently Derek Cooper in his book *Skye* reports that it was so named after a battle between the MacLeods and the MacDonalds where the former were massacred

Facing page: **Sgurr nan Gillean and the Pinnacle Ridge.**

and their bodies piled round the base.

Of more immediate interest to John and myself were Ashley Abraham's comments in his magnificent work *Rock Climbing In Skye*. Here in 1908 he climbed the rock by two different starts writing the following about the most difficult: ' . . . the start is a fine object-lesson in how to trust gabbro as a foothold.' We also climbed the rock by 'the Abraham starts', and I added a more difficult variation (a first ascent?) from the north, before we shouldered our packs to continue up the corrie. As you proceed up the burn you will notice, on top of the black-blue-grey gabbro rocks and pebbles and whenever a streamlet rushes in from the south flanks of Meall Dearg above, an intrusion of red rocks; an interesting meeting of the Black and Red Cuillin. As the valley tightens, small waterfalls are encountered and while we were there, whether from the blueness of the sky or from the colour of the gabbro rocks, the clear waters took on the translucence of a Glacier Mint sweet.

In a few of the many boulders now tumbling across the path and into the stream I noticed a concentration of shiny black metallic crystals. Sure enough, on placing the compass near to the rock I could watch the needle deflect visibly from magnetic north. Magnetite is the reason why the compass cannot be relied upon in the Cuillin and it should be carefully noted that, in the advent of poor visibility, you are on your own.

From here you follow on up a number of small waterfalls and cross the burn to enter Upper Harta. Confronting you now is a long curtain of impenetrable rock. Vertical for 300 ft (100m), it separates the Harta and Lota Corries. On its right a long and elegant waterfall marks a break in the defences; immediately to its right (the eastern edge of the corrie) the rocks are broken and a reasonable path can be followed leading into the upper sanctuary. The walking becomes strenuous from here to the head of the pass and rises steeply for almost 2000ft (610m).

Observe that this is the only way from Harta to Lota and vice versa. From below, the cliffs can be easily picked out and recognised. From above they cannot be seen. For this reason I do not recommend that the route is taken in the reverse order to that described. I will repeat that from above, the vertical cliffs cannot be seen and their tops are rounded with no indication of what is below — the consequences of misnavigation would be dire.

Gain the ground to the right of the fall and scramble up until an easy rock path takes you back left, spectacularly over towards the top of the fall. This is marked by the occasional small

cairn. You are now in a total mountain environment with scenery that can only meaningfully be labelled 'The Black Cuillin'. You will see not a blade of grass or splash of green, but all around there is rock. Rock piled upon rock; rock smooth and intact; rock tumbled and heaped; flat rock and rock sweeping giddily upwards. But there is colour, its subtleties varying with the ambient light; sometimes black, sometimes purple, sometimes grey-blue but always, intoxicating.

Looking back down the corrie across the lesser, although still dramatic, ridge of Druim nan Ramh, could be seen the black profile of the savage Cuillin Ridge with some of the giants showing their heads above it. Sgurr Thuilm and Sgurr a' Greadaidh were visible and the sight sent a shiver down my spine. More immediately the sweeps of buttresses and interconnecting boiler plate slabs of Sgurr na Bhairnich added further impact to the hostility of the encounter.

Ahead could be picked out some tiny silhouetted figures on the top of Am Basteir; their presence in this alien environment made one feel that they were only abstract. Our minds, conditioned by the solitude and deso-

lation of the scene, tried to tell us they were yet more inanimate stones, but no, movement proved they were alive. Below them and leading up to the obvious gap between Sgorr A'Fionn Choire to the left and the Basteir Tooth and Am Basteir to the right, lay the obvious Bealach nan Lice (Pass of the Flat Stones) — and our route. It looked a long way to its head.

At first we followed a small stream leading into a corridor that headed directly up to the head of the pass. However, we almost immediately quitted this to scramble up the easy buttress to its left. This led conveniently to the scree tumbling from the head of the pass and this was followed on its left-hand side, where the rocks are smaller and safer to negotiate, under the cliffs of Sgurr A' Fionn Choire (not marked on the map but the lesser summit of Bruach na Frithe).

As we neared the top, The Basteir Tooth captured the eye but as we crossed a reasonably substantial snow patch (in mid June!) we had to concentrate solely on upward progress. John, sporting dark glasses was OK, but for me, without, the light reflected from the snow was almost blinding. Then out we pulled onto

Above: **A climber looks to the Basteir Tooth and Am Basteir from the point where Bealach nan Lice bridges the Ridge.**

Facing page, top: **John Cleare crosses the Allt na Measarroch Burn along the Sligachan Valley with Sgurr nan Gillean behind.**

Facing page, bottom: **John Cleare approaching Bealach nan Lice.**

171

John Cleare approaching the Bloody Stone.

the Cuillin Ridge itself and all that effort and sweat to get there was repaid in an instant.

The scene and the panorama is quite wonderful and just to feel the presence of the great Tooth, there by your side, is a powerful experience. One maybe that will live in the memory forever. Perhaps this is so because the Tooth is such a striking feature both from the road and the Sligachan Hotel, now a long, long way below, where you started many hours ago.

We now followed the gentle rise up the arete leading to the summit of Sgurr Bhasteir and today it literally felt like the stairway to heaven. All that could be seen in front was the sure rock path and, beyond a blue space with occasional wisps of white cloud. Below, to the left, lay the gentle scoop of Fionn Choire while right, the inviting rock pools of Coire a' Bhasteir glistened invitingly below the snowline. Looking back along from the Basteir Tooth and Am Basteir the upper walls of the latter corrie curved round to join with the dominating view to our left. Sgurr nan Gillean, with its Pinnacle Ridge falling away towards the north, was absolutely spellbinding. The view of views, the hill of hills on the most perfect day possible. A lone figure stood upright on the very topmost pinnacle. Even John Cleare, traveller, mountaineer, and photographer of all the world's great mountains was almost speechless. Almost, but not quite; the solitary word 'Immaculate' stumbled from his lips.

The descent is mild mannered and the going is made easier by the fact that the rock here is not gabbro but has changed to a smaller crystalline structure similar to that of the Red Cuillin. A little easy scrambling leads you to the horizontal band of Meall Odhar and you continue directly along its back to follow the shoulder below. Detour left towards the bottom to avoid some small rock bluffs, and it's only a short way to the rock pools of the Allt Dearg burn.

'Skinny dipping' in the cooling waters of the burn provided a heaven-sent interlude before the completion of our mountain day; the transparent and cascading white waters contrasting completely with the stark serenity that we had experienced high up on the Black Cuillin Ridge. Then, with the Red Cuillins ahead, we took the well trodden path down past the Alltdearg cottage and back to the 'Sliggy', floating as we did so, through waves of air sweet with warmth.

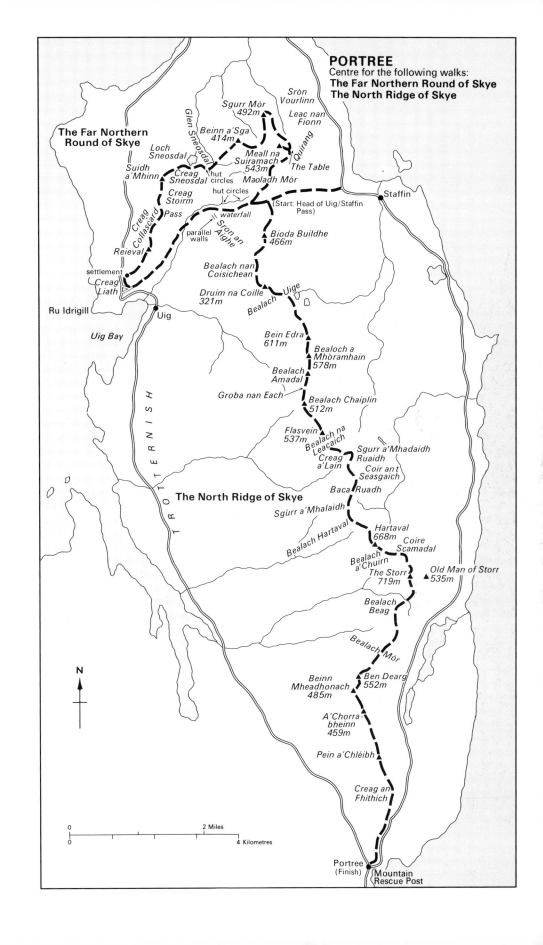

PORTREE
Centre for the following walks:
The Far Northern Round of Skye
The North Ridge of Skye

Sròn Vourlinn

Sgurr Mór
492m

Leac nan Fionn

The Far Northern Round of Skye

Beinn a'Sga
414m

Quirang

Glen Sneosdal

Loch Sneosdal

Meall na Suiramach
543m

The Table

Suidh a'Mhinn

Creag Sneosdal

hut circles

Maoladh Mór

Staffin

Creag Stoirm

hut circles

Creag Collascard

Pass

waterfall

(Start: Head of Uig/Staffin Pass)

parallel walls

Sròn an Aighe

Bioda Buildhe
466m

Reieval

settlement

Bealach nan Coisichean

Creag Liath

Druim na Coille
321m

Uige

Ru Idrigill

Bealach

Uig

Uig Bay

Bein Edra
611m

Bealoch a Mhòramhain
578m

Bealach Amadal

Groba nan Each

Bealach Chaiplin
512m

Flasvein
537m

Bealach na Leacaich

Sgurr a'Mhadaidh Ruaidh

Creag a'Lain

Coir an t Seasgaich

Baca Ruadh

T R O T T E R N I S H

The North Ridge of Skye

Sgùrr a'Mhalaidh

Bealach Hartaval

Hartaval
668m

Coire Scamadal

Bealach a'Chuirn

The Storr
719m

Old Man of Storr
535m

Bealach Beag

Bealach Mór

Beinn Mheadhonach
485m

Ben Dearg
552m

A'Chorra-bheinn
459m

Pein a'Chléibh

N

Creag an Fhithich

0   2 Miles
0   4 Kilometres

Portree
(Finish)

Mountain Rescue Post

The Walk: The Far Northern Round of Skye, Trotternish.
Accommodation Base: Portree (see p163).
Maps: OS L23-Northern Skye.
Start and Finish: Uig, at the junction of the A855 and Uig to Staffin Road (map ref. 388644).
Length: 14mls (22.5km), or 9¹/₂mls (15km) to head of the Uig to Staffin Pass.
Approx Time: 7 hrs.
Ascent and Descent: 4600ft (1400m).
Difficulty: An increasingly strenuous mountain walk first over short heather then over damper, more difficult peat terrain. No marked way. The return finish is down a metalled road. Escape from the circuit to the road is possible at most stages.
Access: Car to start or bus to Uig.
Seasons: April to October.
Observations: Backpackers will wish to link this round. It is the logical start to the North Skye Ridge which I have described as starting at the head of the Uig Staffin Pass (map ref: 440679 and 5¹/₂hrs to the Pass). However the return down the metalled road is not unpleasant though one could arrange a car pick-up at the head of the pass.
Summary of Peaks: Reieval: 951ft (290m), Suidh 'a' Mhinn: 1148ft (350m), Beinn a' Sgá: 1358ft (414m), Sgurr Mór. 1614ft (492m). Meall na Suiramach 1781ft (543m)

SCOTLAND: The Far Northern Round of Skye by Bill Birkett

The Route

From the junction gain the summit of Reieval (951ft, 290m). Starting left of the wire fence avoids crossing fences. Continue along the top to skirt the cliffs of Creag Collascard and drop into the obvious bealach (pass) (689ft, 210m). Contour left and up to the trig point on the summit of Suidh 'a' Mhinn (1,148ft, 350m and 1¹/₂hrs). Cross to the flat top of the huge cliffs of Creag Sneosdal (care!). Drop down to the stream of Lòn nan Earb at the head of Glen Sneosdal (558ft, 170m). Cross the stream and continue down to another tributary — cross this climbing up to what appears to be a well formed diagonal track raking up the hillside (it is actually a land slip fracture). Continue up to the indefinite summit of Beinn a'Sgá (1358ft, 414m and 2hrs) and take a circular contour to reach the summit of Sgurr Mór (1614ft, 492m). Continue on to the edge of the cliff (care!). Keep to the eastern side of the summit (for the views), along the cliff tops, then up to the summit of Meall na Suiramach (1781ft, 543m and 1hr). Return to the cliff edge and overlook the Quirang (care!) then contour round to turn back right aiming for Maoladh Mór. Drop steeply down to path leading to picnic area at the head of the pass (853ft, 260m and ³/₄hr). Down the road to starting point. (l³/₄hrs, total: 7hrs).

The Walk

To a casual observer, eyeing this walk from the lonely Uig to Staffin Pass, there will be little increase in the heart beat. True, it forms an integral part of the marvellous and desolate scenery of this ancient area of Skye but it doesn't readily display its secrets, or reveal its unique charisma. These are only to be discovered by the walking of this superb round of the far north.

The motorist viewing from the Pass will get a sight of the Quirang and its mysterious and fantastic pinnacles, a glimpse of The Prison and The Needle, and from the main road (Uig to the north), you will realise that, that which you previously regarded as bland upland is in fact a mighty and precipitous shoulder. But these are only hints of what makes this walk an outstanding adventure.

The Far North Round is a mountain walk but it offers more than one could reasonably expect of a walk so defined and holds a wealth of contrasting form and interest. Underfoot the terrain varies from short rolling heather through peat, to golf course grass that suddenly, unexpectedly, terminates at huge vertical cliffs. Ultimately the physical geology leaves one feeling humbled by its complexity and scale.

On another level it reveals something of the tale of ancient Skye, from ruined crofts to weird conical mounds and works of pre-history. But overriding all this, its position above the shore and sea of this magical island give you some of the best seascapes to be encountered in Britain: from the west, to the western Isles; north across the northern tip of Skye to Lord Macdonald's Table, Shiant Islands and beyond; finally across The Minch to the great wild areas of the north-west mainland.

We were keen to get going, despite the incessant wind that was gusting to gale force, and we set off for Reieval, the first summit above Uig, impatient to explore the secrets of this forgotton land. After only a little way the sharply angular wings of an Arctic Skua held the bird motionless, fighting the gale just above our heads. Its stony eye fixed on us unblinkingly and there seemed to be no hint of fear as it hung there. A few more yards and the reason became obvious: amongst the prolific clumps of yellow primroses lay the corpse of a tiny calf. Food for the hungry.

The going on this initial section is very pleasant with short firm heather, for the most part, giving easy walking. Soon you are standing on the first top and already you command a powerful view looking down to the table and seat formation of Creag Liath guarding the now storm-lashed port of Uig Bay and then across Loch Snizort to the Ascrib Islands and the Waternish headland beyond. We gazed across those stormy waters as heavy blackness alternated with the dazzling silver brilliance of the sun breaking through. We observed that the Hebridean ferry had again set off on its journey. Previously it had bobbed back into the harbour and anchored some way off the jetty to sit out the storm. This was a good sign and we set off again, confident that the weather was going to improve.

You now move across to skirt the top of the cliffs of Creag Collascard and begin to feel the elation of your position. Spread out far below, the brilliantly white crofts tumble out across the plain into the sea, contrasting sharply with the blackness of the ruined crofting village that lies below the crags of Creag Stoirm a little way ahead.

These crofts serve as a timely reminder that there had once been over 30,000 people living and working on Skye. Now there are only just over 7000. As Willie (Hunish) McCloud, who lives in the most northerly croft on Skye, had said as he kindly sat us down to his strupach (a light tea or snack): 'There were 17,000 Skye men sent off to fight in the Napoleonic War, but I don't think they'll be going again'.

Cutting the ridge in front and once, no doubt, serving as the main access to the community below, is a well constructed but now deserted, pass. After dropping down into it you continue skirting leftwards above the cliffs to make a long haul up to the concrete trig point on the top of Suidh 'a' Mhinn (which apparently means the place of the court, or the locality where wrong-doers were tried). The going here became noticeably more difficult with the introduction of peat hags and corresponding boggy areas but the vista spread below was unforgettable.

You start to break east now, heading for the cliffs of Creag Sneosdal and move through an area where the peat hags stand above you capped, like thatched cottages, with a roof of grass. I remember that for this section the sun shone and the exposed peat, wet from the rain, was displayed rich brown with the texture of a chocolate flake. It was that kind of light, brief but intense, where colour and form are heightened and exaggerated. Even the frequent black pools whipped by the gale glimmered like horizontal slabs of polished marble.

Over to our right we were puzzled by two very distinct dead parallel lines that were running straight down the distant shoulder of Sron an Aighe. At a distance of some one and a half miles away they obviously had to be of some consequence and although we both put

Facing page: **The Table and weird Pinnacles of the Quirang.**

forward theories as to their origin we were in truth baffled.

Then quite suddenly you arrive on grass as cropped and as smooth as a putting green. Equally suddenly, and it's easy to be caught unawares you find there is nothing but space below your feet. A 700ft (213m) cliff plunges vertically and immediately into the black Loch Sneosdal. Below, and separated from the settled coastal strip with its white crofts there is a barren and deserted raised plain. Only vacant troughs, where the peat has been cut, indicate that man has had any influence on the area.

At the head of this deserted Glen a waterfall tumbles and to its left, on the back of Beinn a' Sgà, there is a huge land slip. An area of the mountain has moved visibly forward and down, leaving a hollow above, a parallel situation to the Quirang on the opposite side of the mountain, perhaps not quite as spectacular as its famous brother but still, by virtue of its size alone, an impressive sight.

As if all this was not enough to captivate your imagination, your position now commands an unbroken view across to the northern point of Skye that is Ruba Hunish, and on to the Western Isles. Even though the wind howled and battered us we lingered to take it all in and John brought out the map to name the features spread before us. Refolding it proved to be difficult: I worked on the folds and John simply hung on to it to stop it being blown away. Eventually we got it into some semblance of order and crammed it back into the sac. Despite all the beauty surrounding us it was a relief to descend into the little valley below and take shelter from that fearsome wind.

In a number of respects it was like discovering a Shangri-La. Sheltered from the buffeting wind it appeared to have its own micro climate and, without the cooling effect of the wind, the warmth of the sun could be appreciated. The little burn of Lòn non Earb ran sprightly and on its banks clustered yellow primroses. We were just admiring the scene when we began to notice perfectly circular mounds, obviously man made; three at first, high above the burn on the western bank, and one noticeably larger than the others. But as we looked closer they were also down below us, situated between the meanders of the burn. All were circular, up to about twelve feet high and indented at the top. Still remaining in some of these indentations were circular stone walls standing around three feet high and three feet in diameter. As we crossed the burn and moved along the opposite bank we discovered yet more of these curious earthworks.

I feel that these most probably date back to prehistory and know of no record detailing them. If so they owe their remarkably preserved state, complete with standing walls, to their remoteness and the absence of man's influence in this secretive and deserted valley. Hopefully no one will do anything to change this unique site.

We followed the burn down until we intercepted a further burn sited in a subsidiary little gorge. Here, sheltered from the wind, we took a break and ate lunch. We simply sat listening to the music of this little burn and watched its peaty brown colour turn to milky white as it tumbled over a series of rock slides; it was an effort to get going again. We crossed the burn to take a steep and direct line up to what had appeared to be an obvious trackway. On arrival we found that this veritable motorway of a track was no such thing but was in fact a substantial land-slip fracture raking up the hillside. We walked along this with an uneasy feeling, even though we knew there was no likelihood of our weight precipitating another slip! Near its end we took a more direct line up the hillside, passing a further parallel fracture line, then to head northwards to the indefinite summit of Beinn a Sgà.

We then took a high contour round the head of Glen Scamadal to follow a long flat walk across to the summit of Sgurr Mor (The Big Mountain). This is a long drag and it is very tempting to cut it short and directly gain the summit of Meall na Suiramach (above the Quirang). It took us just under the hour from the little burn but I can assure you that the panorama gained is more than worth the effort of getting there. From a fairly flat and featureless terrain the summit is marked by a rock outcrop rising abruptly from the peat to form a natural cairn, but walk on past this to the end of the plateau — now there is absolutely nothing to interrupt the splendid views to the east, the north and the west.

From here along to Meall na Suiramach we skirted above the cliffs. This route offered us slight shelter from the wind, which was partly the reason for taking it, but mainly it was chosen so we could observe and enjoy the varied and exciting rock scenery of Sròn Vourlinn and Leac nan Fionn. Viewed from here they are, if anything, more impressive than from the road far below. Seen in this relief, high above the sea, they appear as impenetrable strongholds, particularly the latter, set as they are against a wild and hungry landscape. In point of fact this may well have been their function — one name is of Norse origin and the other Celtic. Sròn Vourlinn means the nose of Vourlinn — most probably a Viking chief, and the gaelic Leac nan Fionn also relates to a person's name.

Of the two influences on Skye, Alexander Smith wrote evocatively in his classic book, *A Summer In Skye:*

To this day in the islands the Norse element is distinctly visible — not only in old castles, the names of places, but in the faces and entire mental build of the people. Claims of pure Scandinavian descent are put forward by many of the old families. Wandering up and down the islands you encounter faces that possess no Celtic characteristics; which carry the imagination to 'Noroway ower the faem;' people with cool calm blue eyes and hair yellow as the dawn; who are resolute and persistent, slow in pulse and speech; and who differ from the explosive Celtic element surrounding them as the iron headland differs from the fierce surge that washes it, or a block of marble from the heated palm pressed against it.

The summit of Meall na Suiramach (Head Sheriff) is indistinctive in itself, although it commands a fine position at the head of this far north round; but just below and to the east lies the fantastic and famous Quirang. To look down is to experience an almost overpowering sense of mystery. In the foreground there is the absolutely flat cricket-field-like Table and beyond, a series of separate standing rectangular and perpendicular buttresses and pinnacles. The Needle is over to the right, and further along the cliffs one can look down to The Prison below. The top of the Quirang is marked by a small cairn but take care; there is little other warning and the sheer rocks drop away immediately. As we gazed down two figures scrambled onto the Table from below and it seemed reminiscent of a scene in the Giant's castle from Jack and the Beanstalk. Leaning over the edge to take a photograph I was hit by a gust of wind so strong that I only just managed to stop myself from being blown over. It was time to go!

Keeping high we contoured along to Maoladh Mór then plunged directly down to the well-trodden path that takes one from the head of the pass to the Quirang. We sought some shelter behind rocks beside the road and had a further bite to eat. Then it was the long walk back down the road to Uig. The sun shone and the going was blissfully easy. On the way back, below a little burn and then for a long way down the main stream, there appeared many of the earth mounds with the indented tops that we had first seen around Lòn nan Earb; and passing under the shoulder of Sron an Aighe we could plainly see, coming down to the road and continuing along down below it, the parallel lines we had seen so clearly from above Creag Sneosdal. The most southerly of these continued, raking in straight lines, right across towards Lon nan Earb. On examination these

The hut circles by Lòn nan Earb with Beinn á Sgà behind.

were definitely not of geological origin but were man-made and consist of a constructed stone base with sod and earth topping. Looking east, running up above the road, they were parallel (about 30ft apart) until they disappeared from sight. Perhaps the name gives us a clue as to their origin; Sron an Aighe means nose of the beast and possibly these lines could have been some system of containing or collecting cattle. Perhaps not, but puzzling over what their origin may have been, occupied our thoughts until we ended our walk at Uig.

One thing we were both certain about however, was that this walk is a magnificent way to view the amazing and spectacular environment of this ancient region of Skye.

SCOTLAND: The North Ridge of Skye by Bill Birkett

The Walk: The North Ridge of Skye, Trotternish, Isle of Skye, Scotland.

Accommodation Base: Portree (see p163).

Maps: OS L23-North Skye.

Start: Head of the Staffin/Uig Pass (map ref: NG 440679).

Finish: Portree or just above where the A855 turns a right angle and makes a junction with the minor road to Achachork (NG 488454).

Length: 19mls (30km).

Approx Time: 10hrs.

Ascent and Descent: 10,730ft (3270m).

Difficulty: Although the walking is easy and the going good underfoot the full mountain ridge is a long and energetic expedition. Always to the east lie great cliffs and the walk should only be tackled in good visibility. Additionally the ridge takes one through the heart of a barren and desolate landscape — difficult terrain and some considerable distance separate you from either the west and east coast roads or civilisation (make careful note of the escape passes).

Access: This walk is described from north to south and a car drop off is necessary at the head of the Staffin/Uig Pass (no public transport to this point),

Seasons: April to September.

Escape Points: There are a number of passes (bealachs) where escape from the ridge is reasonably practical. These are worth noting in case the weather deteriorates or fatigue takes its toll. They are as follows:

Bealach Uige (approx 1¹/₂hrs from start). Follow path to Uig.

Bealach á Mhòramhain (approx 2¹/₂hrs from start). Follow path to Uig.

Bealach Chaiplin (approx 3hrs from start). Descend to a plateau and cross to follow the stream to Loch Cuithir. It is possible to leave/be collected by car from this point but the walk out along the road is long.

Bealach Beag (approx 7hrs from start). Descend a ravine by following the stream to a car park alongside the main road.

Observations: Longer than the famous Black Cuillin Ridge (which is a mountaineering expedition not suitable for walkers), this great mountain walk is thoroughly practical because of the excellent conditions underfoot. A tremendous day out for the fit walker.

Summary of Peaks: Bioda Buidhe; 1530ft (466m), Beinn Edra: 2006ft (611m), Mhòramhain: 1896ft (578m), Flasvein: 1959ft (597m), Creag á Lain: 1995ft (608m), Sgurr á Mhadaidh Ruaidh: 1926ft (587m), Baca Ruadh: 2091ft (637m), Hartaval: 2192ft (668m), The Storr: 2358ft (719m), Ben Dearg: 1812ft (552m), Beinn Mheadhonach: 1591ft (485m), A' Chorra-bheinn: 1506ft (459m).

Previous pages:

Left: **Storr and the Old Man.**

Right, top: **Looking to Sgurr a' Mhadaidh Ruaidh (left) and Creag a' Lain (right).**

Right, bottom: **Approaching Bioda Buidhe.**

The Route

From the road (853ft, 260m), follow the obvious track leading up and across to the edge of the cliffs overlooking Loch Leum na Luirgin. The simple rule now, for the most dramatic cliff scenery, is to follow along the edge of the cliffs for the length of the ridge. Go gently up to the summit of Bioda Buidhe (1530ft, 466m) and along to the flat plateau between Bealachs nan Coisichean and Uige to follow a wire fence along and up to the summit of Beinn Edra (2006ft, 611m and 2hrs). Along via Bealach Mhòramahain and Bealach Chaiplin to gain the summit of Flasvein. Down and up to the summit above the huge coire of Cuithir to eventually drop down to 'the table' giving views across the cliffs of Creag a' Lain. Down a little further (a hidden stream can be found here if one requires water) and then up to the separate summit of Sgurr a' Mhadaidh Ruaidh. Continue to Baca Ruadh (2091ft, 637m, and 2½hrs). The next summit is Hartaval (2192ft, 668m) and after the dip into Bealach a' Chuirn a steepish slog takes you to the summit of The Storr (2358ft, 719m and 2hrs). Drop to Bealach Beag and along the flats to a very steep rise to Ben Dearg (1812ft, 552m and 1½hrs). Take the long slow drop to Portree (2½hrs, total: 10hrs).

The Walk

'That is an incredible walk, in fact it's absolutely brilliant', enthused the big man breaking into a run to finish. The rest of us, now beginning to feel the pace that had been set throughout the walk agreed in spirit, but were too breathless to air our agreement. At the time we were convinced that we had completed what, in many respects, must be the finest upland walk in Britain. Now, retrospectively mulling over the details and remembering its experiences, that conviction remains.

This walk takes the 22-mile (35-km) North Ridge of Skye from the pass at the head of the Uig to Staffin road and Portree. A walk taking you through some of the wildest country, providing some of the most spectacular rock scenery and giving superb views to some of Britain's most incredible mountains. To cap it all, it does it with conditions underfoot that are best likened to walking on your lawn at home — close cropped greensward. Surely a unique and masterful combination.

Although a long day's walk, it is a thoroughly practicable proposition because of the ease of the walking. The backpacker, or the walking elite, will want to logically link this ridge with the Far North Round where they merge at the head of the Uig/Staffin Pass. However, the ridge takes you down the centre of Trotternish and into the midst of some extremely wild and remote country; directly below you to the east are huge cliffs, and below these and to the west are uninterrupted miles of bog. Reasonable escape can only be undertaken at selected bealachs (as outlined in the fact sheet) and these should be carefully noted before this great ridge walk is embarked upon

It's a bit of an embarrassment telling you the time of morning we six lads (Mike Ansell, Martin Battersby, Mike Feeley, John Hargreaves, Stewart Sykes and myself), actually embarked from the big man's bus to begin this marathon adventure. Suffice to say that Ted Lean, the volunteer driver and 'dropperoffera', fully missed the morning rise and consequently had no brown trout to offer us on our return. Still, he had caught three dozen the previous day and it was all in a good cause.

Well, to be honest, it was actually past midday when we began along the path leading from the road to gain the east edge of the ridge overlooking Loch Leum na Luirginn and little Loch Cleat. Before the edge is reached you walk along what is, effectively, a single flat plain tilted gently upwards, and today with the edge perched against the blue of the sky it gave the illusion of the world ending here, in space, at that edge. As the eye travels up and along its intricacies towards the summit of Bioda Buidhe there is nothing to shatter the illusion.

Once there, however, three dimensional reality hits you hard and fast; first the large remote pinnacle of the Cleat is observed and then the mini Matterhorn-like combination of Dùn Dubh and Druim an Ruma which together quickly dispel the flat earth theory. Impressive cliffs these, and believe you me you 'aint seen nothing yet!' Before the summit, in one of the many recesses of the edge, you can observe ancient earth and stoneworks now handed over to the sheep to graze and scratch upon.

The top of Bioda Buidhe may be unexciting in itself but the cliffs below, and the superbly panoramic views more than make up for its lack of form. The Western Isles, the Quirang and the multi-coloured patchwork of grass, bog and heather leading to Staffin make a wonderful scene. But for us the clouds were building and the wind had quickly risen so we continued without lingering, rapidly down to Bealach nan Coisichean.

Here the wind lost some of its edge and down below this lesser cirque of cliffs, lay green lands and green-leafed birch, where a cuckoo called and sheep grazed. Before we had reached the levels between this bealach and Bealach Uige we again detected an ancient earth and stone wall running straight over the shoulder of Bioda Buidhe to end abruptly on the edge of the cliff. The end was marked by the remains of a small stone building and I observed a two-inch diameter post hole scooped from one of these stones. For all intents and purposes it appeared that this long forgotten man-made artefact was the single continuation of the mysterious parallel walls that run down the shoulder of Sron an Aighe. (See 'The Far North Round Of Skye'.) Why it should be there, apparently situated randomly, in this wilderness area gave us food for thought as we continued on our journey.

Mike who had been looking distinctly green since we launched out was now experiencing the advanced stages of nausea. A halt was called, for a rest and black tea from Johns' giant flask. This did the trick and we all set off again feeling as though the 'job was on'. If there had been any reasonable doubt as to Mike's or anyone else's fitness, now would have been the time to quit as Uig can be reached on a reasonable path descending from Bealach Uige via Glen Conon, in about two miles.

Crossing this low level area one picks up a wire fence running along above the cliffs. The driest ground and best views are gained by following this as it skirts the eastern edge of the ridge, on towards the summit of Beinn Edra. This is the least of the three 2000ft (610m) summits on the ridge and effectively marks the quarter-way point. The fence actually disappears some little way before the summit and if mist or cloud descends then extreme care must be taken with navigation, for great cliffs lie below. Before the summit is gained the strange effects of wind and erosion can be noticed as the grass gives way to expose allotment beds of pea gravel. Again, because of the wind, this was no place to linger and Martin and I who had been taking photographs near the trig point had to run full tilt to catch the others. A very late lunch was called for in Bealach a' Mhòramhain, huddled behind a small boulder and above the foundations of yet another long-forgotten wall. It had taken us two and a half hours to reach this point (including our previous stop). We noted that a reasonable path led down westwards from here via Glen Uig to Uig.

It is from this point south, to Storr, where the most interesting and dramatic sections of the ridge lie. The way now becomes noticeably narrower and, possibly for the first time conveys the feeling of being a true ridge. Keeping along the edge of the cliffs to the east brings one along to the low point of Bealach Chaiplin and dropping down (east) from here

would lead safely to the shelf of Dubh-chàrn and in turn along to the stream, falling down to Loch Cuithir. There is a good track (possible to drive up to this point) leading from here as the Loch and the deep little lochans above it are actually the site of a diatomite mine. This is why, surprisingly, there is a railway track in the middle of this wilderness area.

'Mine' really conjures up the wrong impression, for diatomite is a fine grained sedimentary earth, on a microscopic scale, made up from the skeletons of once-living organisms. Diatomite is mined by simply digging it out of the ground. If you should visit the mine you will be impressed by the trouble and expertise taken to construct both a railway and a track to this remote site, but diatomite is a valuable inert material. One of its uses is in the manufacture and stabilisation of high explosives such as dynamite.

Pulling up to Flasvein it is difficult to decide whether to stick to the edge or to wander further west, for the views are magnificent on both sides. My notebook records 'wind howling clag' at this point, but if the wind was constant at least the clouds and mists came and went very quickly. We worried that the weather would worsen and those incredible views would be lost, but fortunately it didn't.

The next bealach, Bealach na Leacaich, was marked by the remains of an ancient wall and then up above it a more modern stone wall (but still of ancient origin). This wall, and on Skye such stone walls are an exceptional rarity, was beautifully built with superbly regular, almost rectangular, blocks of masonry. If it had been elsewhere one could have imagined that these blocks had been purpose cut in some quarry, but up here I assumed they were a feature of regular jointing in the local geology. The wall and its origins became the subject of much discussion, the conclusion of which was that they had been constructed to direct beasts down from the open hills where, trapped by the cliffs on one side and blocked by the wall ahead the cattle were forced to move along the wall, to their destination. A word of warning about this bealach — it did not appear that there was any safe way down the cliffs to the east and so on to the diatomite mine track.

The cliff scenery now becomes particularly fine and, although a complex of different colours, the strata was dominantly horizontal giving very much the appearance of limestone country. You are now in a world of very big cliffs and awe inspiring steepness and form. I remarked knowledgeably to Martin that this was surely golden eagle country, although in truth I had never seen an eagle in all my many visits to Skye. The descent from Creag a' Lain revealed a great amphitheatre of cliffs with, in its centre, a throne-like rock table from which could be seen a kingly view sweeping right across the cliffs to the fearsome pillar and separate summit of Sgurr á Mhadaidh Ruaidh.

The 'big man' was first on the throne and I waved him back to photograph the occasion. By the time John and myself arrived the others were gone, eagerly heading off for the summit of Sgurr á Mhadaidh Ruaidh (peak of the red fox). We posed a while, taking in the view and experiencing the atmosphere of this wonderful place.

It was John, keen eyed as ever, who spotted

it first. A great bird with huge wings, feathers upturned with fingers playing the wind, gliding nonchalantly past those great cliffs as though they were mere pebbles strewn on a beach. A golden eagle is one of nature's most impressive creatures and this was the perfect setting in which to view the monarch of our skies. Having inspected us, the eagle settled on a spur running down the far side of Creag a' Lain and remained perched there until we left. Despite its not inconsiderable distance away from us it still appeared as a great gargoyle, black and menacing. We set off with some eagerness to tell the others.

From the summit of Sgurr a' Mhadaidh Ruaidh, it takes about two hours to reach the summit of Storr, via the summits of Baca Ruadh and past the forlorn cairn on Hartaval. This is the *piece de resistance* of this constantly amazing walk. But undoubtedly, it is standing at the top of Storr that is the highlight, which outshines everything else. At the end of the strip of blue that is the Sound Of Raasay, the Cuillin (both the Red and the Black), beckon irresistibly, and across Raasay and the Inner Sound the individual jewels of Applecross and Torridon shine. Westwards, Macleod's Tables rise distinctly above the distant backdrop of the Hebrides. And below, if you dare approach the edge of the cliff (extreme caution is required if you do), lies the climax of the sheer, exposed cliffs along which you have been walking for so many miles. Absolutely vertical for some 800 unbroken feet, looking over is a mind blowing experience, for the rock, banded lava, looks absolutely rotten.

Interestingly it can be seen that the main top of the cliff is actually detached from the true summit, in some ways reminiscent of the strange collection of pinnacles below. The most obvious of these is the Old Man of Storr. Over 200ft high and an extremely difficult rock climb (first pioneered by Don Whillans), it can be seen from the road even before the motorist arrives at Portree. Unfortunately these cannot really be seen to any effect from the 'ridge' itself but they are easily accessible from the road (best to approach alongside the little plantation) and are well worth a separate visit.

There is still a way to go but the next bealach, Bealach Beag, serves as a convenient descent from which to quit the ridge should it prove desirable so to do. Really the essence of the walk now lies behind you and the going is fairly flat until a steep drag gains the summit of Ben Dearg. A long plunge down to Portree picks the road up by the junction and a final foot slog down through the lights brings you back to civilisation. Sometimes, it's not unwelcome.

Facing page: **Near the summit of Storr.**

Below: **On the flanks of Beinn Edra looking back across the wilderness to the Quirang.**